LOST AT SEA

ALSO BY JOHN WUKOVITS

Chesty Puller: A Marine Legend in World War II

American Commando:
Evans Carlson, His WWII Marine Raiders,
and America's First Special Forces Mission

One Square Mile of Hell: The Battle for Tarawa

Pacific Alamo: The Battle for Wake Island

LOST AT SEA

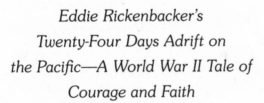

*Eddie Rickenbacker's
Twenty-Four Days Adrift on
the Pacific—A World War II Tale of
Courage and Faith*

JOHN WUKOVITS

CALIBER

CALIBER

An imprint of Penguin Random House LLC
penguinrandomhouse.com

LIBRARY OF CONGRESS CATALOGING-IN-PUBLICATION DATA

Names: Wukovits, John F., 1944– author.
Title: Lost at sea: Eddie Rickenbacker's twenty-four days adrift on the Pacific—a World War II tale of courage and faith / John Wukovits.
Other titles: Eddie Rickenbacker's twenty-four days adrift on the Pacific—a World War II tale of courage and faith
Description: [New York]: Dutton Caliber, [2023] | Includes index.
Identifiers: LCCN 2022038131 (print) | LCCN 2022038132 (ebook) | ISBN 9780593184844 (hardcover) | ISBN 9780593184868 (ebook)
Subjects: LCSH: Rickenbacker, Eddie, 1890-1973. |
World War, 1939–1945—Search and rescue operations—United States. |
United States. Army Air Forces—Search and rescue operations. |
World War, 1939–1945—Search and rescue operations—Pacific Ocean. |
World War, 1939–1945—Pacific Area. |
Aircraft accidents—Pacific Ocean—History—20th century. |
United States. Army Air Forces. Air Transport Command. |
United States. Army Air Force—Biography.
Classification: LCC D810.S45 W85 2023 (print) |
LCC D810.S45 (ebook) | DDC 940.54/49730922—dc23
LC record available at https://lccn.loc.gov/2022038131
LC ebook record available at https://lccn.loc.gov/2022038132

Printed in the United States of America
1st Printing

BOOK DESIGN BY KATY RIEGEL

To Moe,

You know why

CONTENTS

PART I

Background to the Pacific

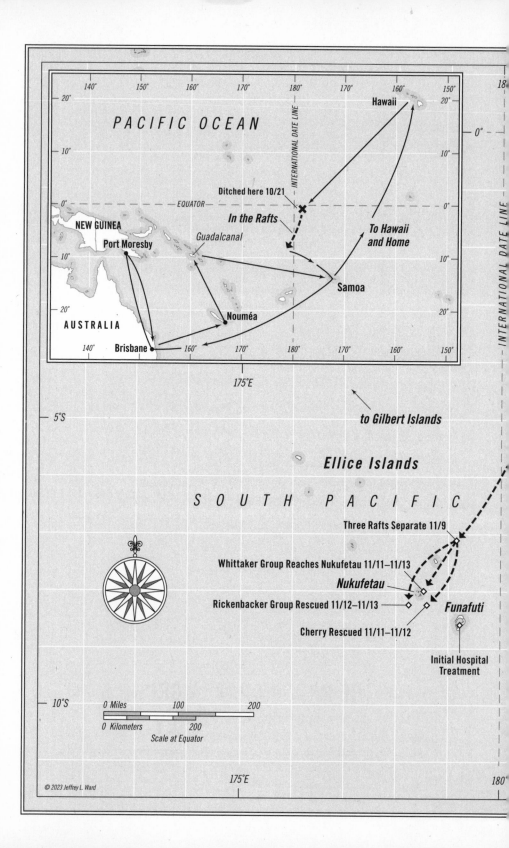

PACIFIC OCEAN

20°

140° 150° 160° 170° 180° 170° 160° 150° 18

Hawaii 20°

0°

10° 10°

Ditched here 10/21

EQUATOR 0°

NEW GUINEA

Port Moresby

Guadalcanal

In the Rafts

To Hawaii
and Home

10° 10°

Samoa

Nouméa

20° 20°

AUSTRALIA

140° Brisbane 160° 170° 180° 170° 160° 150°

175°E

5°S

to Gilbert Islands

Ellice Islands

S O U T H   P A C I F I C

Three Rafts Separate 11/9

Whittaker Group Reaches Nukufetau 11/11–11/13

Nukufetau

Rickenbacker Group Rescued 11/12–11/13

Funafuti

Cherry Rescued 11/11–11/12

Initial Hospital
Treatment

10°S

0 Miles   100   200

0 Kilometers   200

Scale at Equator

175°E 180°

© 2023 Jeffrey L. Ward

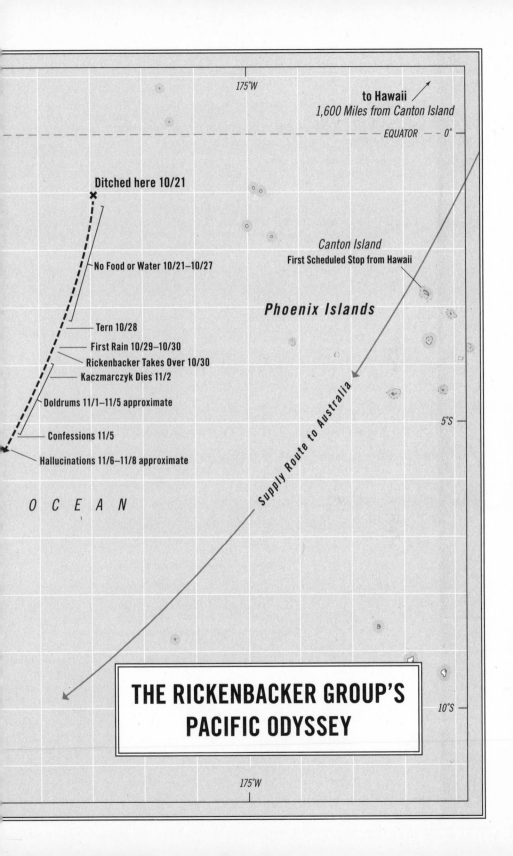

to Hawaii
1,600 Miles from Canton Island

175°W

— EQUATOR — 0°

Ditched here 10/21
✕

Canton Island
First Scheduled Stop from Hawaii

No Food or Water 10/21–10/27

Phoenix Islands

Tern 10/28
First Rain 10/29–10/30
Rickenbacker Takes Over 10/30
Kaczmarczyk Dies 11/2
Doldrums 11/1–11/5 approximate

Confessions 11/5

5°S

Hallucinations 11/6–11/8 approximate

O C E A N

Supply Route to Australia

THE RICKENBACKER GROUP'S
PACIFIC ODYSSEY

10°S

175°W

LOST AT SEA

PART I

Background
to the Pacific

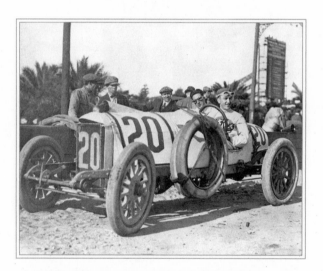

US Air Force photo courtesy of the National Museum of the United States Air Force

CHAPTER 1

"He Has Cheated
the 'Grim Reaper' About as Often
as Any Living Man"

1890 to 1940

THEY WOULD SOON be dead. How could they think otherwise? The eight men, ranging in age from twenty-two to fifty-two, alone on the ocean, crammed into three tiny rubber rafts, had drifted for so long that they could not be certain where they were or how long they had been afloat. In a day or two, at most, they would undoubtedly join the countless unlucky voyagers lost forever to the Pacific.

They had survived multiple challenges. Each day, the sun's glare bounced off the ocean surface to emit "billions of sharp splinters of light; no matter where one looked, it was painful." The blistering sun had so burned their skin that one of the group compared it to "being turned on a spit." They had prayed for nighttime's welcome relief, only to shiver in the dark from the chilling ocean swells that drenched them. "Daytimes we prayed for the coolness of the nights; nights we craved the sun," wrote one of the eight.

Men had lapsed into stupors, bobbing in the ocean with their mouths half open and fatigued heads drooping on sunburned chests. They had battled both extreme hunger and severe thirst, and had grimaced from constricted muscles caused by squeezing into rafts hardly big enough for two people, let alone three. "Our bodies, our minds, the few things we had with us were slowly rotting away."[1] Intensifying their anxiety was that they would perish without a trace, denying family and other loved ones details that could help bring closure. They could hold on awhile longer, but eventually the Pacific would wield the upper hand.

Except for one, the eight men had led routine lives. They had attended school, dated girls, played baseball and football, and afterward commenced careers they hoped would bring long and pleasant lives. The one exception, however, enjoyed a lifestyle the others could only envy. His name dominated the nation's headlines, and he had packed more thrills into his fifty-two years than the other seven combined. He enjoyed fame as a race car driver, dated gorgeous women, and basked in the limelight of being the nation's preeminent hero of World War I. He had eluded death so often on the racetrack and in the skies that an adoring public believed nothing could stop him.

"No man of this living generation has seen death more closely and more often than Eddie Rickenbacker," wrote popular author W. L. White. "He has learned to look the Old Fellow right back in the eye, as one man to another, returning his steady gaze." *Time* magazine turned to legendary figures from ancient Rome in depicting Rickenbacker as a man whose core was built upon "a gladiator's indomitability."[2]

In October 1942 eight men crafted a rousing saga at sea that inspired their fellow countrymen and enhanced the legend of a man who had long captured the nation's adulation.

"I DIDN'T GO TO SCHOOL—I WENT TO WORK"

Eddie Rickenbacker's youth in Columbus, Ohio, provided few hints of the extraordinary path he would follow. In 1879 his father, William Rickenbacher (the last name contained the letter *h* until Eddie changed it later in life), joined tens of thousands of Europeans who sought a better life across the Atlantic than that offered by the hardscrabble existence prevalent in their native countries. William said goodbye to family and friends in the small village of Zeglingen, Switzerland, nestled in the foothills of the Jura Mountains, determined to join his uncle in Columbus and begin work as a railroad laborer. Two years later, Elizabeth Basler crossed the ocean from Switzerland to settle in the same city, where her two brothers resided. The confident, assertive woman, called Lizzie by everyone in Columbus, adapted quickly to her new surroundings, and four years after her arrival, she married William.

Life with William, who waged a constant battle with financial problems, was never easy. The birth of their third of eight children, Edward Vernon Rickenbacher, on October 8, 1890, added to William's burdens. Hampered by his inability to provide for the family, the father vented his rage by whipping the children for the slightest misdeeds.

Eddie inherited his mother's grit, and, before he was five years old, he was scouring the city's streets for walnuts, rags, or pieces of coal that dropped from railroad cars as they rumbled by. He awoke before sunrise to walk two miles to collect the newspapers he would hawk for the *Columbus Dispatch*, and to milk goats to sell to neighbors.

Eddie could be counted on to help despite frequent mishaps, beginning with his being struck by a horse-drawn streetcar at the age of four. He suffered only minor injuries, but more serious misadventures followed, such as the time he tumbled down a well, knocking himself out, or slipped from a tree, scarring his chin. Another time, he got his foot caught in some railroad tracks and watched in terror as a steam engine approached. Fortunately, his brother freed him just in time for the train to barrel past. At age eight, as he raced down a steep hill his out-of-control cart flipped over on top of him and slashed his leg to the bone. He smoked when he was just five and organized a group of roguish youngsters known around the neighborhood as the Horsehead Gang, specializing more in fights and stealing cigarettes than in major crimes. Eddie lacked the comforts that kids from wealthier families took for granted, but his Columbus hardships honed an iron determination to outlast his foes and forged a foundation for his subsequent accomplishments.

Eddie's life changed drastically on July 18, 1904, when his father suffered a fractured skull and lapsed into a coma after brawling with a fellow worker. When William Rickenbacher died the next month, the embarrassed son chose to suppress memories of the incident, and for decades, Eddie claimed that his father died when a large piece of timber smashed into his skull.

The night following the funeral, thirteen-year-old Eddie awoke upon hearing noises from the kitchen. He walked in to find his sobbing mother, head in her hands, wondering how she, as the sole parent, would provide for the children. Eddie hugged Lizzie and vowed that he would take care of her and would never make her cry. He then stepped over to his father's chair at the head of the table and sat down as a sign that, henceforth, he was the man of the family.

The next morning, instead of walking to school, the seventh-grade student abandoned his education and traipsed out to find a job. Within hours, he started the first of his six nights a week, twelve-hour shifts, earning $3.50 each week for his labors at the Federal Glass Company, even though he had to walk four miles to and from work. Eddie later claimed that the moment he handed his mother his first paycheck "was the proudest day of his life." He added, "I changed from a boy to a man," and said that "I didn't have to be told what we were up against. The day after my father's funeral, I didn't go to school—I went to work."[3]

Even though dropping out of school was then not uncommon, Eddie considered his lack of education an embarrassing deficiency. Fearing that people might try to take advantage of him, he masked his shortcomings by charging straight into matters before anyone had time to discover that he could not read or write as well as they could.

"GET OUT IN FRONT AND DRIVE LIKE HELL"

A crowd in downtown Columbus altered the direction of his life. Eddie wandered over to find out the source of their interest and muscled his way in to see a gleaming new Ford two-passenger automobile, the first of its kind in Columbus, with a salesman touting the benefits of owning such a revolutionary vehicle. When the man finished his pitch, Eddie, never one to shy from an adventure, asked if he could take a ride in the vehicle. "Sure, kid. Hop in, and we'll go around the block." The exhilaration of driving by strolling couples at ten miles per hour electrified Eddie. "That thrill would remain vivid all the rest of my life," he wrote in his autobiography. "And it had a direct influence on the course I would follow for many years."[4]

Cars became Eddie's passion. If ten miles per hour was grand, how much better would twenty or thirty be? His knack for repairing broken bicycles and carriages came to the attention of Lee Frayer, one of the founders of the Buckeye Motor Company in Columbus. With automobile racing rapidly gaining popularity, Frayer asked Rickenbacker to accompany him as his riding mechanic to the 1906 Vanderbilt Cup Races on Long Island, the most renowned car competition then staged in the United States.

Whereas Frayer at least had the steering wheel to help prevent him from being thrown out of the machine, Eddie occupied the most treacherous, exposed spot in the car, where he contended with dust, dirt, pebbles, and other debris kicked up by cars to their front. Rickenbacker sat next to Frayer, keeping his eye on the gauges and relaying information about where their competitors stood.

Before 200,000 spectators, Frayer and Rickenbacker drove onto the track for their trial runs. During the second run, Frayer lost control of the car when the front tire blew on a sharp turn.

The vehicle swerved off the track, bounded through a ditch, and finally smashed into a sand dune. The impact hurled both riders from the vehicle.

Frayer suffered a dislocated shoulder, but, miraculously, Eddie walked away with only mild bruises. The close call with injury and death bolstered Eddie's burgeoning belief that fate smiled kindly on him and that no harm would come his way if he took proper precautions. "Frightened?" said Rickenbacker. "Frayer tried to talk me out of continuing this dangerous experimental sport, but I wouldn't listen. I was a part of progress. I was going to live. Hadn't I just escaped? I had faith."[5]

In 1909, however, an unfortunate incident with a cinder almost swiped away his future. As he watched a train rumble along the tracks, the wheels kicked a red-hot cinder into Eddie's right eye. Although a physician removed the particle, the incident left a permanent blind spot that he religiously kept hidden from others so that he could continue racing and, eventually, flying.

To promote sales of the 1909 Firestone-Columbus automobile, Frayer sponsored drivers to compete in races staged on a variety of surfaces, including county fair races conducted on rough and rocky back roads. Rickenbacker soon made a name for himself. Frayer saw the promise of his young protégé and, in the spring of 1911, asked him to be his relief driver in the first of what would become the sport's most influential race in the United States, the Indianapolis 500. On Memorial Day the duo finished eleventh in an electrifying spectacle that thrilled 80,000 spectators.

Encouraged by his performance at Indianapolis, Eddie turned to racing full time. He quickly rose through the ranks, gaining the respect of fellow drivers with a daring style summed up by his motto "Get out in front and drive like hell." Though aggressive, he was far from reckless, spending countless hours preparing carefully for each race. In 1915 Rickenbacker earned $40,000 to rank fifth in the standings. *Motor Age* magazine heralded him as "one of the greatest American drivers," and one driver labeled Eddie "the nerviest and most unerring of them all."[6]

"That was a golden period of my life," he would write. Rickenbacker enjoyed the adulation of fans, loved that newspapers dubbed him "the Baron," "the Speedy Swiss," and "the fastest

Eddie Rickenbacker sits behind the wheel of a Mason race car during an Illinois event around 1914. The riding mechanic, Eddie O'Donnell, sits on his right. Accidents during competitions in those early days were common, and deaths were not infrequent.

thing on wheels," and was proud that "We were front-page news."[7] In 1914, when war rent Europe into two camps, pitting Germany and other Central Powers against Great Britain and her allies, Eddie, concerned that his last name might cause his fans to think he was of German origin, amended it from Rickenbacher to Rickenbacker in hopes that it sounded more American.

The sport offered excitement and rewards, but it came with a price, as danger and death hovered over every track. Reporters claimed that Eddie lived a charmed life, and Lowell Thomas, famous in his own right for his coverage of celebrated world figures, including T. E. Lawrence, a British officer better known as Lawrence of Arabia, became enamored with Rickenbacker's eagerness to face "the maelstrom of life, dreaming big dreams, unafraid to test himself against the roughest and toughest."[8]

Rickenbacker's intrepid style, in which he all but taunted the Grim Reaper, reaffirmed his belief in his invulnerability to death. He said, "It came to me that I could control that machine with my mind, that I could hold it together with my mind, and that if it finally collapsed, I could run it with my mind. It was a feeling of mastery, of supreme confidence." He added, "I believe that if you think disaster, you will get it. Brood about death, and you will hasten your demise. Think positively and masterfully, with confidence and faith, and life will be more secure, more fraught with action, richer in achievement and experience."[9]

His racing days brought Rickenbacker fame and money, but a more imposing test—flight—would soon command his attention.

"SLID TO A STOP IN A CLOUD OF DUST"

In November 1916 Rickenbacker traveled to California to participate in a series of West Coast races. As he drove to Riverside during one free afternoon, a single aircraft resting on a grass runway grabbed his attention. Since he had never seen an airplane up close, he stopped to examine the machine. When he neared the hangar, a man about his age ambled out and introduced himself as Glenn Martin, the designer and builder of the aircraft. Martin recognized Eddie from newspaper photographs and asked if he would like to go for a ride. Though afraid of heights, Rickenbacker accepted the invitation and hopped into the tandem seat for a thirty-minute flight above the California countryside.

An entire new realm opened to him that day, one in which he was no longer bound by gravity or the inconveniences of traveling America's roads. When Martin, a former student of aviation pioneers Orville and Wilbur Wright, asked if Rickenbacker would like to take the controls, Eddie readily agreed and quickly veered the aircraft into a smooth bank. That moment hooked the young man, and Rickenbacker decided that his future lay in the air rather than with auto racing.

The next year, with his nation now embroiled in a European war, Eddie volunteered for air service, but the military informed the twenty-seven-year-old that he was too old for the rigors of the skies and that he lacked the necessary college degree to join its air arm. Taking note of his skill as a racer, however, in May 1917 they swore him in as an Army sergeant and agreed to ship him overseas to serve as a chauffeur for high-ranking officers. His prospects for aerial service brightened when Colonel William "Billy" Mitchell, an ardent advocate of air power, asked to have the car racer as his chauffeur.

While strolling along the Champs-Élysées in Paris one day, Rickenbacker met New York banker James E. Miller, a fan of his and a captain in the Army's Aviation Section. Miller, who commanded a flying school in Issoudun, near Tours, France, offered Eddie a post, and after passing the required physical with the help of a doctor who ignored his eye injury and advanced age, Rickenbacker assumed his new position as an engineering officer.

Rickenbacker received his commission as a first lieutenant in the Army Signal Corps and left for Issoudun. After a brief stint there, in March 1918 he received orders to join the 94th Aero Squadron, a unit of American fliers formed in Texas the previous August. Along with Rickenbacker, the squadron arrived at the front in April to support American and French forces operating near Toul, close to the German border. With this assignment, the 94th became the first American pursuit squadron to operate at the front and engage in combat.

Eddie found that German fliers posed only one of numerous menaces to his safety. Since the United States had not yet built its own air arm, the military had purchased the outdated French Nieuport 28 aircraft, a plane so badly outclassed by German fighters that the French had rejected it. Once in the air, pilots feared for their lives. Fabric ripped from the wings during steep dives, guns frequently jammed, oil lines ruptured during hard

Eddie Rickenbacker stands beside his airplane in France in October 1918. The "Hat in the Ring" emblem of his famed 94th Aero Squadron is visible on the aircraft's side.

NATIONAL ARCHIVES PHOTO #50126

landings, and enemy bullets ignited exposed fuel tanks. The unreliable, poorly constructed Nieuports, fashioned from wood and cotton fabric treated with a highly combustible fluid applied to tighten the fabric, burst into flames at the slightest spark, forcing airmen into making the hideous choice of death by fire or by leaping from the burning aircraft.

A parachute could have solved the dilemma, but military superiors condemned their use as cowardly and concluded that the life-saving devices made pilots more likely to abandon an aircraft they might otherwise be able to fly back to base. Understandably, Rickenbacker and his fellow fliers held a contrary opinion. He mentioned that for aviators, "Death by burning was

the death we dreaded more than any other," but superior officers forced them to face an impossible quandary. "It was abso-
lutely criminal for our higher command to withhold parachutes
from us."[10]

At least Rickenbacker had a good luck charm. Eddie was not
a deeply religious individual, but he never went anywhere without making certain that his Catholic crucifix—safely inserted in
a leather case—rested in his pocket. The ten-year-old daughter
of a racing friend from Detroit had given it to Rickenbacker
shortly before he left for the war. If he kept that crucifix with
him, the girl told Eddie, he would never be harmed. Whether
storming into aerial combat or walking the city streets back
home, Eddie Rickenbacker made a constant companion of that
crucifix for the rest of his life.

RICKENBACKER DOWNED HIS first plane one month after joining
the squadron and bagged three more within the next few weeks.
First Lieutenant Reed M. Chambers, another talented flier in
the 94th, credited Eddie's success to the former car racer's coolness under fire and his ability to focus on the task at hand. According to Chambers, Rickenbacker "wasn't the best pilot in the
world. He couldn't put as many holes in the target that was being towed [in gunnery practice] as I could, but he could put
more holes in a target that was shooting at him than I could."[11]

By late May 1918, only one month into his tenure over France,
newspapers in the United States trumpeted the feat that Rickenbacker registered his fifth kill, making him one of America's

aces. "Rickenbacker Gets Fifth Hun Plane" and "Daredevil Racer Is New Ace," proclaimed headlines, and the *Chicago Tribune* reported that "America's daredevil auto race driver and now an aviator with the American armies has become America's second ace."[12]

On May 17, when he and Chambers lifted off to patrol enemy lines northwest of Toul, Rickenbacker spotted three German planes at lower altitudes. He dove toward the trio, positioned his plane behind one of the targets, and with an accurate volley sent one German spiraling to his death. He next maneuvered his aircraft to evade his two pursuers, but the severe twists and turns

Eddie Rickenbacker relied on keen instincts and accurate aim to become the nation's top World War I ace. Pictured here in his Spad aircraft near Rembercourt, France, in 1918, he is standing behind his plane's machine guns, which helped bring down twenty-six enemy aircraft during the war.

ripped the fabric of his upper right wing from the frame. As his plane twirled toward the ground, the fabric flapping in the wind, Rickenbacker utilized every trick he could think of to regain control.

"It was death," he later wrote. "I had not lost my willingness to fight to live, but in that situation there was not much that I could do. Even birds need two wings to fly." He said "the good things I had done and the bad things" flashed through his mind, and he wondered if his Nieuport would hit the ground and shatter into a hundred pieces, or if he would plummet toward a cluster of trees and be impaled on their branches. More poignantly, he thought of his mother receiving word of his death. With the plane only a few hundred feet above the ground, Rickenbacker, certain he was about to die, muttered a quiet prayer. Seconds later, in desperation, "Without thinking, almost as though I were moved by something bigger than myself, I pulled open the throttle." The last-ditch maneuver having halted his downward momentum, Rickenbacker pulled on the joystick

Eddie Rickenbacker often skirted dangers in the European skies during World War I. His Nieuport 28 sustained damage during a May 1918 dogfight with three German planes. Here he stands beside a wing that had broken off his plane moments after he had landed.

and reversed the rudder, a combination he guessed had no more than a million-to-one chance of success. His Nieuport suddenly coughed and sparked to life.

When Eddie finally regained control, he still had to navigate a deadly two-mile gauntlet bristling with German antiaircraft batteries, machine guns, and rifle fire standing between his crippled plane and friendly lines. With his plane groaning to remain above the treetops and sputtering toward his airfield, Rickenbacker miraculously evaded a torrent of enemy shells and bullets. "I grazed the top of the hangar, pancaked down on the ground, and slid to a stop in a cloud of dust,"[13] he recounted. Eddie whispered a short prayer of thanks, then leapt from the bullet-riddled Nieuport and strutted toward the hangar, grateful that he had once again outfoxed the Grim Reaper.

In the European skies, the daredevil of the racetrack was further embellishing his record and solidifying his spot as one of the United States' most popular heroes.

HIS PERFORMANCE HAD SO impressed his superiors that when the post as commander of the 94th Aero Squadron opened, on September 24 they handed the promotion to Rickenbacker. Many of the college-educated men barely concealed their disdain for someone with little education and often snidely commented about Eddie's poor grammar and his German-sounding name. Undeterred, the new commander warned his pilots that he would brook no foolishness in the air, and he dictated a list of actions he expected all to follow: aggressiveness in seeking out the enemy, thorough knowledge of every strength and weakness of both their aircraft and the enemy's, readiness to fly at every opportunity, and the understanding that while he demanded the utmost from them, they could expect the best from him.

In the coming months, Rickenbacker logged more hours in the air than anyone in his squadron, frequently returning from one mission only to lift off for another following a brief rest and a coffee break. On his first day as commander, Eddie hopped into his Nieuport for a solo flight over German-held territory. He flew near Verdun when tracers from seven German aircraft ripped into his plane. Despite damage to his propeller, Rickenbacker turned to attack and dove directly through the enemy formation, shooting down two before eluding the other five and limping back to the airfield. When he landed, mechanics stared at the splintered propeller and twenty-seven bullet holes that riddled his Nieuport, each within six feet of Rickenbacker's seat. "Eddie Rickenbacker Has Narrow Escape,"[14] proclaimed the *Akron Beacon Journal*'s headline two days later. His exploits that day earned Rickenbacker the French Croix de Guerre, and twelve years later the United States belatedly awarded him the Medal of Honor for the same attack.

Eddie's example in the air, combined with his firm leadership, brought cohesiveness to the 94th Aero Squadron, which soon posted more kills than any other American unit. One of his fliers, Lieutenant J. L. Maloney, said of Rickenbacker that "he cheered his pilots, and he cussed them. In his quiet, yet forceful and incisive talks to us by candlelight at the mess table, before the big map in the operations room, and on the field before the takeoff on patrol, he inspired us." According to Maloney, Eddie frequently told his men, "Follow my order and advice, profit by my experience, and I will take you back with me in victory to see the Statue of Liberty."[15]

Reed Chambers, as talented a flier as any man Rickenbacker commanded, said that as the days and missions piled up, the squadron's loathing of their new commander turned to open admiration. Chambers explained that, at first, "he was just an uneducated, tough bastard who threw his weight around the wrong way," but through actions and words, "he developed into the most natural leader I ever saw."[16]

In 1930 Eddie Rickenbacker proudly displays the Medal of Honor he received for his exploits during a September 1918 melee in which he shot down two of the seven German planes that attacked him.

Just before dawn on November 11, 1918, Germany acceded to an armistice with the Allies and agreed that a cease-fire would take effect at eleven o'clock that morning. Rickenbacker, because of his prominent standing, was given the honor—dubious though it might have been because of the inherent risks—of making the final flight over German lines. He had flown 300 combat hours, more than any other American aviator, and had survived 134 encounters in the air. Rickenbacker received the Distinguished Service Medal with nine oak leaf clusters—each cluster representing an episode in which the flier exhibited outstanding courage in moments of extreme peril—the French Croix de Guerre on five separate occasions, and the Medal of Honor.

The press compared Rickenbacker and other daring aviators to knights of yore, and the public showered the same adulation on the cocky fliers as they did on the president or a beloved baseball star. Since he had earned the designation of "Ace of Aces" by notching twenty-six kills, more than any American flier, an adoring nation bestowed the most acclaim on Rickenbacker. Combined with his exploits as a car racer, Eddie's military success earned him widespread fame throughout the United States as a bona fide hero. He had become the most celebrated American aviator since the Wright Brothers ushered in the age of flight fifteen years earlier—a status unsurpassed until Charles Lindbergh's solo transatlantic flight aboard the *Spirit of St. Louis* a decade later.

"ONE OF THE TRUEST KNIGHTS OUR COUNTRY HAS EVER KNOWN"

A festive public greeted Rickenbacker on January 31, 1919, upon his return to the United States. New York City's automobile plants blew their whistles, and the city's journalists flocked to the ship to scribble down the hero's words.

In the first week of February the American Automobile Association feted Rickenbacker at a lavish dinner at the Waldorf-Astoria Hotel. Renowned people from the worlds of politics, racing, and the military attended, including former president William Howard Taft and Secretary of War Newton D. Baker, who in a speech called Rickenbacker "one of the truest knights our country has ever known." After Baker's rousing tribute, the association gifted Rickenbacker, called by the *Los Angeles Times* the "beloved American 'ace of aces,'"[17] a sparkling pair of platinum and gold wings sporting more than two hundred diamonds and sapphires.

The following week he appeared at the Capitol in Washington, DC, where Congress gave him a standing ovation. He then boarded a train for his hometown, signing autographs along the route for the lengthy line of passengers seeking to get near the hero. In Columbus, people stood along the tracks to greet the local boy who had added luster to an already-established national reputation, and when he stepped from the train, men cheered and women kissed him on the cheeks. A parade through packed city streets ended in a meeting with the governor and other top officials.

In the coming months, cities across the nation honored Rickenbacker with similar welcomes and gifts. In June he traveled to Los Angeles for a three-day gala in his honor. More than 300,000 people jammed city sidewalks to get a glimpse of the war hero. As bands played patriotic tunes and trucks packed with war veterans slowly passed by, aircraft from Rockwell Field in San Diego flew over and dropped flowers on the spectators. "Eddie Rickenbacker is in Southern California again after two years spent in accumulating Hun scalps and Allied war medals," blared the *Los Angeles Times* of the man who was now "feted and honored more than any one man who has ever visited Los Angeles." Comic actor and filmmaker Charlie Chaplin attended the festivities, and on the final day, popular actor Douglas Fairbanks honored Rickenbacker with a lavish luncheon at his Beverly

Hills home, followed by a tour of the star's film studio. "That Los Angeles celebration outdid them all," Rickenbacker wrote in his autobiography. "The official program had full-page advertisements from all the movie stars."[18]

A song titled "I'm Glad to Be Back in the USA," with Rickenbacker's image on the cover of the sheet music, amassed astounding sales figures, with 10,000 copies sold in the flier's hometown alone. Promoters begged him to endorse commercial products, star in movies, or embark as a speaker on a vaudeville tour, but he declined every offer because he felt they were simply trying to take advantage of his war heroics. The sole exception, meant to augment his depleted finances, was his consent to publish a memoir. Titled *Fighting the Flying Circus* and written for Rickenbacker by a ghostwriter, the book enhanced Rickenbacker's image, provided financial stability, and cemented his role as America's number one hero. He had already triumphed on the ground during his racing days; he now earned additional fame for doing the same in the air.

Once the warm receptions ended, Rickenbacker shifted his focus to more sedate occupations. He was ready to conquer new worlds, realms that offered financial security and a comfortable life, but inevitably contained dangers both familiar and new.

WHILE THE UNITED States turned to flappers, bootleg gin, gangster Al Capone, and the Great Depression, the 1920s and 1930s offered Rickenbacker a time of triumphs and setbacks. Once home from the war, Eddie rejected financially lucrative offers to return to the racetrack, and instead concentrated on promoting aviation in his country. He embarked on a series of cross-country flights, stopping in various cities to talk to crowds about aviation while simultaneously trying to establish speed records along the way.

Rickenbacker faced risks each time he headed skyward, including as a passenger. In one 1920 takeoff from Omaha, the plane hit a ditch at the end of the airfield, bounded over a road, and smashed into a house. A two-by-four punctured the side of the cabin, missed his head by inches, and exited out the back of the aircraft. Before his thirtieth birthday, Rickenbacker had already illustrated multiple times that he lived a charmed life. "In more than twenty-five years tinkering with speed," wrote one reporter, "Captain Rickenbacker figures that he has cheated the 'grim reaper' about as often as any living man. He has cracked up in racing cars and fighting planes."[19]

Newspaper columnist Henry McLemore wrote of the time he had nearly perished in an aircraft with Rickenbacker. "I looked Mr. Death in the eye with Rick" when accompanying the aviator in his attempt to set a new cross-country speed record. The engine quit as they flew over the Rocky Mountains, forcing McLemore and two other passengers to prepare for a crash. With his heart pounding and his palms sweating, McLemore worried that he was about to meet a shattering demise when his friend suddenly emerged from the cockpit. "Then, over the big drum of gasoline that took up most of the fuselage, crawled Rick. I can see his grinning face now."

Rickenbacker, assured as ever, said to McLemore and his two

associates, "Boys, you had better adjust your safety belts. We may have to make a forced landing." McLemore glanced at his seat belt, thinking there was no way a device that small would help him survive a crash, and then looked at Rickenbacker. "His old friend of many years, Mr. Death, was just outside the windows, but he was laughing at him,"[20] said the columnist. Fortunately, the engine restarted, and they continued the flight, but the incident illustrated for McLemore not merely Rickenbacker's calm, confident response to crises, but also that fate appeared to smile on this uncommon man.

The World War I ace kept his name in the headlines by setting cross-country speed records. He once raced from coast to coast in a little over thirteen hours, and topped his own record by dashing from Los Angeles to New York City in just over twelve hours. A crowd of five hundred cheering fans greeted him as the plane touched down, and publications gushed that the aviator ate breakfast in Los Angeles and dinner in New York.

Combined with his prior accomplishments in racing and in World War I, the feats lifted Rickenbacker to a lofty stratosphere of celebrity occupied heretofore only by Charlie Chaplin, Charles Lindbergh, and New York Yankees baseball slugger Babe Ruth. Like those three, he gave Americans mired in the Great Depression a cause to celebrate, and in the unsteady economic times, he became a role model in how to face life's daily challenges. Women had considered him one of the nation's most eligible bachelors before his 1922 marriage to socialite Adelaide Frost, and men longed to enjoy the fame and adulation the aviator received from an adoring nation.

Eddie Rickenbacker married Adelaide Frost in 1922. Her tenacity matched that of her famous husband and helped play a role in his rescue from the Pacific Ocean twenty years later.

Reporter Walter Kiernan, a friend of Rickenbacker's, wrote that Eddie possessed traits that every American desires, and listed them as "Iron nerves, a steady hand, never flustered, confidence in his machine and, if his machine failed, the kind of confidence in himself that could outweigh the disadvantage." He added that "Rick believed that if a man knew his business and was certain of his equipment, the element of chance was reduced proportionately to a fraction."[21] People from coast to coast, then battling severe problems of their own, saw a bit of themselves in the aviator and figured if Captain Eddie could surmount his obstacles, perhaps they could, too.

"THE TOUGH GUY HAD RECOGNIZED SOMEBODY WHO WAS TOUGHER"

While Rickenbacker electrified the country with his record-setting speed jaunts across the nation, he took steps to stabilize his financial status. With the backing of three prominent automobile executives, Rickenbacker became vice president and director of sales for the Rickenbacker Motor Company. The initial Rickenbacker cars appeared in 1922, offering an attractive package that included a four-wheel braking system and impressive speed of sixty miles per hour. However, during an economic recession a few years later—this prior to the Depression—his company suffered from slumping sales and financial difficulties.

With the company in a death spiral, and finding himself shackled to a quarter-million-dollar debt at age thirty-five, Rickenbacker moved into smaller quarters and sought other economic opportunities. Friends urged him to declare bankruptcy, but he vowed to repay his creditors and planned his comeback. "I was not ashamed and not afraid," he wrote of the dismal time. "Failure was something I had faced before and might well face again." He contended that instead of branding failure as a calamity, it can rejuvenate a person if he is willing to work hard and learn from it. "Here in America, failure is not the end of the world. If you have the determination, you can come back from failure and succeed."[22]

Rickenbacker's personal fortunes brightened when he purchased the Indianapolis Motor Speedway, the track that had helped cement his career as a top car racer. Eddie ordered significant improvements to the fabled track and arranged for radio coverage of the annual Indianapolis 500 Memorial Day race.

His outlook brightened further in January 1935, when Rickenbacker took the helm at Eastern Air Lines, a firm with great potential but beleaguered with fiscal woes. Eddie modernized an outdated fleet, added new routes to enhance ease of travel for passengers, and increased wages for better productivity. With future prospects improving, in 1938 he and several associates purchased the firm, with Rickenbacker as its president and

Eddie and Adelaide Rickenbacker pose for a photograph around 1935 with their two adopted sons, William (left) and David.

general manager. Under his guidance, Eastern turned into the most profitable airline in the United States.

Rickenbacker relied on an adroit, if sometimes unpopular, managing style. He worked far into the night, seven days a week, to inspect facilities, become acquainted with the employees, and determine the changes that could transform the airline. He flew 200,000 miles during his first year alone, and, according to *Time* magazine, "poked his nose into every airplane, every ticket office, every hangar, and every repair shop."[23] He had a series of "Captain Eddie Says" posters mounted in every office that bore different Rickenbacker slogans pertaining to the value of quality workmanship, thrift, and safety. Rickenbacker's insistence on doing things his way enraged many of his subordinates, and his brusque personality annoyed others, but once he outlined a path to success, Eddie would not be swayed.

For a time, Charles Lindbergh's landmark 1927 transatlantic flight from New York to Paris had catapulted the aviator to the national prominence that Rickenbacker had previously enjoyed. However, the public still retained a love for the tough, nononsense hero of World War I, and, within ten years, his success at Eastern once again put him in the public eye. One 1938 poll named Rickenbacker "the greatest living human being," and his fame extended to every level of society. One evening Eddie entered a popular New York restaurant for dinner. As he ate, a group of notorious mobsters at a nearby table looked over and chatted to one another about the aviator's presence. Suddenly one of the gangsters, infamous for the long list of rivals he had supposedly murdered, walked over and sheepishly asked Rickenbacker for his autograph. As the popular columnist Ed Sullivan recounted about the moment, "The tough guy had recognized somebody who was tougher."[24]

Stubborn in dealing with his rivals and subordinates, Rickenbacker displayed a sentimental side when it came to youth. He believed that young boys and girls needed heroes, and he loved his stature as a role model to legions of teens and preteens. He turned to a popular format—the Sunday newspaper comics—to deliver his message to American youngsters that a combination of hard work and clean living brought about success. The popular strip *Ace Drummond,* based loosely on his own aviation career, featured a dashing flier who rescued people in distress, and from 1933 to 1939, the comic appeared in more than 100 newspapers across the United States.

ONE FAN OF the strip, a teenager from New Jersey named Johnny Bartek, loved reading about Rickenbacker's deeds. Eddie was Bartek's childhood hero, and the youth hoped to meet the aviator one day.

Johnny's parents, born in Czechoslovakian villages only a few miles apart, immigrated to the United States, married, and settled in Bayonne, New Jersey. They were a loving and nurturing couple whose words and actions were anchored in a deep religious foundation and in the simpler things of life. Charles provided a stable life, while Mary maintained a spotless home filled with family photographs and the aroma of stuffed cabbage. The most prominent photo was that of a castle entrenched on a rock, with the biblical quote "The Lord Is My Rock and My Fortress and My Deliverer."[25]

After Johnny's father lost his job due to Depression-era cutbacks, the Barteks moved to Freehold, New Jersey, where Charles began working in a rug mill. Both parents believed that despite the setback, their Baptist faith would sustain them through their travails. Each morning, Mary either attended church or listened to religious services on the radio, and no matter the weather, at dusk she could be found in her favorite pew for that evening's service. Bartek loved and admired his mother, who had named him after the Apostle John, but like many boys his age, he used to sneak out of the house to avoid what he concluded was time wasted listening to a sermon.

The freckled youth with thick red hair was never comfortable in the classroom, either, and consequently dropped out of high school following his freshman year. He worked assorted odd jobs before looking up to where his idol, Eddie Rickenbacker, had become master of the sky. Bartek enrolled in a four-month course in an aircraft mechanic school, and before long he could inspect any plane to ensure that the engine functioned properly.

Like Rickenbacker, he saw glory and nobility in soaring through the sky, once the sole domain of starlings and robins, hawks and eagles.

Bartek never suspected that in a few years, fate would cast him and the man he so admired in an epic sea odyssey.

CHAPTER 2

"Would Have Been at Home with Lance and Armor"
February 1941 to October 1942

BLINDED BY THE mystique associated with flight, Johnny Bartek overlooked the dangers that accompanied Eddie Rickenbacker each time he lifted off the ground. By the late 1930s, the senior executive of Eastern Air Lines still regularly boarded airplanes on frequent trips to inspect factories and hangars throughout the nation.

"HE WAS COOL THROUGHOUT"

Rickenbacker's nighttime flight from New York's LaGuardia Field to Atlanta on February 26, 1941, seemed to be one of those routine trips. He was among thirteen passengers, including popular political columnist Drew Pearson and Maryland congressman William D. Byron, aboard the Douglas DST Silversleeper, called the "Mexican Flyer." After delivering a speech to the city of Birmingham's municipal aviation committee the next day,

Eddie would board a second flight to Florida in hopes of persuading his board of directors to approve $5 million for the purchase of new equipment.

Pilot James A. Perry Jr., age twenty-nine, and copilot Luther E. Thomas, thirty-one, prepared for takeoff as steward Clarence Moore directed passengers to their seats. Perry's inexperience—he had captained Eastern planes for only one year—bothered Rickenbacker, but the famous flier's unease paled compared with Perry's discomfort in having the nation's most celebrated aviator, and his ofttimes irascible boss, looking over his shoulder.

Perry lifted off at 9:05 p.m., with weather reports cautioning against low cloud cover and possible heavy rains. Rather than adopt the normal air route to Atlanta, Perry followed a path that skirted the worst storms, but deteriorating conditions followed the Silversleeper. Information also suggested that severe weather was fast closing in on the Atlanta airfield. Concerned over what he might encounter in Georgia, and knowing that he carried illustrious passengers, Perry walked back to inform Rickenbacker to expect tricky weather as they descended into Atlanta.

Near the town of Stone Mountain, eighteen miles northeast of Atlanta, Perry contacted the Atlanta tower operator, who notified the pilot that the cloud cover stood at just 300 feet, the minimum height for a safe landing. He also told Perry that Delta Air Lines had rerouted two flights away from Atlanta because of the weather, but that a third plane had landed safely only moments ago. Upon receiving the tower's clearance at 11:44 p.m., Perry continued his descent.

With Atlanta's Candler Field drawing closer, the pilot dropped into a thick overcast. Closer to the airfield, Jonesboro chief of police O. L. Roberts reported that residents saw a big plane flying westward over his town, but rather than turning south toward the airfield, it seemed to head toward a sparsely settled area with poor roads.

With visibility no more than one mile, the twin-engine aircraft droned on into a rain that was fast turning into sleet. Perry dropped from 500 to 300 feet, hoping to dip below the cloud cover and gain sight of the airfield, but the sleet, one of the most hazardous threats to flying, obstructed his view.

Rickenbacker had just put away his work and was chatting with Moore when Perry lowered the left wing to enter a turn toward the airfield. Rickenbacker felt the wing hit against something—he later learned it was the tops of trees—which flipped the left wing up and the right wing down. As the cabin lights extinguished, Rickenbacker, knowing from his past experience that the best place to be in a crash was the rear of the plane, jumped out of his seat and hurried back. "In a surprise crash, the plane sometimes breaks in two," he later explained. "If you're in the rear, you will be thrown out. It may break your neck, but you won't run the hazard of burning up."[1] Fortunately, someone in the cockpit, moments before he perished, had cut the electrical system to prevent fires from consuming Rickenbacker and the other passengers.

The plane started disintegrating before he could reach the back of the cabin. Perry had overcompensated for brushing the foliage by raising the left wing, but that also further lowered the right wing, which hit and became entangled with large pine trees. The collision ripped the right wing from the fuselage, sent the aircraft into a wild somersault, and knocked it directly toward other trees.

The plane smacked into the forest south of Atlanta near the small town of Morrow with such force that the noise awakened residents in the area. The plane cartwheeled, sliced the tops from a cluster of trees, and came to rest on its roof as it burrowed into the earth. The impact shoved the plane's nose and cockpit backward under the inverted top of the fuselage, instantly killing both Perry and Thomas. The tumbling sheared the nose section from the plane, sliced off the tail section, uprooted trees in its path, spiraled debris inside and outside the aircraft in every direction, tore loose and hurled one motor seventy-five feet away, and thrust Rickenbacker and the other passengers against seats, armrests, and the floor. The plane, according to Rickenbacker, twisted "like a paper bag,"[2] and broke in two, with him lying on the floor between the cockpit and cabin compartments.

The darkness masked a nightmarish scene. The front third of the plane was embedded in the earth, while the cabin housing Rickenbacker and the other passengers protruded at a 45-degree angle. Sleeping in his seat at the cabin's rear section, passenger George Feinberg suddenly found himself lying on the upended ceiling. Miraculously suffering only minor injuries, he crawled out of the wreckage through a crack in the plane's side, one of the eight fortunate passengers who survived the mishap.

Rickenbacker suffered the worst injuries, particularly to his left side. He fractured his left hip when the impact of hitting the terrain smacked him against an armrest, and experienced excruciating pain from multiple cracked bones, including his ankle, left elbow, nose, and several ribs. A gruesome slash oozed blood above his left eye, and his shattered left hip socket and pelvis shot waves of pain throughout his body. With the bulkhead and a gas tank resting inches from his head, and barely able to move his right leg even a few inches, Rickenbacker had survived the impact because he had immediately left his seat for the rear.

Plane parts and shattered tree limbs littered the ground. Jesse S. Rosenfeld, who had been hurled from the plane, heard survivors inside the aircraft moan for assistance. "For God's sake, help!"[3] A fully alert Rickenbacker, held in place by debris tossed about by the impact, covered in his own blood, and soaked from the gasoline dripping from the fuel tank, feared dying in an explosion if he could not extricate himself from the tangled mess.

As freezing rain pelted him, Rickenbacker concluded he had no choice but to try to free himself from the metal that tightly encased him. "What the hell," he said later. "If you have to die, you might as well die trying to get out as laying there and letting the thing happen."[4] He twisted his body and forced himself upward a few inches, but a jagged piece of aluminum directly above sliced into his face and popped the left eyeball out of its socket, leaving it dangling on his cheek. Rickenbacker tried again, but slumped back when he cracked more ribs, which produced a sound that reminded him of popcorn popping. He now had no choice but to lie in the debris, accept his pain, and hope that someone came to his rescue before the plane exploded and fires engulfed him.

Despite his own precarious condition, Rickenbacker shouted encouragement to others, and even apologized on behalf of his airline. "I'm sorry this happened to you boys," he kept repeating. When one of the passengers who had exited the plane suggested that they should build a fire to ward off the cold, Rickenbacker, aware of the fuel gushing out of the damaged aircraft, shouted, "No! Don't light a match. You'll set the gasoline on fire. For God's sake, don't light a match!" He added, "Just sit tight and wait. Somebody will come and get us."[5]

Philip Brady, a mechanical engineer from New York en route to the Canal Zone, could hardly believe that anyone, especially the horribly injured Rickenbacker, could have maintained his composure throughout the ordeal. "Rickenbacker was swell," Brady said. "As long as he was conscious, he kept calling out to us to be careful. He was cool throughout."[6]

Some of the other survivors tried to locate help. N. Hansell of the Bronx, New York, stumbled from the wreckage and wandered around until he encountered a dog. As dawn approached, he followed the animal to a home belonging to farmer J. T. Lee, who called the airport. Jesse Rosenfeld also staggered through muddy woods until he reached a home belonging to a second farmer, who took him to a nearby telephone.

"YOU'LL HAVE TO SHOOT ME TO GET RID OF ME"

Unaware of the drama to their north, Eastern Air Lines and airport officials worried when they were unable to make contact with the aircraft. Shortly after midnight, the officials called for ambulances. Bishop Simpson, one of Eastern's airport mechanics, and fifteen other workers divided the area around Jonesboro into five sections and organized a comprehensive search of the terrain. For more than six hours, in rain, fog, and sleet, they slipped on treacherous ground and stared into a darkness illuminated only a few feet at a time by their flashlights. The men talked to area farmers to see if they had heard or seen something. At one point, they came within 300 yards of the plane without spotting it, due to the thick vegetation and fog.

Atlanta newspaper reporter William Key wrote of the rescue party's frustrations and concluded that the men staged as thorough a search as possible "over country at its worst with rain making the roads and the fields slithering masses of red clay. Through the night, men from Candler Field, from police departments, from nearby farms, and from Jonesboro and Morrow sought to blanket the territory in which the ship was believed to have fallen."[7]

Near dawn, they finally stumbled onto the outer edges of the crash site. For 400 yards, rent trees with their tops shorn off pointed to an isolated spot tucked into dense foliage and deep ravines 700 yards off a dirt road. "Large trees were flattened and broken," wrote one of Atlanta's premier reporters, Ralph McGill. "The sylvan dell had become a coldly stark and bloody hell." Bodies of the dead and injured "were strewn in grotesque positions near the ship,"[8] and rescuers doubted that anyone could have survived such a violent collision between machine and terrain.

"Those who came gasped, for they saw it suddenly, as though

in turning a corner," wrote another reporter. "Even from nearby the wreckage seemed more the handiwork of an irate giant than of man." One of the motors, "its cowling battered and the propeller blades bent backward across it,"[9] rested on the soil, and beyond it lay the airplane, smashed into the ground amidst clothing, airplane parts, and suitcases.

Ravines made it impossible for cars and ambulances to reach the site, forcing men on foot to traverse the slippery slopes and wind through charred trees to enter the area. Shocked workers halted when they spotted Rickenbacker, lying helpless and bloody, still wedged in the rubble with the body of one of the victims draped over his feet. Broken bones protruded from his skin, and the eye dangling gruesomely down his cheek caused some rescuers to turn away and vomit. Some were certain the national hero was dead, but a doctor at the scene inspected him and concluded that while Rickenbacker's chances of survival were grim, "He still breathes. There is some life."[10] Optimism rose when Rickenbacker, though lying helpless on the ground and in excruciating pain, directed rescuers to other survivors and joked with his company's mechanics while they cut a hole through the plane's side to remove their boss.

After freeing Rickenbacker, and after a physician had administered a shot of morphine, the rescuers wrapped him in blankets, placed him on a stretcher, and gingerly carried him to an ambulance. Each jolt shot searing pain through his body, but the only time Rickenbacker spoke during the arduous journey was when the four stretcher bearers struggled down one ravine, tilting the stretcher. "Easy, boys, don't dump me," said Ricken-backer in a voice barely above a whisper. He admitted later that "every step hurt," and that it "was all I could do to keep from crying out with the pain."[11]

The ambulance transported the still-conscious Rickenbacker to Piedmont Hospital in Atlanta, where doctors initially con-cluded he was unlikely to last through the day. "He's more dead than alive," said one intern. "Let's take care of the live ones." When the hospital's Catholic chaplain prepared to give Rickenbacker the Last Rites, the aviator summoned enough strength to object that he was "a god-damned Protestant, like most people."[12]

A Baptist pastor arrived to console Rickenbacker in what the cleric assumed were his final moments, but Eddie, even though he lay helpless in a hospital surgical unit, was having none of that. "You can say for me that I am bruised in my body, but not broken in my spirit,"[13] Rickenbacker told the pastor.

When the hospital's chief surgeon, Dr. Floyd W. McRae Jr., strode in, nurses held Rickenbacker down on the surgical table as the doctor pushed the flier's eye back into its socket and sewed shut the wound to the eyelid. Eddie cursed and threatened McRae, but the physician, who could not use an anesthetic as it might weaken the eye muscles and further complicate the proce-dure, outcussed his stubborn patient and ordered him to be quiet. McRae continued without further objection from the aviator, as did the other surgeons who subsequently wrapped Rickenbacker in a cast that, save for one arm, covered his body from head to toe.

ADELAIDE LEARNED OF the crash while visiting her friend Mrs. O. Y. Kirkpatrick in Charlotte, North Carolina. Charlotte's city traffic manager, Marton Funkhouser, whisked her to the Georgia–South Carolina border, where the Georgia State Patrol escorted her at top speed to the hospital. Along the way, Adelaide listened to a radio report announcing her husband's death, while other police escorted their sons, sixteen-year-old David and thirteen-year-old William, from school in Asheville, North Carolina, to join their mother in Atlanta.

At the hospital, Dr. McRae brought Adelaide up-to-date. When she learned that her husband, despite his severe injuries, tried to help the other survivors at the site, she turned to Mrs. Kirkpatrick and said, "We knew he'd be like that, didn't we?" Adelaide waited by Eddie's side until he regained consciousness, and when her husband saw her, he attempted to make light of the grim situation. "I'm sorry I interrupted your work, dear," he apologized. "I guess you'll have to shoot me to get rid of me." To allay fears among the public that he would never recover, he told the medical team, "Tell the boys I'll be out in three or four weeks."[14]

According to Rickenbacker, "The next ten days were a continuous fight with the old Grim Reaper,"[15] which forced Dr. McRae to order transfusions of blood and plasma each time Eddie seemed to be slipping away. Two days after the crash, Rickenbacker took a sudden turn for the worse and teetered on the brink of death. He would say later that he felt as if he were standing at the gates of Heaven, experiencing his final moments before succumbing.

"Dying is the sweetest, tenderest, most sensuous sensation I have ever experienced," he wrote. "Death comes disguised as a sympathetic friend. All was serene; all was calm. How wonderful it would be simply to float out of this world. It is easy to die. You have to fight to live." Rickenbacker, however, summoned every fiber of strength and relied on the discipline he had developed during his racing days and in World War I to keep battling. "I fought death mentally, pushing away the rosy, sweet blandishments and actually welcoming back the pain."[16]

Spite welled up when he heard the voice of Walter Winchell, an influential national newspaper columnist who also hosted a popular radio news program, announce that Eddie Rickenbacker was dying. Irate over Winchell's premature statement, the aviator lifted a water pitcher next to his bed and hurled it at the radio. "The radio flew apart, and Winchell's voice stopped," said Rickenbacker. "Then I got well."[17]

Excruciating pain caused Rickenbacker to hallucinate, and during one wild episode, he tore off

After enjoying a ride through the countryside with his wife, Adelaide, Eddie Rickenbacker slowly emerges from his automobile during his recovery from the harrowing 1941 air crash near Atlanta.

AUBURN UNIVERSITY, SPECIAL COLLECTIONS & ARCHIVES

the cast on his left wrist with his teeth. Dr. McRae placed him in an oxygen tent and told Adelaide to prepare herself for the worst, but once again Eddie pulled through. After ten days, Rickenbacker had improved sufficiently that the doctor felt free to finally set his patient's hip.

Over the coming weeks, Rickenbacker slowly regained use of his body. He walked for hours at a time, leaning on crutches at first, then discarding them eventually for a cane. An outpouring of affection from people around the country boosted his spirits, as almost 20,000 letters, cards, telegrams, flowers, and assorted gifts swamped Piedmont Hospital, including notes from prominent aviators, politicians, and friends.

Eight people—three crew members and five passengers—perished in the crash. A subsequent investigation determined that the pilot and copilot had failed to properly adjust their altimeters to the barometric pressure reading given them by the airfield, causing the plane to approach in the fog at a dangerously low altitude.

On Wednesday, June 25, almost exactly four months after an ambulance rushed Rickenbacker to the hospital, Dr. McRae discharged his patient. Walking unsteadily with the aid of a cane and a specially designed shoe—the accident had left his damaged leg shorter than his right—and still in great pain, Rickenbacker boarded a plane for a return flight to New York's LaGuardia Field. Looking pale and thin, and accompanied by Adelaide and his two sons, he gingerly stepped off the aircraft to a rousing welcome from a crowd of 200 friends and Eastern Air Lines workers, including old buddies from his World War I squadron.

The warm welcome convinced him that, injured as he was, he had more to contribute to his country. Adelaide joined her husband in believing that his time in the limelight had not yet ended. "I guess his number wasn't up yet,"[18] she said after the crash.

Popular opinion appeared to agree that the hero's place in the spotlight was far from over. One of the first rescuers to reach the crash site and help pull Eddie out of the plane, LaVerne Raymond, said of Rickenbacker, "Boy, there's a man! Not many men could have stood what that man took." The *Atlanta Constitution* called him "A debonair figure always, direct of speech, dynamic of answer, but pleasant and personable," declaring that "Edward Vernon (Eddie) Rickenbacker is the beau ideal of an aviator" whose personality "would have been at home, with lance and armor, riding in the van of William the Conqueror's host at Hastings. His clear-cut features, sharp, intelligent eyes, and wiry body would have caught most certainly the attention of the chroniclers of the times, and of the great captains, and for centuries his saga would have been a mighty legend."[19]

Noted columnist Ralph McGill claimed that "Eddie always has been made of tough stuff," and that "Looking at the wreck and at those who lived, one could be fatalist enough to say that one goes when one's number is up. Not before." Henry Vance employed a humorist's view in his *Birmingham News* column when he wrote, "As I understand it, th' Grim Reaper loses his temper and flies off th' handle every time he ketches [*sic*] Eddie Rickenbacker thumbin' his nose at him."[20]

With his recovery from the plane crash, Rickenbacker's popularity had reached a peak to rival that of his return to the United States in 1919. As Charles Lindbergh waned in public favor during the 1930s with his uncomfortable flattery of Adolf Hitler, Rickenbacker's fame soared.

A plane crash was not about to slow Rickenbacker. He planned to continue his work, for Eastern as well as for his nation, as soon as possible. He said that the more mishaps with death he faced, "the more reasons I found for not fearing him," and that the event reinforced his belief that he had survived spectacular race crashes, death-defying dogfights, and now this most recent event "for some good purpose. I was being tested for some great opportunity to serve, a privilege that might come at any time."[21]

"NO. KEEP THAT YOURSELF."

His opportunity arrived suddenly and violently with the December 7, 1941, Japanese surprise attack on the US Pacific naval base at Pearl Harbor, which catapulted America into World War II. Young men swamped recruiting centers, while the rest of the nation prepared to meet the new challenges to daily life that war would inevitably bring. "Now there was more reason than ever to get fit again,"[22] thought Rickenbacker. Although too old to hop into a fighter and duel Japanese fliers, Rickenbacker figured that the aviation knowledge he had accumulated through the years might be valuable to the government in the coming days.

Lieutenant General Henry H. "Hap" Arnold, the commanding general of the Army Air Forces, agreed. In a March 1942 meeting with the World War I ace in Washington, DC, Arnold expressed his concerns that morale among aviation units needed a boost since Pearl Harbor. "I'm told that they are indifferent, that they haven't got the punch they need to do the job they're being prepared for," he explained. "I want you to go out and talk to these boys, inspire them, put some fire in them."

He figured that Rickenbacker, a combat veteran with legendary status among airmen, would be welcome at every base. Arnold said that the mission, which entailed amassing 15,000 air miles while visiting forty-one bases in the United States in thirty-two days, might tax Rickenbacker, but he felt that urgency overrode any concerns. Rickenbacker hesitated to embark on such a grueling mission so soon after his recovery from the Atlanta crash the previous year, but Hap was adamant. "Some of these units will be on the way overseas in ten days. If you won't go right away, there's no point in your going at all. The situation is that serious."[23] When Rickenbacker accepted, Arnold offered him the rank of major general, but the aviator preferred to remain a civilian so that he could speak without worry that the Army might try to censor his remarks.

Eddie arranged to have a friend of his, Colonel Hans Christian Adamson, accompany him. The soft-spoken, bookish Adamson had been a pioneer aviator and, in the 1920s and 1930s, an ardent promoter of air power. The visionary worked for the assistant secretary of war for aviation under Presidents Calvin Coolidge and Herbert Hoover and, in the mid-1930s, had even forecast space probes and moon landings. He had written for New York newspapers and, as the director of public relations for the American Museum of Natural History, had helped spread word of its spectacular dinosaur collection, instilling in countless young boys and girls a fascination with the prehistoric creatures. The fifty-two-year-old Adamson, only three months Rickenbacker's senior, would give Eddie a companion who shared not only a similar age but also a love of aviation.

The pair, accompanied by an osteopath and a masseuse to ease Rickenbacker's pain-wracked body, commenced their tour on March 10. Speaking as often as eight times a day, Rickenbacker brought his message to young airmen soon to be in combat. He emphasized the importance of teamwork and told them that victory in the air always began with thorough preparation on the ground, especially in understanding every intricacy of their aircraft as well as those of their foes. He explained that while in the first war he flew against the Germans with only two machine guns, a less potent engine, and no parachute, "You are going into combat with a big advantage over our 1918 squadron, both in training and equipment. One of your fighters has more fire power than our whole squadron had. And you have more training than we."[24]

In one Los Angeles speech attended by retired baseball great Babe Ruth, Rickenbacker cautioned that the nation faced a long, exhausting conflict during which every citizen would have to temporarily forgo certain freedoms, including the right of unions to order labor strikes. He said bluntly, "We've got to wake up" to a new reality that included death and injury. "It is cruel, but that is what war is for—to kill," he told one group of airmen. He said in sparse, blunt words that the airmen had to become killers, and added, "If you don't kill them first, they will kill you."[25]

A *Los Angeles Times* reporter wrote, "Eddie Rickenbacker gave his own countrymen hell yesterday. He said they are trying to win the war in their spare time. He said this public attitude is letting down the men in the armed service." Rickenbacker emphasized, "The men and women of America must realize this is a life and death struggle."[26]

An editorial in the *Spokane Daily Chronicle* asserted that apathy had set in among some civilians, that union strikes had plagued industries vital to the war effort, and that some industrialists were more concerned with profit than with producing the weaponry needed to win the war. The editors argued that people "need some of the prodding of a Rickenbacker. Lay on, 'Eddie,' you are serving your country that way as truly as you did in 1918." A letter to the editor in a Los Angeles newspaper stated that Rickenbacker "was doing his part in saving us from destruction as he limps his way with his tortured body throughout the land to arouse us. He is grim, powerful, and determined."[27]

Rickenbacker ended his tour on April 12 with a final talk at Mitchel Field on Long Island, New York, but his work was not over. The government called on Rickenbacker two months later when Secretary of War Henry L. Stimson asked that he embark on a second tour to reassure the American people about the quality of the aircraft being sent to the fighting zones. Rickenbacker spoke in multiple locations, and in three national radio broadcasts assured listeners that their sons were not being sent to war in deathtraps.

In September Stimson dispatched Rickenbacker to England so that he could visit the bases of the American Eighth Air Force stationed in that country and determine their most urgent needs. In addition, Rickenbacker enjoyed a lunch with the British prime minister, Winston Churchill, and met with General Dwight D. Eisenhower, the new commander of American forces in the European theater. Eisenhower handed him one of only three sets of secret plans for the upcoming landings in North Africa and asked that he hand deliver it to Stimson and Army Chief of Staff General George C. Marshall.

While Rickenbacker addressed the country's concerns, Adamson visited an old Army friend, Freddie Brisson, at his home in Hollywood, California. The two, who had been officers in the Army Air Corps (redesignated as the Army Air Forces earlier in 1941), shared a love of reading and discussing topics such as religion and philosophy. Freddie, by then a respected film producer, befriended the popular actor Cary Grant. The heartthrob introduced Brisson to a woman Grant felt was perfect for Freddie,

Colonel Hans Christian Adamson in early 1943. His friendships with Eddie Rickenbacker and with actress Rosalind Russell played important roles in the Pacific saga from which he returned.

AUBURN UNIVERSITY, SPECIAL COLLECTIONS & ARCHIVES

Actress Rosalind Russell (left), Colonel Hans Christian Adamson's friend, holds a guest register at a charity event to benefit Chinese war orphans in Los Angeles on October 7, 1941. Next to her are two other famous actresses of the 1930s and 1940s, Jane Withers and Mary Pickford (right).

actress Rosalind Russell, a devout Catholic who had starred alongside Grant in the 1940 comedy *His Girl Friday*. The two began dating, married in October 1941, and settled into their Hollywood home.

Despite Adamson's agnosticism, Russell had grown fond of her husband's friend. She said that Adamson "was one of the best-read men I have ever known, which is why Freddie and I took so seriously his views on religion." The man who neither believed nor disbelieved in an almighty being often exchanged ideas with the actress, but while he admired Russell's Catholic faith, he could not embrace it. "I try to understand your churches and your little medals and things," he told her, "but I cannot. So I cannot believe."

Adamson surprised Russell during this July visit by reaching into his pocket and retrieving a religious medal of the seventeenth-century Franciscan priest St. Joseph of Cupertino, the patron saint of aviators. Adamson had purchased it as a gift for Freddie, but Russell grabbed his hand and said, "No. Keep that yourself."[28]

Adamson tried to protest, but Russell refused to let him hand over the gift to her husband. As she would explain later,

The medal of St. Joseph of Cupertino, the patron saint of aviators, helped Hans Christian Adamson endure the ocean travails. Actress Rosalind Russell asked Adamson to keep it with him during his trip across the Pacific.

she sensed not only that it was the right thing to do but also that their friend might need it. Adamson, not wanting to offend the actress, tucked the medal in his pocket, figuring its presence could not do any harm.

"TAKE THAT MEDAL OUT AND PUT IT IN YOUR HAND"

The tours to boost morale among American airmen were preludes to Rickenbacker's next endeavor. He had been back in the United States only a week when Secretary Stimson asked him to deliver a secret message to General Douglas MacArthur, then guiding the fighting in New Guinea as commander of the US Army Forces in the Far East. The message was so sensitive that Stimson refused to put his request in writing and asked Rickenbacker to memorize the dispatch before he left the secretary's office. Both men, as well as MacArthur, never subsequently divulged its contents, but the message was most likely a stern rebuke of the general for his harsh criticism of President Franklin D. Roosevelt and top military leaders for prioritizing the European war over the Pacific conflict. The message also likely contained a request for the general to reduce his public appearances, which some, including Roosevelt, considered an indication that MacArthur intended to oppose the incumbent in the 1944 presidential election.

Rickenbacker was the perfect messenger to relay the rebuke. His prominence in the country—as a racer at Indianapolis, as a Medal of Honor recipient, and as a survivor of multiple plane crashes—was more than a match for the imperial, arrogant general, another Medal of Honor recipient who never shied from referencing his impressive military record. MacArthur would not intimidate him.

Stimson asked Rickenbacker to leave for New Guinea immediately and said

General Douglas MacArthur's fame rivaled that of any other American military commander. Eddie Rickenbacker was on his way across the Pacific to see the leader when his B-17 disappeared.

that while he could bring Adamson along, he would have to forgo the masseuse and osteopath. Eddie, weary from the previous tours and still recovering from the Atlanta crash, hated the thought of sitting in cramped, cold military aircraft for hours at a time, but he considered Stimson's request a summons to duty in wartime and was certain that he could muster enough strength to endure the journey.

On October 17 Rickenbacker and Colonel Adamson left on an overnight flight from New York City to San Francisco, where he visited his mother, Lizzie, and brother Dewey. Lizzie had never been comfortable with the death-defying antics of her son, but this trip bothered her more than his previous feats. She begged Eddie to stay home, but the aviator promised he would be back before she knew it. "My mother felt that something was going to happen to Eddie and asked him not to go," said Dewey, "but he just laughed and reassured her that everything would be all right."[29]

Adamson needed reassurance of his own. Earlier that month he had telephoned his Hollywood friend, Freddie Brisson, in the middle of the night to inform him and his wife, actress Rosalind Russell, of his concern about accompanying Eddie Rickenbacker on a secret mission to the Pacific. "Hans kept saying that he felt nervous," Russell explained. "He had never talked that way before. There is not a bit of cowardice in Hans Adamson yet he kept saying the trip had a fatality to it."

The actress concluded that Adamson sought words of comfort before leaving on what he thought might be a hazardous assignment. She sat upright in bed and asked him, "Hans, do you have that medal that you tried to give Freddie some time ago?" As if embarrassed, Adamson hesitated before saying, "Yes. I've got it in my pocket with my change."

"Now, mind you," replied Russell, "I don't think anything is going to happen. But if it does, if something should go wrong, you take that medal out and put it in your hand and hold on to it."

Adamson remained silent a few seconds before answering, "Yes."[30]

ON OCTOBER 19 Rickenbacker and Adamson boarded a plane in San Francisco for the fifteen-hour flight to Hawaii. Even though Eddie could move about the aircraft and flex his muscles, the lengthy time aboard aggravated his stricken body. His discomfort took a back seat, however, to what he saw when the plane descended for its landing in Hawaii. Even now, ten months after the Japanese attack had all but shattered the Pacific Fleet in Pearl Harbor, the sight of ruined facilities and sunken ships stunned Rickenbacker and Adamson.

After inspecting air units on the island into the afternoon of October 20, Rickenbacker headed to Hickam Field to board what he had been assured would be a newer-model aircraft manned by a top-notch crew. Instead of a spacious, shiny B-24 bomber, he was driven to an older B-17 that had been retired from combat operations to be used in training in the United States.

Disappointed with the plane, Eddie hoped that the crew, at least, would meet his expectations.

"SOMEDAY YOU'LL PRAY FOR HELP"

One of those crew members, Johnny Bartek, had enlisted in the Army and was dispatched to Hawaii as part of a coastal artillery unit. Along the way, he took up photography as a hobby. He purchased an expensive camera with which he took photos of luxurious Hawaiian scenery and tourist attractions, and subsequently sold copies of those photographs to his buddies.

While Rickenbacker leaned on karma and good fortune to pull him through rough moments, Bartek had religion. As a youth, he had attended a Baptist church, but more from a sense of duty and obedience to his mother than from any spiritual benefits. Mary noticed Johnny's lukewarm attitude toward church services and Bible reading, and warned him that one day he was going to land in trouble and need God's assistance. "Yonko [Slavic for John], someday you'll pray for help because man himself won't be able to help you, only God."[31] He dutifully attended church in Hawaii, once again mostly to appease Mary Bartek.

The engineer aboard the bomber, Private Johnny Bartek, considered Eddie Rickenbacker his childhood hero. He was ecstatic at the opportunity to fly with his idol.

After a year in the coastal artillery, Bartek, passionate about flying and airplane mechanics, asked for a transfer to the Army's aviation branch. The Army granted the request, with the proviso that Johnny remain in the Army another three years. Unwilling to accept those terms, Bartek completed his tour and returned to Freehold, New Jersey, where he worked as a freelance photographer at weddings and other ceremonies.

The attack on Pearl Harbor pulled Johnny back into the service, and the youth reenlisted in the Army Air Forces on January 8, 1942. He hoped to be posted to a bomber crew, but the Army assigned him instead to the newly established Air Transport Command as a flight engineer. Rather than combat, in the ATC he would serve as part of a crew tasked with delivering new aircraft to the front, an unexciting prospect that to him offered nothing but boredom and dull routine.

Before Johnny left Freehold for the Pacific, in April the town's First Baptist Church gave him a New Testament containing an appendix filled with popular prayers and selected verses from the Old Testament. Bartek carried it with him in his travels and occasionally flipped through the pages, but he rarely used it to gain insight. Its value lay in the connection to home and family.

In the first week of October, Bartek received orders to join a B-24 bomber crew for a flight across the Pacific. Johnny wrote his mother that she should not worry if she failed to hear from him for the next three weeks, but could add little more as he then knew no details of his upcoming flight. Once the plane was airborne, officers told Bartek and the crew that along with three other B-24s, they were journeying to Brisbane, Australia.

Shortly before the plane took off, a letter from home informed Bartek that his sister Ruth, age seventeen, had collapsed and died while walking to school, apparently the aftereffect of an accident she had suffered the day before. Bartek briefly thought of asking for permission to go home for his sister's funeral, but he concluded he should obey orders and remain in the Pacific.

The four crew members with whom Bartek would fly, all members of the ATC, offered an excellent mixture of Army veterans with relative newcomers like Bartek. Twenty-seven-year-old Texas native Captain William T. Cherry Jr. had studied at Hardin-Simmons University in Abilene, Texas, where his leadership talents led to his being voted freshman class president. However, before receiving his degree, Cherry left college, obtained his wings, and joined American Airlines as a copilot of large passenger planes. That experience, which included a few flights from Hawaii to Australia, aptly prepared him for flying the ATC's massive, four-engine bombers over Pacific waters. Awaiting him at home were a wife and a two-year-old daughter.

Cherry presented a dashing figure, replete with a Vandyke beard and cowboy boots. According to his copilot, Second Lieutenant James C. Whittaker, Cherry was the epitome of an aviator, "a sturdy, drawling Texan." The broad-shouldered Cherry transfixed people with his steely blue eyes and with his habit of speaking deliberately, as if each word was essential. "As a copilot, I have flown thousands of miles with Bill Cherry, and I've never had a better partner," said Whittaker. "He is calm in crisis, stoical in adversity, and possessed of a drawling humor that saved many a situation in the blazing days to come."[32]

Captain William T. Cherry Jr. in early 1943. His skill as a pilot enabled him to safely ditch the B-17 Flying Fortress in the Pacific. However, during the twenty-four days adrift, he and Eddie Rickenbacker clashed over who was in overall command, a dispute that irreparably drove a wedge between the two.

Forty-year-old Whittaker, a Missouri native, started a three-year stint in the Navy in 1919. Upon being discharged, he worked in the construction business and took up flying as a hobby in 1927, the year Charles Lindbergh conquered the Atlantic Ocean. Like Bartek, Whittaker entered the Army Air Forces shortly after Pearl Harbor in hopes of flying combat aircraft, but as his age disqualified him for that duty, the Army assigned him to the Air Transport Command. Whittaker brought a wealth of flying experience to the crew, as in the last few months, he had conducted numerous trips to the Southwest Pacific.

The resident of Burlingame, California, sported dark eyes that beamed from a chiseled face beneath a crop of gray hair. Whittaker scorned religion and claimed to be an atheist who believed that the power of the human mind controlled man's fate, not some notion of a distant, invisible God.

Everyone liked affable, smiling Staff Sergeant James W. Reynolds, the plane's radioman. The resident of Oakland, California, took a bit of teasing from the other crew members about his engagement, announced shortly before leaving on this mission, but the good-natured Reynolds laughed it off and said he could not wait to return to the United States and marry his sweetheart.

The fifth crew member, twenty-four-year-old Second Lieutenant John J. De Angelis, loved his Italian heritage, sports, and dancing. The native of Nesquehoning, Pennsylvania, graduated from the Citadel military college in South Carolina. Handsome, dark haired, with piercing eyes and pencil mustache, De Angelis reminded people of the swashbuckling movie star Errol Flynn. When exams and classwork did not

Second Lieutenant James C. Whittaker in early 1943. The Flying Fortress copilot, a lifelong atheist, experienced a religious conversion while on the ocean, and later embarked on lengthy tours to speak to church groups and other organizations about his experiences.

intrude, he dazzled onlookers as he glided about the floor at the Lakewood and Lakeside dance halls in Nesquehoning to popular romantic ballads crooned by Frank Sinatra and Bing Crosby, or jitterbugging to the big band music of Glenn Miller, Benny Goodman, and Duke Ellington. Colonel Adamson described him as having "the nervous and impatient energy of a fox terrier."[33]

After being commissioned an officer, the former Catholic altar boy studied navigation and was assigned to the Air Transport

Command. He had extra motivation to return home as soon as possible, as only two days before leaving the West Coast for the Pacific, De Angelis married his fiancée, Mary Yuskanish, in a civil ceremony. He vowed that when he returned, they would be properly married in a Catholic church.

The transpacific flight unfolded smoothly until the approach into Brisbane, when suddenly the landing gear light warned Captain Cherry of a problem. He ordered Bartek to inspect the equipment, and the young engineer discovered that while the nose wheel had correctly moved into position, it had failed to lock and would most likely collapse upon hitting the runway. The crew sat silently as Cherry descended, hoping that their first sight of Australia would not also be their last. "Captain Cherry gently touched down on the main landing wheels," recalled Bartek, "dragged the tail skid to slow the plane's forward momentum, and then gently let the nose down, causing superficial damage, scraping the paint from the bottom of the nose wheel area. A perfect landing, nobody hurt."[34]

Bartek, Whittaker, and the rest of the crew had avoided a close call, and witnessing Captain Cherry so calmly land the B-24 reassured them that his reputation as a skilled pilot was well deserved. They agreed, however, that they had no desire to experience that kind of landing again.

After a brief layover in Brisbane, the crew left Australia for the easterly route back to Pearl Harbor. The vastness of the Pacific Ocean fascinated Bartek, who for much of the time saw nothing but water as the bomber hummed toward the islands. He reminisced about a trip two years earlier, when he was aboard an Army transport ship traveling from Hawaii to Panama, "and how depressing it was for just one week or so at sea, surrounded by only sky and water."[35] His thoughts drifted to anyone in peril in that immense body of salt water and how difficult it would be to survive such a predicament. He thought of how, in 1937, the acclaimed aviatrix Amelia Earhart had vanished without a trace midway across the Pacific while attempting to fly around the world in a twin-engine monoplane, and of how grateful he was to be flying in a modern B-24 with four crew members accompanying him. The last place he wanted to be was in that unfriendly ocean.

In contrast, copilot James Whittaker referred to the Pacific as viewed from an altitude of 5,000 feet above the surface as "a beautiful sight." Nature's gorgeous vistas never failed to surprise him, and the blue ocean, so serene from his vantage high in the air, did not disappoint.

During a break Lieutenant Whittaker stretched his legs and checked on the crew in the cabin. He glanced at Bartek, whom he described as "a serious kid of 20 from New Jersey; red haired and freckled." Aside from Cherry and himself, the young man was the busiest person on the plane because he had to monitor the gasoline levels, know when to switch tanks during the flight, and, in their approach to Hawaii, make certain that the landing gear had lowered and locked in place.

Whittaker also noticed that whenever possible, Bartek read from a small, khaki-covered New Testament. Whittaker never gave much credence to the lessons of the Old or New Testament and remarked that "the sight of that little Bible and Johnny's serious red face as he read from it invariably handed me a chuckle."[36]

Flying in a sturdy bomber with an excellent crew was faith enough for him. He would leave the prayers and Bible readings to others.

CHAPTER 3

"It Was Obvious to All of Us That We Were in Grave Danger"

To the Ditching, October 20–21, 1942

UPON LANDING AT Hickam Field late in the afternoon of October 18, the five men were told that they would be part of a unit flying four obsolete B-17 bombers to the continental United States for use in training. The good news meant that they would soon receive time off to see families and girlfriends.

In the early afternoon of October 20, Bartek drove to Hickam to check on the B-17D they were to use later that day. Upon arrival, he was delighted to see Cherry already on the scene, carefully inspecting his plane. The pilot greeted Bartek and then shared a secret. Instead of heading home, they were reversing course and flying west on a special assignment that he was not at liberty to discuss. Cherry added, however, that Bartek would be thrilled about the famous passenger they were to transport.

Bartek peppered Cherry with names, including President Roosevelt and Charles Lindbergh, hoping to learn the identity of the mysterious traveler. He considered mentioning Eddie

Eddie Rickenbacker and his seven companions left Hawaii in a B-17D similar to this one, nicknamed "the Swoose." Rickenbacker looked out at the ocean through a small window on the aircraft's right side as the plane, short on fuel, descended toward the surface.

Rickenbacker but omitted him because he knew the aviator was still recuperating from his Atlanta crash. Bartek loved the notion of flying an important figure to his destination, but hated the thought of delaying a visit home, where he could comfort his grieving parents.

Bartek was working at the bomber when a staff car deposited two Army officers and a civilian at the airfield. The civilian, wearing a Burberry coat, business suit, and fedora, leaned heavily on a cane as he walked awkwardly toward the young mechanic. Bartek wondered why the Army would be transporting an infirm individual until he recognized the passenger. "To my surprise I was being introduced to and shaking hands with the ace of aces Captain Eddie Rickenbacker," said Bartek. "I was at a loss for words and could only muster 'nice to meet you.'"[1]

Rickenbacker looked old and nothing like the flamboyant aviator Bartek imagined. He wondered if Rickenbacker should still be in a hospital recovering from the crash instead of boarding an aircraft for a lengthy transpacific flight, but nonetheless, here Bartek was, staring at his idol. He made a mental note that somewhere along the route, he should query Rickenbacker about his wartime experiences in Europe. "All my life up until that point, that's all I wanted to do,"[2] he said.

"MY NAME IS RICKENBACKER"

When Whittaker and the other crew members arrived at the bomber, they learned that their plans had been altered and that they would instead transport an important person across the Pacific. Disappointment masked their faces, but orders were orders.

That discontent faded, however, when they discovered they were flying Eddie Rickenbacker to Brisbane. "There was not one of us who did not know all about Eddie Rickenbacker, America's No. 1 ace of World War I, who knocked down more German war planes than any other American," said Whittaker. Each man had read about Rickenbacker's fame on the racetracks and his feats during the first world conflict, but something more attracted them to the flier, and Whittaker knew that the entire crew "wanted to meet the man who had survived so many thrilling escapes from death both in war and in civilian life. Being a flying man myself, I think I was most thrilled by his courage

Sergeant Alexander Kaczmarczyk in 1942. He, Eddie Rickenbacker, and Colonel Hans Christian Adamson were the three passengers flying aboard the B-17 with its crew of five.

Auburn University, Special Collections & Archives

while lying pinned beneath a wrecked airliner in Georgia, seriously injured and soaked in gasoline, yet directing the rescuers."[3] The mission would delay their return home by only a handful of days, and they could wait to see family until after they had concluded this relatively routine flight across the Pacific.

One other passenger accompanied Rickenbacker and Colonel Adamson. Twenty-two-year-old native of Torrington, Connecticut, Sergeant Alexander Kaczmarczyk, a veteran in the Air Forces who had served in Panama, Guatemala, and Hawaii, boarded the plane to rejoin his unit in the South Pacific after a seven-week stay in the hospital while recovering from yellow jaundice and an appendectomy.

While in the hospital, Kaczmarczyk had written a bundle of letters to his girlfriend, Coreen Bond, whom he nicknamed Snooks. They had first met in the late 1930s at a popular Connecticut roller-skating rink, and after he enlisted in the Air Corps in 1939, they exchanged letters. In July 1942, shortly before he was to leave for the Pacific, Alex and Coreen announced their engagement and made plans to marry the next time Kaczmarczyk came home. After writing the letters, Kaczmarczyk arranged for a friend to mail them, one by one, so that Coreen would receive a note every few days while he was in the Pacific.

Shortly before leaving the United States for the Pacific, Kaczmarczyk, a devout Catholic, had tried to comfort his mother. "Don't worry mother," he wrote. "God is good to me." Mrs. Kaczmarczyk appreciated her son's thoughtfulness and said, "He knew I used to worry about him because he was in the Air Forces. I would tell him I thought it was dangerous up in those airplanes. He told me often not to worry."[4]

RICKENBACKER HAD EARLIER asked Brigadier General William E. Lynd, who as commander of Hickam Field had arranged for a bomber to be prepped and ready to whisk the ace off the island, his opinion of the five crew members who would fly him westward. Lynd replied that they were part of the Air Transport Command with excellent records and experience in aviation both before and during the war.

His introduction to the crew, though, left Rickenbacker unimpressed. He liked that Captain Cherry had flown as a copilot for American Airlines but wondered why, despite his years with the company, he had never been elevated to pilot. His unease spiked with an initial glance at Cherry, who looked nothing like the crisp military aviator he had expected. Instead, Rickenbacker discovered "that my pilot was a Texan with a goatee and highheeled cowboy boots. But there wasn't much for me to do but go aboard."

He held similar reservations about the others. He thought

Whittaker was too old to still be a copilot and lacked experience in four-engine aircraft. When he learned that Sergeant Reynolds, the radio operator, planned to marry his sweetheart in two weeks, he worried that the fellow might not be as focused on his job as he should be.

Rickenbacker appreciated that Lieutenant De Angelis "had crossed the Pacific a half-dozen times as navigator and was considered to be very good,"[5] but he was uncomfortable that De Angelis had not logged the required hours of training with the sensitive equipment aboard the plane. He lacked practice with the intricate octant, whose multiple mirrors and prisms had to be perfectly aligned to produce accurate readings from the stars and sun, and the chronometer, which calculated air and ground speed. From his own experience, Rickenbacker knew that even a minor miscalculation in location or speed could easily cause Cherry to miss their first island layover on the way to Brisbane.

While concerned that Whittaker might be too old, Rickenbacker thought that Bartek might be too young. Eddie had succeeded because he learned how to overcome obstacles and endure rough times, but according to Rickenbacker, Bartek, naïve in the ways of the world, had "no worldly knowledge at all, an innocent youngster, very nice character, but like most youths he hadn't suffered during his early life or never had any particular failures"[6] from which he could absorb valuable lessons. Rickenbacker thought that Sergeant Kaczmarczyk's background in servicing bombers would help Bartek, but how effective would the sergeant be after spending so much time in a hospital? Rickenbacker nevertheless kept his reservations to himself, but he was uncomfortable lifting off in a cramped, older-model B-17 bomber manned by what he considered an inexperienced crew.

CHERRY AND WHITTAKER finished their preflight routines in the cockpit and prepared to start the engines as soon as their celebrated passenger boarded the aircraft. By 10:20 p.m. five crew members sat in their assigned positions, with Cherry in the left cockpit seat and copilot Whittaker in the right. To chart courses, Lieutenant De Angelis, the navigator, had squeezed into the nose compartment below and forward of Cherry and Whittaker, the location normally occupied by a bombardier on a bombing mission. Sergeant Reynolds sat amidships at a desk in the radio compartment of the bomb bay, while Bartek occupied his engineering post by the generator controls. Sergeant Kaczmarczyk, technically a passenger, sat in the bomb bay.

"Well, we're ready whenever he is," Cherry said to Whittaker, after their passengers' bags, containing high-priority mail and personal belongings, had been placed in the cabin. A few moments later, Whittaker felt a hand on his shoulder as two individuals sat down on jump seats just behind them. "My name is Rickenbacker,"[7] said one.

"ANYBODY HURT? ANYBODY HURT?"

Problems confounded Captain Cherry and the crew from the flight's onset. After leaving Hawaii, the pilot planned to stop first at Canton Island, the northernmost part of the Phoenix

Islands group. Located three degrees south of the equator and eight degrees east of the international date line, Canton, 1,900 miles southwest of Hawaii, extends a mere nine miles long and five miles wide. The tiny speck in the midst of the Pacific posed a significant problem for Lieutenant De Angelis, who would have to rely on his octant and other instruments to locate an island all but dwarfed by the ocean. However, the veteran of previous transpacific flights had accomplished the task before and was confident he would execute it again.

With the bomber idling on the airstrip and its interior darkened due to an island-wide blackout, Cherry waited to receive the tower's assent to depart. When the approval arrived at 10:30 p.m., Cherry opened the throttles and started down the runway. The pilot maintained pressure on one brake to counter the effects of a crosswind that threatened to nudge the aircraft off its path, but as he reached seventy-five miles per hour and was about to lift the plane from the runway, the brake expander tube on the starboard wheel burst, locking the landing gear and swerving the aircraft into a sudden lurch. In the bomb bay to the cockpit's rear, Rickenbacker felt the plane twirl wildly toward a cluster of hangars.

In his front-row seat in the plane's nose, where he had a clear view of the takeoff, Lieutenant De Angelis watched

Second Lieutenant John J. De Angelis in early 1943. He served as the navigator aboard the B-17 taking Eddie Rickenbacker to Australia.

AUBURN UNIVERSITY, SPECIAL COLLECTIONS & ARCHIVES

the runway spin beneath him as Cherry struggled to bring the plane back on its path. Should the pilot fail to halt the momentum, the B-17 would career straight into those hangars, with De Angelis witnessing the cause of his probable demise charging directly at him. Only Plexiglas and a few yards separated him from those hangars, and as the buildings neared, De Angelis realized that whether he would see his new bride again now rested in Captain Cherry's skills to regain control of the plane.

Cherry's quick reflexes averted a close call with the hangars, but in dodging the structures, he now lacked enough runway to lift off before plunging into the harbor waters up ahead. Navigator De Angelis held on for dear life as the bomber skidded down the rapidly disappearing strip, and wondered whether the inordinate strain placed on the bomber's wheels by Cherry's abrupt maneuvering might cause them to collapse and crush him beneath a disintegrating plane.

Down to his final options, Cherry switched off the ignition, waited for the plane's speed to drop, and, near the end of the runway, cut the rudder hard to the left to swing the tail about and put the bomber in a desperate spinning motion called a ground loop. The tactic, which rotates the plane in tight circles to halt momentum, placed excessive strain on the tires and gave everyone aboard a few anxious moments, but the ploy succeeded. The plane suddenly halted short of the runway's end with, according to Colonel Adamson, "a snap that should have cracked the necks of all aboard."[8]

Cherry's adroit moves prevented Rickenbacker from enduring yet another air disaster and possibly saved everyone's life. "The

Captain William T. Cherry Jr., pilot of the B-17, impressed even Eddie Rickenbacker with his ability to bring the large aircraft out of a dangerous ground loop while lifting off from Hawaii.

DRAWING COURTESY OF DUTTON

pilot, by clever manipulation of the engines, managed to swing back onto the runway," said Rickenbacker in praising Cherry's skills. After taking so many calculated chances in his life, Rickenbacker welcomed Cherry's willingness to purposely "risk a violent ground loop, which saved us from plunging into the bay."[9] He had avoided death once again, and with any luck, the remainder of his journey to visit General MacArthur should unfold calmly.

When the plane stopped its spin, Rickenbacker spoke up that he never thought the tires would hold. "You and me both," admitted Cherry. In his calm Texan drawl, the pilot turned to his famous passenger and said, "We got more of these, Captain. The crew and I will stand by until another plane is ready." Eddie said nothing but thought what everyone else was thinking: "Well, it had better not be like the first."[10]

Emergency crews in ambulances and crash trucks quickly arrived. Brigadier General William Lynd entered the bomber, frantically yelling, "Anybody hurt? Anybody hurt?" Rickenbacker answered, "Nobody's hurt, Bill! Everything is O.K."[11] Eager to begin his journey to Australia, he asked if another bomber could be rushed out to the runway.

Before the second aircraft taxied out, Lieutenant De Angelis checked his navigational equipment and noticed that the impact of the ground loop had thrown the octant across the plotting table and against a section of Plexiglas. If he were to accurately gain a fix on the bomber's position while flying the vast stretches of the Pacific, devoid of landforms and other navigational markers, he needed this delicate instrument to work properly. An octant, which calculated locations through a complex combination of airspeed, wind velocity, weather, and the angles between the sun, stars, and horizon, proved difficult to manage in normal conditions, but if its prisms and mirrors had been jarred out of alignment, De Angelis would be at a severe disadvantage. He was about to inspect his octant when the second bomber arrived, and with Rickenbacker's impatience to take off, De Angelis lacked the time to recalibrate the instrument. To reach Canton, he had to trust that the earlier mishap had not damaged the octant or other delicate equipment.

"I FLEW WITH RICKENBACKER AS MY PILOT. WOW!"

Captain Cherry assumed that when they received a second bomber, which happened to be another outdated B-17, to fly Rickenbacker to Australia, the plane would undergo the customary preflight check to ensure that everything worked properly. Lynd, however, bowed to his prominent passenger. Since Rickenbacker insisted on promptly lifting off rather than waiting two to three hours for the ground crew and others to approve the second aircraft, the general told Cherry to depart as soon as possible.

Cherry objected. As the pilot, he bore the responsibility for the safety of his passengers and crew, and he reminded Lynd of the risks involved in flying an uninspected aircraft on a lengthy flight over the Pacific. When Lynd abruptly terminated the exchange and threatened to replace Cherry if he continued to protest, the pilot, wishing to avert an end to a promising career, suppressed his objections and reluctantly agreed.

Irritated at being overruled by an aging businessman who had made his name as a flier more than two decades earlier, Cherry pegged Rickenbacker as a prima donna. Cockiness and arrogance were certainly not uncommon among aviators, and Cherry would be the first to admit that he, too, possessed those traits, but on this flight Rickenbacker was only a passenger, not the pilot in command of the aircraft. General Lynd should have ceded to Cherry's wishes, but the officer had already yielded to Eddie's requests. Would the national hero now expect Cherry to do his bidding? The first few moments of this flight created an unspoken tension between the two that would fester over the coming weeks.

Shortly after midnight, once the baggage and mail had been placed aboard and two cots had been added for Rickenbacker and Adamson, the Flying Fortress was ready for takeoff. When Rickenbacker asked Captain Cherry about weather conditions along the route to Canton Island, Cherry answered that he expected a smooth flight in a clear sky sparsely punctuated with a few scattered clouds. At 1:30 a.m. on October 21, Cherry guided the B-17 down the runway, lifted off beneath a beautiful moon, and climbed to 10,000 feet for the ten-hour flight to Canton, almost 2,000 miles to their southwest. De Angelis entered the cockpit to give Cherry the latest navigational information, while Rickenbacker and Adamson stepped back to the bomb bay to see if they could catch a brief nap on the cots. Because of the cold temperatures encountered at high altitudes, however, they only sporadically drifted off.

During Rickenbacker's flight from the mainland to Hawaii, and now again westward toward Australia, the Pacific's vastness mesmerized him. The Atlantic Ocean shrank in comparison with the Pacific's immense reaches and its long stretches devoid of land. For fifteen hours, his plane from California had droned over nothing but water, and that leg to Hawaii comprised not even a third of the distance he must now travel to meet General MacArthur. He faced a ten-hour flight southwest to Canton, 1,300 miles southwest to Suva in the Fiji Islands, followed by two similar 900-mile flights southwest to New Caledonia and Brisbane.

Captain Cherry estimated that they would reach Canton by 9:30 a.m. Normally, planes flying the Hawaii–Australia route stopped at Johnston Island or Christmas Island closer to Hawaii, but since Rickenbacker was in a hurry to reach MacArthur, they opted to fly 1,200 miles beyond Christmas Island directly to Canton. This alteration alarmed no one, as numerous flight crews had charted that route before, but it placed them closer to one of the most isolated portions of the Pacific, not far from the area where Amelia Earhart had disappeared. Should they miss Canton, they risked flying into a remote sector that saw sparse air and surface traffic and contained few accessible islands.

Before heading to his cot, Rickenbacker had briefly chatted with Cherry and Whittaker, and all agreed that the bomber operated smoothly on a beautiful night for flying. Once he slid under the blanket, though, something the pilot had mentioned nagged at him. According to Cherry, the plane was being nudged along by a ten-mile-per-hour tailwind. Rickenbacker was certain, however, that the tailwind was as much as three times more powerful. He knew little about the pilot, but, through the years, Rickenbacker had developed a keen instinct about air and ground travel, and as he lay on his cot, those instincts had triggered an alarm. He said nothing to the pilot, but if his estimate was correct, De Angelis would rely on faulty information that would cause Cherry to increase his speed to compensate for what he thought was a milder tailwind. If so, that would place the plane farther to the southwest than Cherry thought. The ace's instincts would prove accurate, as records from other aviators flying at the same time registered tailwind speeds of up to thirty miles per hour.

Cherry climbed to 10,000 feet to remain above a cloud cover. Approximately halfway to Canton, the bomber passed near Palmyra Island, and De Angelis's readings indicated they were on course. At 5:00 a.m., Cherry asked Whittaker to take over the controls so that he could go back for a nap, but after a fruitless attempt to drift off in the cold—"It makes little difference whether you are flying over the equator or over Chicago in January,"[12] Whittaker said—Cherry returned to the cockpit and resumed flying.

When the sun peeked over the horizon an hour and a half later, Rickenbacker rejoined Cherry and inquired about the flight. While they breakfasted on coffee, orange juice, and sweet rolls, the pilot brought him up-to-date on what had been a routine trip. Following that exchange, Whittaker asked the ace, "Would you like to fly her a little, Captain?" Rickenbacker accepted the offer, although, he admitted, "I've probably forgotten how to fly by instruments." Eddie took the controls for an hour, all the time regaling the crew with the differences between piloting the B-17 and the World War I fighters he had flown two decades earlier. "I'm really lucky," thought Bartek. "I flew with Rickenbacker as my pilot. WOW!"[13]

What could go wrong with the famed World War I ace at the controls?

"IT WAS PLAIN NOW THAT WE WERE LOST"

At 8:30 a.m., Captain Cherry took the controls from Whittaker to begin the long, gradual descent for a 9:30 landing on Canton. When he leveled off at 1,000 feet, the crew searched for the island but saw only water in every direction to the horizon. Cherry attempted to obtain a bearing with the plane's direction finder, a device resting outside the fuselage and directly above the pilot that locks onto radio station beams to help determine location, but he could move the crank that turned the direction finder only one inch instead of a complete rotation.

"Jim, did this thing work okay during the takeoff this morning?" a puzzled Cherry asked his copilot. "It won't budge an inch now."[14] That simple method of plotting their position had been eliminated from his arsenal because no one in Hawaii had time to check the direction finder.

Whittaker took his turn with the crank, to no avail, as Cherry and the other crew members anxiously combed for Canton Island. "Bill, this doesn't look good to me,"[15] De Angelis said to Cherry. The navigator worried that their failure to recalibrate the octant and inspect the bomber before departing Hickam Field had now come back to haunt them in the middle of the Pacific, with no land in sight and with engines depleting their fuel supply every second.

Sitting behind Cherry, Rickenbacker sensed the familiar tension he had experienced before every near-calamity. Chaotic situations were nothing new to Eddie, but Cherry, not he, occupied the pilot's seat and would determine any reaction. Rickenbacker asked the captain how much gas he had left, and when Cherry answered that about four hours' worth remained in the tanks, Rickenbacker concluded that they had to locate Canton Island soon, or else they would run out of fuel. Adding to his apprehension was the fact that if he had correctly assessed the tailwind's strength, the plane might have already flown past Canton Island. Rickenbacker told Cherry that he thought the pilot had underestimated the tailwind's actual strength by twenty miles. "I believe we've overshot the island," he said. "I think we ought to get cross bearings in order to find out just exactly where we are."[16]

Transpacific air travel in 1942 was hardly routine, but an excess of mishaps had plagued this flight from the start. A faulty brake expander almost caused a deadly crash into Hickam's hangars, in the process damaging a valuable octant that led Lieutenant De Angelis to obtain incorrect navigational fixes. Rickenbacker's impatience to depart in the second bomber left no time for Cherry or the ground crew to inspect the aircraft, or for De Angelis to check that his octant, a device that each navigator carried from plane to plane, worked properly. A stubborn crank thwarted their attempts to gain a precise fix on Canton Island with the direction finder, and an errant estimate of the tailwind's strength had likely pushed them beyond their destination. "It was plain now that we were lost," Rickenbacker wrote later, "and the first sight of nervousness appeared in the crew."[17]

One hour after their expected arrival time, Cherry contacted Canton Island and asked to establish a "lost plane" procedure. In that technique, the ground station on Canton takes two bearings, fifteen minutes apart, based on information sent from the plane to the base. Lines are drawn on a map from those two bearing points to the station, which enables the station to plot the plane's position and provide the pilot with the proper course for a descent into Canton Island. Unfortunately, the island operator could not provide any bearings as the equipment needed to conduct the procedure had only recently arrived and had not yet been removed from its shipping crates.

"That's cute,"[18] Cherry muttered sarcastically upon hearing the message. Rickenbacker silently observed the events and wished he were flying in one of his Eastern Air Lines planes, which carried up-to-date radio and weather aids in the cockpits that military aircraft lacked.

Cherry handed the controls to Whittaker and went below into the nose compartment to confer with De Angelis. The navigator suggested that his octant might have been damaged at Hickam Field, and as a result, each time he had attempted to gain a fix since leaving Hawaii, he received incorrect readings, possibly by as much as several degrees. Cherry understood that even if the octant yielded minor miscalculations, those inaccurate figures could cause them to miss Canton Island, either to its west or east, by hundreds of miles.

In the cockpit, Rickenbacker and Whittaker hushed when Cherry returned and explained that as they had now gone past their estimated time of arrival, they had undoubtedly flown by Canton Island. Rickenbacker agreed with Cherry's summation when the Texan added glumly, "We're lost."[19]

Cherry ordered Reynolds to contact the radio operator on

Palmyra Island, situated to their northeast, midway between Hawaii and Canton, and request that they transmit a radio signal. If Palmyra could not help, the eight men would be faced with flying in a sparsely used region of the Pacific without proper navigational bearings. No one dared mention that somewhere to the northwest lay Howland Island, Amelia Earhart's destination in her tragic 1937 around-the-world flight, which resulted in her disappearance. If it could happen to that famous aviatrix, the probability that it might again occur, this time to them, seemed all too real to the eight men aboard. "By then, it was obvious to all of us that we were in grave danger,"[20] said Rickenbacker.

Everyone hoped Palmyra had the equipment that Canton lacked, and when its radio operator replied he would relay a proper course, tension in the bomber eased considerably. Unfortunately, the island's radio operator mistook the Rickenbacker B-17 for another bomber arriving on a different path and relayed to Reynolds a reading intended for that B-24, further compounding the situation.

SINCE EACH MOMENT used in trying to determine the proper course of action consumed more of the bomber's precious fuel and took them farther from Canton Island, Cherry had no time to waste. He asked Reynolds to see if he could raise other island bases, but the only response came from one that stood 1,000 miles away, too great a distance to be of any aid. Cherry faced a multitude of dire issues—a steadily depleting fuel supply, lack of contact with air bases that could lend a hand, and flying blindly into an unfamiliar region of the Pacific where assistance would be doubtful. He had endured other tight spots before, including the recent near mishap in Brisbane, but he had never been confronted with one offering so many uncertainties.

Cherry turned to the box procedure in hopes of locating Canton. He announced he would fly forty-five minutes in one direction before turning 90 degrees to the right and doing the same. Two additional repetitions would complete the box, thereby permitting the crew to scan a broad area of the ocean on each leg. Fortunately, the cloud cover had begun to dissipate, yielding a decent view of the ocean surface from 5,000 feet. The pilot estimated that upon completing the maneuver, they would have about one hour's worth of fuel remaining.

Cherry had just commenced the first leg when Rickenbacker remembered a World War I tactic he and other aviators in distress had used. He was probably grasping at a last-ditch measure with scant chance of success, but with time running out, it offered their best hope. He suggested that Cherry should request that Canton fire antiaircraft shells, whose bursts might create beacons to guide them in. Cherry ordered Reynolds to send a query asking the island base to fire shells at five-minute intervals, set to explode at 8,000 feet. Canton's radio operator responded that they would immediately begin firing, as well as scramble planes to begin searching for the lost B-17.

WHILE CHERRY ASCENDED to 10,000 feet to take the bomber above any shell bursts, the crew and passengers scanned the sky for any signs of antiaircraft fire. "I strained my eyes for the grayish black shell bursts that would locate our island and for the planes that would lead us in," said Whittaker, who sat beside Cherry. "I searched the far rims of the cloud bank, the blue vault of the sky above me, and the watery blue floor far below." Eight pairs of eyes scoured the ocean and the heavens, but only clouds and blue sky stretched for miles from both sides of the plane. "Never had I seen a world so ominously empty,"[21] added Whittaker.

The plane droned on after Canton ended its firing. Running out of both time and remedies, their sole remaining hope was that someone on the B-17 would locate the island. Should that fail, Cherry would have to consider ditching the massive bomber in the ocean, something that no pilot had ever accomplished with an aircraft of that size.

The crew again stared out the windows, praying that Canton would suddenly materialize. Men gazed so intensely that a phenomenon called "island eyes" tricked them into seeing an island where no landform existed. White-capped waves became water crashing against reefs surrounding an island, and shadows cast upon the Pacific's surface from clouds above assumed land-like shapes. Cherry turned into the second leg and then the third, but again only water spread before them. The immensity of the Pacific Ocean, so awe-inspiring earlier, had morphed into a life-threatening entity.

"Well, we flew the whole course and in the meantime we saw nothing out in the vast Pacific," recalled Bartek. "We covered hundreds of miles and still nothing. I figured we would at least find somebody trying to get away from the war in some ship out there, some little sailboat or something, find the Japs or something, but there was nothing out there. But we realized how big the ocean was."[22]

"RICK, I HOPE YOU LIKE THE SEA"

Captain Cherry bore a heavy burden, but just as big was the responsibility Rickenbacker and Adamson faced. From their September meeting with General Eisenhower, both knew the details of the early November assault against German forces in North Africa. Should the Japanese capture either man, the enemy would subject him to torture, and if he revealed what he knew, the Japanese would pass it along to their ally Germany, which would then prepare defenses and plan countermoves to repel the US offensive. Hundreds, possibly thousands, of American lives would be lost, and the Allied war effort against Hitler would suffer a grievous setback. The two quietly agreed that, should capture appear imminent, they would jump from their life rafts and drown in the ocean rather than being taken alive. They kept this decision to themselves in case American units rescued them, which would make their choice moot, and to prevent the others from trying to talk them out of it in the event that Japanese forces closed in.

While the crew continued to look for an island refuge, Cherry cut power to the two outboard engines to save fuel and prolong their time in the air. He figured that even ten additional minutes might deliver the opportunity to spot an island or come across a ship's wake. Cherry, certain that some radio operator would receive their transmission, told Reynolds to begin sending the distress signal and to keep broadcasting the SOS until moments before the bomber hit the surface.

When the SOS transmissions elicited no response, the group faced a nearly hopeless predicament. Once they ditched, not only did the eight men have no clue about their location, but potential rescue planes or ships could not possibly know where to begin looking for them either. "Wherever we were, no American could hear us," Rickenbacker wrote later. "That meant that, even if we made a successful crash landing on the water, nobody would know which way to look for us."[23]

Staff Sergeant James W. Reynolds in early 1943. The radioman aboard the B-17 weighed less than 100 pounds after enduring twenty-four days drifting on the Pacific Ocean.

AUBURN UNIVERSITY, SPECIAL COLLECTIONS & ARCHIVES

A sense of isolation and distance from all that could be helpful, from all that was friendly and familiar, enveloped the eight people aboard the B-17 as it hummed above the Pacific Ocean. Until now, they had simply been on their way to their next destination, which in turn would lead them back home to loved ones and all that was comfortable. Suddenly everything in the

United States, including their parents, wives, children, and futures, all but disappeared. If they could not locate Canton Island, the men knew that finding their way back home might be nearly impossible.

"Rick, I hope you like the sea," Adamson dryly remarked to his friend. "I think we're going to spend a long time on it." Rickenbacker agreed and then suppressed his irritation when he thought of Cherry. "Well, my young friend," he mused, "your cowboy boots and goatee are going to look pretty damn funny in the middle of the Pacific."[24]

While friction simmered between the veteran aviator and the young bomber pilot, from his seat beside Cherry, Whittaker appreciated Cherry's coolness under stress. Eight lives depended on his ability to place a 35,000-pound bomber atop an ocean. If the Texan succeeded, they had a slim chance of being located and rescued, but if he failed, eight men would most likely be dead in moments.

Cherry knew that ditching the Flying Fortress would tax every talent he possessed, but once he determined his method, his anxieties dissipated. He would execute his plan and leave the outcome to fate and to God.

He first had to lighten the bomber's weight before attempting the emergency landing, for each ounce of material tossed overboard could mean the difference between a successful landing and one that terminated with either a shattering impact onto the surface or a sudden plunge below the waves. Cherry ordered every piece of luggage thrown out of the plane, as well as any loose items that might, when they hit the ocean, endanger the men by rocketing about the inside of the plane. Rickenbacker and De Angelis loosened the bottom hatch in the bomber's rear section while the others grabbed their belongings and brought them to De Angelis near the hatch. De Angelis handed each piece to Kaczmarczyk or Rickenbacker, who tossed the luggage and cherished mementos overboard. Suitcases packed with favorite articles of clothing and briefcases stuffed with important documents littered the skies, and high-priority mail, the aircraft's toolbox, cots, blankets, and empty thermos bottles tumbled from the B-17 like a string of bombs.

One by one, men let go of personal possessions they only moments before had assumed were safe, or keepsakes they might have handed down to children one day. The loss of each item further frayed the imaginary bond with home and reinforced the crushing sense of aloneness above the ocean. Bartek

Johnny Bartek's copy of the New Testament that he took with him from the B-17 as the bomber was sinking. At first scorned by a few in the rafts, the book gradually became a crucial ingredient in helping the men survive more than three weeks without sufficient food, water, and other basic needs.

Monmouth County Historical Association

stared at his expensive Leica camera, and then at the New Testament his church had given him, and decided that his faith, however tenuous it had been in his young life, was more important. "I thought for a split second," he wrote, "and the camera went overboard." The young engineer handed the Leica to De Angelis for disposal, for as he explained, "Material things aren't worth anything when your life is at stake."[25]

Rickenbacker tossed out the new, expensive Burberry coat that he had purchased in London a few weeks earlier, as well as the baggage he had brought with him, including a beautiful suitcase that Eastern Air Lines employees had given him as a Christmas gift two years earlier. Before hurling it out the hatch, Rickenbacker removed a handful of handkerchiefs that Adelaide had purchased for him in Paris and stuffed them in his pocket, figuring they could provide protection from a sun he assumed would, in the unlikely event that they remained on a raft for a day or two, become intolerably hot. He hesitated over his brief-case, which contained important business papers, but it, too, joined the procession of belongings plummeting through the sky. "Let the moment come when nothing is left but life and you will find that you do not hesitate over the fate of material posses-sions, however deeply they may have been cherished,"[26] he said.

"WE WERE IN FOR A BONE-BREAKING LANDING"

While Rickenbacker and the others lightened the bomber's load, Cherry and Whittaker discussed options for setting down the plane. Cherry had to rest the B-17 in precisely the correct spot to avoid a disaster. If he clipped the top portion of a wave, the bomber's nose might plunge into the middle of the following wave and collapse. If he smashed directly into a wave, the impact would rip the plane in half.

After exchanging ideas with his copilot, Cherry chose to fly into a crosswind and gently settle in the trough between two waves. He planned to go in while still under power so that he could better guide the bomber into the narrow opening between swells, and he advised Whittaker to be ready to cut power to the engines upon his order.

Seconds ticked away, each one further depleting the dwindling gasoline supply. Cherry ordered Bartek to pump the remaining fuel into the outboard tanks, at which the pilot cut power to the two inboard engines to reduce the likelihood that rotating propellers would spin off during the landing and slice into the cockpit. He then prepared to hit the surface.

In the bomb bay behind Cherry and Whittaker, Rickenbacker, Adamson, Bartek, De Angelis, and Kaczmarczyk placed emergency rations, including thermos bottles filled with water and coffee, beneath the escape hatch above Reynolds, and then donned their Mae West life vests. Rickenbacker reminded them not to inflate the devices until they had left the plane, and told Adamson, De Angelis, and Kaczmarczyk to lie on the floor, facing the tail section with their feet braced against the bulkhead. Five men who had expected a routine flight across the Pacific to Australia now assumed their positions inside the aircraft for the descent to the ocean surface.

They tried not to dwell on the negative outcomes—a sudden, violent death in a ditching gone wrong, or a tortuous purgatory on the surface until heat, hunger, thirst, or sharks ended their lives while rescue craft fruitlessly searched for them—and for the moment pushed aside thoughts of people back home. Instead, they silently waited for an impact that would determine if their lives ended in the next few moments.

While Bartek opened the emergency hatches above the cockpit, Rickenbacker helped Kaczmarczyk loosen the hatch above Reynolds to prevent it from jamming in the crash. Rickenbacker then stuffed a map, his passport, a chocolate candy bar, and a few important papers in his pockets. Sensing that once on the surface the eight men in three life rafts needed to remain together to increase their odds of survival, he wrapped around his body a sixty-foot length of line with which they could tie together the rafts. He then strapped himself in the right-hand seat by a window where, grasping a parachute to shield his face from the impact of hitting the ocean surface, he faced forward so he could look out the window and call out the diminishing distances to the surface as the aircraft lost altitude.

The five men in the bomb bay waited silently, surreptitiously observing their companions while hoping that the next handful of minutes would end favorably. They assumed a passive role while the bomber descended closer to the ocean, and much like a patient in the waiting room trusted his physician, they had faith that Captain Cherry would bring them through.

While Reynolds remained at his small desk on the left side of the bomber, hoping to receive a response as he continued to radio his pleas for assistance, De Angelis propped a mattress and parachute between him and the bulkhead to absorb some of the force from the landing, and crouched on the floor directly in front of Rickenbacker, facing him with his back to the mattress. Inches to De Angelis's right, Adamson did the same, and sat upright against the mattress while staring beyond Rickenbacker toward the rear. A few feet from the right-side trio of Rickenbacker, De Angelis, and Adamson, Sergeant Kaczmarczyk settled behind Reynolds, inclining his back against the radio operator's chair. The last few months had been trying for the ailing sergeant, who had yet to regain full strength from seven weeks in the hospital, but his bouts with yellow jaundice and an appendectomy seemed trivial compared with what he now faced.

With the bomber continuing its steady descent, Cherry asked Bartek to check that everyone was securely in place. Bartek did not consider it strange that Rickenbacker, in a chair looking out the window, still wore his hat, but he wondered why the man had a coil of rope wrapped around his waist. He saw no purpose in keeping the item but figured that with all the near-death experiences Rickenbacker had faced, including the serious Atlanta crash only a short time before, he must know what he was doing.

Bartek returned to the cockpit and reported to Cherry that everyone was ready. He looked for a cushion to place in front of him so he could better brace for the ocean landing, but Cherry and Whittaker had already wedged the cushions between themselves and the control panel. Expecting a rough ditching, Bartek sat directly behind Lieutenant Whittaker, beneath the life raft releases, and figured that he at least rested behind the copilot, whose slightly bigger frame might offer him extra protection. "If those two get killed, I'm going to use Whittaker as my cushion," he vowed. "I had no other choice."[27] His position near the escape hatch provided him with an excellent chance of exiting the plane before it sank, but only if Captain Cherry nestled the huge bomber on the ocean without it breaking into hundreds of pieces. If Cherry failed, Bartek would no longer have to worry. He would most likely be dead.

With Bartek ready to pull the levers that would deploy the two five-man life rafts, which they could quickly inflate once the rafts were ejected from the compartments, Cherry steadied the bomber in its continuing descent toward the ocean surface. No one knew how long a plane weighing almost eighteen tons would remain afloat—some guessed it would slip beneath the surface within five minutes, while the majority worried that the B-17 would sink immediately. To make it easier for them to swim from the plane, most tossed off their shoes, and some removed their pants, but Rickenbacker, concluding that those items would offer protection from the sun in case they lingered on the surface for a few days, kept everything on. He figured the Mae West he wore would keep him afloat.

As they entered their final approach, Whittaker turned to Cherry, offered his hand, and said, "It's sure been swell knowing you, Bill." Cherry, offering a more optimistic appraisal, gripped his hand and replied, "You're going to know me a long time yet, Jim. It's going to keep on being swell!"[28]

Bartek, who overheard the exchange, had no idea whether he would still be breathing in five minutes, but he was certain that even in the best-case scenario, "we were in for a bone-breaking landing."[29]

PART II

Week 1—Alone on the Pacific

CHAPTER 4

"We Were Truly Alone in the Pacific"

First Days on the Ocean, October 21–22

EVERYONE IN THE aircraft tensed as Cherry pushed the wheel forward and dropped the bomber into its descent. Behind the trio in the cockpit, Adamson knew that no one aboard doubted the pilot's abilities, "but every one realized, too, that unless God had both of his arms around them there was little hope that the impact of a twenty-five-ton bomber on a tossing sea would permit any one to escape unhurt and alive."[1]

Next to the colonel, Rickenbacker sat stoically as the plane approached the ocean's surface. During his racing events and his World War I escapades, life-threatening crises usually arrived suddenly, without warning, leaving him little time to think about what came his way. Now he could only wait as the minutes ticked by and brought him steadily toward his fate. He was not even fully recovered from the Georgia crash, yet here he was, staring at the same peril for the second time in twenty months.

Rickenbacker knew he could maintain his composure but

wondered about his companions. When he glanced at the other four men with him in the bomb bay, however, he saw no evidence of panic. Each man—De Angelis and Adamson at his feet, Reynolds sending SOS messages at his desk, and Kaczmarczyk sitting with his back to Reynolds on Rickenbacker's left—displayed only calm. "We were all silent. There was no panic," he wrote.

Rickenbacker had never thought of himself as religious, but he found himself at this moment turning to the Catholic medallion he had carried for twenty-five years. "I patted my upper left-hand pocket," he remembered. "That's where I have always kept the crucifix that my little friend gave me in 1917."[2]

"HOLD ON! HERE IT COMES!"

To soften the impact of the landing, Cherry feathered the propellers of the two idle engines, a process in which he rotated the plane in such a manner that the propellers' blade surfaces aligned with the airflow and reduced the air resistance. At the same time, Reynolds interrupted his barrage of SOS pleas to transmit the information that they had been flying for fourteen hours on a heading south-southwest of Oahu, and that they might have overshot their destination. He then returned to sending the three-letter distress signal. Somewhere, someone had to receive it, Bartek assumed, with a thought that was more prayer than declaration.

At first glance the ocean appeared serene to Bartek, providing Cherry with a relatively flat surface upon which to set the bomber, but as the B-17 descended, the waves he had assessed as gentle from a higher altitude suddenly transformed into ten- to fifteen-foot swells. His thoughts drifted to his quiet, hardworking father and his deeply religious mother, still grieving for the daughter they had recently lost. He wanted to comfort them in their sorrow but feared that he might instead force his parents to mourn the loss of a second offspring in less than a month.

He knew that his mother would whisper that he must trust in prayer and in God, but at this moment practicality mattered more, and the young engineer placed his faith in Captain Cherry's skills. He had already wit-

Captain William T. Cherry Jr.'s calm demeanor and skill as a pilot helped bring the group through its earliest major threat—death on the ocean from an unsuccessful attempt to ditch the bomber at sea.

THE CHERRY FAMILY COLLECTION

nessed Cherry handle a faulty nose wheel while approaching Brisbane and flawlessly conduct the tricky ground loop in Hawaii, so "I just did as Captain Cherry instructed me to do and trusted he would make all the right decisions"[3] to execute a perfect landing.

Cherry turned southwest in hopes of ditching closer to the air and shipping lanes linking Samoa with Hawaii, which might increase their chances of being rescued. Other than Rickenbacker, whose view out the window offered him a vantage the others lacked, the men waiting in the bomb bay could see nothing outside. Their world had shrunk to the bomb bay confines, a cramped space resting between the cockpit in front and machine gun mounts, cables, and other military paraphernalia to the rear. Unlike the trio in the cockpit, they could neither see the ocean drawing nearer nor watch Cherry as he attempted to land the plane, and as a result, mental specters magnified the threats for which Cherry and Whittaker, busy with the ditching, had no time: Were they minutes from ditching into rough waters, or would they settle onto a calm surface beneath serene skies? Would they have time to exit the bomber, which everyone expected would sink within minutes, or would the ocean water gush into a damaged plane faster than they could move, turning the bomb bay into a ready-made coffin entombing them as the B-17 plunged to the ocean's depths?

A somber, quiet scenario unfolded in the bomb bay as the men, other than Sergeant Reynolds, who kept tapping his SOS signals, sat alone with their thoughts. The steady rap of the distress signal blended with the drone of the two engines as Kaczmarczyk, at age twenty-two the youngest of the group by a year over Bartek and De Angelis, tried to stifle the thought that the next few minutes could decide whether he would have a future with Snooks or whether she would receive a government telegram announcing his death or disappearance. Sitting directly at Rickenbacker's feet, Lieutenant De Angelis hoped that having a national figure aboard at least guaranteed a speedy rescue, and that after a minimal time afloat, he would be winging his way home, where he could once again take his wife to local dance halls and dazzle Nesquehoning onlookers.

Next to De Angelis, Colonel Adamson reflected on the pleasant visit he had enjoyed earlier in the year with Rosalind Russell and her husband, Freddie Brisson. The medal of St. Joseph of Cupertino, the patron saint of aviators, that Russell had insisted he keep, rested in his pocket. Adamson, who delivered lectures on prehistoric creatures and astronomy instead of reading Catholic religious tomes, as the actress did, now retrieved it, placed it in his hand, and clasped it tightly. The man of science had found solace in the medal.

As befitting a man who had survived repeated life-threatening situations, Rickenbacker refused to dwell on the predicament and focused on what he might do to alleviate their troubles. Since the four men with him, blind to everything outside the bomb bay, had no idea when the Fortress was about to hit, Rickenbacker followed the descent outside his window and shouted out the distances.

"Here's a situation where you can admire the guts of Captain Rickenbacker," recalled De Angelis. Instead of bracing himself with mattresses, as De Angelis and Adamson were then doing, Rickenbacker rose in his seat to have a better vantage and calmly relayed an estimate of the footage remaining to impact. "Fifty feet! Thirty!" Rickenbacker shouted as the ocean surface loomed larger out his window. Each time one of the others asked if it was time to brace, Rickenbacker cautioned, "Not yet, not yet." Like Bartek, the aviator noticed that the ocean churned and frothed in a series of angry ten-foot swells, certain to make Cherry's task more challenging. "For the first time, I realized that it was quite rough, with a long, heavy swell,"[4] he wrote.

In the cockpit, Lieutenant Whittaker thought the sea "was leaping up to meet us." With less than thirty seconds remaining, De Angelis asked, "Do you fellows mind, do you mind if I pray?" Captain Cherry, his hands full at the controls, replied, "What in the hell do you think we're doing?" and asked the lieutenant to say a prayer for him too. Strangely, the exchange incensed Whittaker, the lifelong agnostic. "I recall a feeling of intense irritation then at De Angelis' suggestion of prayer. I thought what a hell of a time to talk about praying when we need all our wits to save our lives! How often and how ashamedly was I to remember those brash thoughts in the days to come."[5]

As Captain William T. Cherry Jr. guided the B-17 toward the ocean surface, Eddie Rickenbacker, who had faced life-threatening situations his entire life, called out the distances until impact.

The chatter quieted when Rickenbacker called out that fewer than twenty feet remained before impact. At fifteen feet, Bartek loosened the lugs and freed the escape hatch over the cockpit. The lid whipped off and twirled out of sight, allowing the wind to swish in and eddy around the trio in the cockpit before coursing into the bomb bay, where it blended with the sound of Reynolds's radio and enveloped the quintet in a swirling chill. Bartek scampered to the rear to do the same to the bomb bay hatch, then returned to his position in the cockpit.

"Ten feet!" bellowed Rickenbacker. Johnny Bartek checked that his New Testament was securely in his pocket, but declined when De Angelis asked him to join him in prayer. "Why pray when I'm in trouble?" he asked. "If the Lord wants me He'll see me through this; if He doesn't, well, that's that."[6]

"Five feet!" Rickenbacker shouted. "Three feet! . . . One foot!" At that instant Cherry hollered to Whittaker, "Cut it!"[7]

One engine sputtered and died, dipping the bomber closer to the waves. "Hold on! Here it comes!"[8] Rickenbacker shouted.

"BOY, DID WE GET OUT OF THAT SHIP FAST"

With swells lapping upward toward the bomber, Cherry looked for the smoothest place to ditch. When he selected his best bet, he slowed the plane and shouted to his copilot to pull the main line switch, which shut down electrical power throughout the B-17. The plane glided slowly, the flaps stabilizing the descent as it crossed a high wave, then Cherry cut the engines and pulled back on the wheel to hook the tail in the water, which caused the fuselage to lower directly into a trough between the eight- to ten-foot swells.

Cherry braced for the impact by leaning back in his seat and extending slightly bent arms to the wheel so that he could absorb the shock without breaking his arms. The plane struck the water with such ferocity that Cherry pushed the wheel through the instrument panel.

A terrifying, grinding noise assaulted the men as the nose slammed into the water, immediately plunged under, and, just as quickly, reappeared on the surface. Reynolds's face smashed into the radio set, slicing a gaping wound on his nose that bled profusely, while pieces of his radio equipment broke free from their bolts and slashed through the air like shrapnel. The impact hurled other equipment stored in the tail throughout the bomb bay and so forcefully pressed Whittaker against his safety belt that he feared it would slice him in half. Adrenaline created a vinegary taste in his mouth, and "my eyes seemed to spin around like an already tight spring that is winding up to the snapping point." He added that "the shock and pressure of that landing is almost indescribable to a person who hasn't been thru [*sic*] one."[9]

There was a second impact when the bomber rose from its forward momentum and again smacked back down on the surface and settled ten yards from where it had initially touched down. Green ocean water began to gush in through an open topside hatch.

With a jerk of the ripcords, the three life rafts had automatically expelled and either landed on the wings of the plane or in the ocean. Once outside, the first man to reach each raft yanked a canister containing compressed carbon dioxide, which opened a valve that released air to inflate the raft. Two of the three rafts, stored in cockpit compartments on either side of the plane, supposedly had room enough for five men, while a two-man raft ejected from the rear.

With the plane stopped, Cherry and Whittaker waded through water to the bomb bay to help the others. The pilot insisted that Rickenbacker and Adamson go first, since they were considered passengers and not members of the military. Rickenbacker, still

After impressing his seven companions by successfully extricating the bomber from a ground loop in Hawaii, Captain William T. Cherry Jr. added to his laurels by ditching the huge plane between Pacific swells that could have ripped apart the B-17.

DRAWING COURTESY OF DUTTON

clutching his cane, perched on the arm of his seat, grabbed the hatch, and despite the pain from his previous injuries, lifted himself through the opening as others pushed him up from below. Once out on the wing, with ocean water lapping at his feet and the plane rising and plunging, he struggled to keep his footing. "So, this is the placid Pacific,"[10] he sardonically thought.

Bartek, who had escaped through the forward hatch with Whittaker and was already perched on a half-submerged wing, joined Rickenbacker in pulling others up through the hatch. When Bartek spotted Adamson standing on top of the fuselage, screaming from excruciating back pain, he inched a raft alongside the wing so the colonel could slide down. Adamson would have had trouble maneuvering toward the raft in calm waters, but he somehow found the strength to lower himself from the bomber into a raft bucking in constant motion. "Boy, did we get out of that ship fast," remarked Bartek. "We didn't know how long she was going to stay on top of the water—maybe only for a few seconds."[11]

De Angelis and Kaczmarczyk, assigned to the smallest of the three life rafts because they were the shortest and lightest of the eight, worried that the B-17 would sink at any moment, taking anyone remaining inside down with it. De Angelis was in relatively decent shape, but Kaczmarczyk, not yet recovered from his hospital stay, labored to assist his Army comrade.

The sheer size of the ocean swells was astounding. Waves up to fifteen feet high bounced the rafts against the sides of the bomber and lapped over the wings. The weary, shaken men gingerly worked their way along the partially submerged wings to the life rafts while trying to remain upright against the powerful surges and wind.

Despite his eagerness to step into the relative safety of the raft, Bartek helped Rickenbacker and Adamson in first. He did not attribute it to bravery or selflessness, but rather to the exigencies of war. "See, this is wartime," he said, "and I believed in heroes and you've got to save the top man. It was the colonel, and Eddie first, and then I got in. A private is not going to jump in ahead of the colonel."[12]

While Bartek held on to the raft, a huge wave crashed over

In this drawing, Eddie Rickenbacker helps Private Johnny Bartek into the raft the two would share with Colonel Adamson. Moments before, Bartek had assisted Adamson and Rickenbacker into the raft, which supposedly had sufficient room for the three grown men.

Drawing courtesy of Dutton

the wing and swept him into the ocean. Coughing water and gasping for breath, he managed to hold on to the raft with his right hand and pull himself in, but not before slicing four fingers of his right hand to the bone. Each wave washed away the blood, revealing horrid wounds, but as the wave receded, the blood flowed freely again.

De Angelis and Kaczmarczyk's small raft flipped over, leaving the pair struggling to right it while they choked in the swells. Rickenbacker pulled out a knife, sliced the line attaching the raft to the bomber, and freed it so that the men could bob away from the plane rather than be yanked below the surface. The pair eventually flipped the raft right side up and, tossed by the waves, climbed in.

Still inside the airplane, Captain Cherry hurried through the bomb bay searching for food. He guessed that he had a few minutes before the plane sank, but one minute stretched to two and beyond until he finally located three oranges. He stuffed them into his pockets before emerging from the Fortress.

As befitting the captain, Cherry was the last man to leave the B-17. He joined Reynolds and Whittaker, who were resting in the larger raft that had been ejected on the opposite side of the bomber from Rickenbacker's. They pushed the raft away from the wreckage and used oars to paddle toward the others.

When all the rafts were together, Rickenbacker unwound the line wrapped about his body, handed one end to Cherry and the other to De Angelis, and linked the rafts together, approximately twenty feet apart, so that they would avoid being separated by the waves and currents. "A strong man may last a long time alone, but men together somehow manage to last longer,"[13] Rickenbacker wrote.

Gulping air and thankful to be alive, the men slumped inside their rafts. They assumed they had survived the worst part of their ordeal and now only had to wait until the inevitable search soon located them and plucked them from the ocean.

Whittaker's wristwatch read 4:32 in the afternoon. The eight men had no idea where they had ditched. They guessed they had to be at least 200 miles from Canton Island and most likely, if their failure to spot anything while Cherry flew the box formation was any indication, from any landforms at all.

Even though it mattered little who occupied the lead raft as ocean swells and currents tossed and twisted the eight men at whim, it was appropriate that Cherry, the captain, sat in the first raft with Reynolds, the radioman, and copilot Whittaker. Rickenbacker, Adamson, and Bartek trailed in the second large raft, while the navigator, De Angelis, and Sergeant Kaczmarczyk brought up the rear in the smallest raft. Most, per military protocol, looked to Cherry for guidance, but were comforted that if matters worsened, they had Rickenbacker to provide counsel. Command issues at this point seemed to be moot as they expected to be rescued before the next evening arrived.

More disconcerting was the ocean, with swells that Lieutenant Whittaker described as mountainous. "When we were down in a trough we were cut off from the world, even from the other rafts, our taut line disappearing into the heart of a wave. From up on the crest we could see the other boats, stringing steeply downhill into the next trough."[14]

The heavy swells dumped water into the rafts, requiring the occupants to bail them out with cupped hands to avoid sinking. Rickenbacker used the old hat he had worn for years. "Adelaide had threatened a dozen times to throw it away," he said, "well, it certainly proved itself in those first few minutes."[15] Seeing no need for his cane, he tossed it over the side.

They had drifted fifty yards from the bomber when someone asked if anyone had grabbed fresh water. In the frantic moments trying to abandon the sinking vessel, however, no one had. They discussed going back, but decided not to out of concern that whoever returned would be caught inside when the plane finally sank.

That decision came back to haunt them. The plane remained afloat longer than expected, and failing to extract additional items left them with only Cherry's three oranges and one that De Angelis had brought, as well as a few chocolate bars, which quickly turned to mush in the ocean water. The lack of food and water alarmed no one, as they were confident that with every available search plane and ship looking for the nation's hero, they would not be at sea for long.

Safely in their rafts, the men gazed back at the bomber that had taken them to such an isolated spot in the Pacific. Powerless to prevent the inevitable, she swayed upward with the swells and dropped into the troughs. The swells "were giving our plane hell," according to Whittaker. "She was rolling from side to side, skidding into and off crests, and being washed by deluges of blue water. I wondered how long she could last." Whittaker observed the stars on the aircraft's wings, the symbol of the country for which they fought and to which they hoped to return, and was gripped with despondency "as she struggled with an element for which she never had been intended. I thought the old gal deserved better than this."[16]

The B-17 resisted the steady thrashing of the waves for a time, but her demise was imminent. Rickenbacker, bailing water with his hat, suddenly heard someone mutter, "There she goes." He turned to see the tail swing upright, stop in midair for a brief moment, and then slide below the surface to begin her final journey to the bottom of the Pacific. Only six minutes had elapsed since Cherry had ditched the Flying Fortress. "Then we were truly alone in the Pacific," reflected Rickenbacker, "and we felt that our best friend had left us."[17]

"WE WERE IN FOR HARD TIMES"

Eight men floated alone at sea, without sufficient food or water, buttressed only by their comradeship and their own physical and mental strengths, which at this moment stood at a fragile point. Adamson, quietly moaning from back pain, told Rickenbacker that each time the raft swayed, it felt like someone had kicked him in the kidneys. Blood from Reynolds's smashed nose gushed through his fingers and covered his face, and salt water heightened the pain in Bartek's sliced fingers. Sergeant Kaczmarczyk, already weak from previous ailments, had worsened from swallowing salt water while swimming to reach the raft.

Seasickness, brought on by the relentless bobbing of the life rafts, quickly added to their discomfort. One by one, the eight survivors retched over the sides. Rickenbacker later claimed that he had developed an immunity to seasickness while flying in World War I, but Whittaker was certain he saw everyone, including the hero, succumb. "Rickenbacker maintained with a straight face that he had not been upset in the least," Whittaker recalled. "I am under the distinct impression, however, that I saw three heads bent over the gunwale of the raft occupied by Rick, Bartek, and Col. Adamson."[18]

Their physical ailments receded to the background once they

spotted gray, triangular fins circling their rafts. Most likely drawn by the scent of blood from Reynolds's nose and Bartek's fingers, sharks became a constant presence, swishing by the rafts and at times knocking into them. While they posed little threat, and even appeared playful at times, the men's innate fear of those "long, ugly, evil-looking monsters"[19] as Rickenbacker called them, did not abate.

Everyone found it impossible to get comfortable. In the two larger rafts, one man stretched out along the bottom while his two companions sat with their legs across his. After trying a number of positions in the smallest raft, De Angelis and Kacz-marczyk reclined opposite each other, with each man draping his legs over the other man's shoulders.

The rafts drifted with the currents, bumping into one an-other as a swell rising to the crest shoved them one way, then back in the opposite direction in its descent into another trough. Bobbing in their oceanic roller coaster, they figured that every-one, even Rickenbacker, still recovering from the Atlanta crash, could muster the strength to endure the discomfort for a day or two.

Their main concern that first afternoon was whether they would be rescued before darkness forced them to spend an un-easy night alone on a turbulent ocean, in uncomfortably under-sized rafts. When Rickenbacker offered $100 to the man who first spotted the ship or plane that rescued them, everyone exam-ined the sky and the horizon, but as the afternoon wore on, neither came into view.

With darkness fast approaching, Rickenbacker cautioned everyone to talk only when necessary, as it was important to retain saliva to battle their thirst. The men alternated two-hour watches in case rescue craft appeared, but even as nightfall neared, Bartek was not overly worried, "because I knew in my heart that we would be rescued within three days; we had Eddie Rickenbacker on board so the sky would be overrun with planes from the United States Air Corps." Lieutenant De Angelis agreed that their prospects of a speedy rescue were excellent with such an important national hero aboard.

As the sun began to dip, Bartek hedged his earlier optimism. "I didn't have even the remotest idea of what to expect," he said. "I had no training for survival, I only knew that we were alone in our three tiny rafts. And soon the sun would set. I just wanted to cry out for help so loud that the whole world would hear me, but I knew it was useless."[20]

The eight men were about to exist in complete darkness, floating on an angry ocean whose swells could toss them into shark-infested water.

NIGHT CAME SWIFTLY. The men had only begun to organize the rafts when the sun suddenly plunged below the horizon, casting them into a blackness that, had it not been for the faint light from a three-quarter moon, would have been total. "It was as if an electric light had been snapped off, so quickly did the equatorial dusk descend,"[21] marveled Whittaker. A cold mist wrapped them in a surreal blanket in which they could only barely discern the outlines of men and rafts, and which deepened the sense of isolation that had begun when they abandoned the Flying Fortress.

The group established two-hour watches to ensure that someone would be awake at all times in case air or surface craft appeared. Men periodically shouted upon spotting a light in the distance, only to be disappointed each time when their discovery turned out to be a bright star rather than blinker signals from ships. When firing one of the flares revealed only emptiness, they abandoned expectations for rescue that first night and pondered a sobering thought—how could help arrive in the dark, or even in the daylight, when neither the eight men nor the rescue forces had any idea where in the Pacific they might be? They assumed that they had ditched west or southwest of Canton Island, but otherwise could only guess their location.

The men squirmed and twisted in the darkness, trying to find enough comfort for sleep, but they could do little but contort themselves into one painful arrangement or another. As waves tossed them from side to side, nothing eased their discomfort, but with their bodies cramped together, they at least gained a little warmth. Every few hours they had to bail out four or five inches of seawater swirling around in the bottom of the rafts, leading Rickenbacker to recall that everyone, that first night and each ensuing night, was "wet and miserable."[22]

The nighttime air buffeted their wet clothing and chilled them. Rickenbacker said that "it was like being doused with a bucket of ice water, in spite of the fact that the air was warm and the sea was warm." As a result, "We were soaked constantly." They expected the drenching, but were stunned at being so cold while drifting near the equator. The men trembled throughout that long first night, and "even with my suit, shoes, socks and leather jacket, I was colder than I had ever been in my life,"[23] wrote Rickenbacker.

Bartek altered positions with Rickenbacker every hour to relieve tightened muscles and to find a more comfortable spot. He thought about the moment before their plane left Hawaii, when he decided not to ask to be relieved of this assignment and return to the United States. Now, after surviving the ditching and the hurried evacuation of the Flying Fortress, Bartek wished he had submitted that request.

Lying next to Bartek, Rickenbacker was plagued with stiffness, numbness, and poor circulation from the Atlanta injuries. While resting at home, he turned over often in bed to soothe his muscles, but in the confining rubber raft, he was forced to remain in an awkward stance in wet clothes. "But I had no choice," he said. "I simply had to lie there and take it. It was a matter of survival."[24]

Sharks continued to follow. Throughout the long first night, and in subsequent days and nights, sharks, trying to scrape their backs clean of barnacles, smacked against the rafts' undersides and terrorized the men inside, who assumed the predators could easily slice through the rubberized surface. Rickenbacker said that "the water seemed full of them," and that "you could feel his hard body through the thin canvas bottom. The force of the blow was enough to lift you three or four inches."[25]

Rickenbacker knew that someone would have to step forward and lead them through their ordeal. The US Navy might mount a widespread search, but he now feared it could be days, even weeks, before they were located, if at all. He admired the traits displayed by his comrades, but saw nothing to make him believe that anyone but himself could keep them alive for a lengthy period. "They had their strengths, and they had their weaknesses. Somebody was going to have to hold them together, and that somebody would have to be me,"[26] he later wrote. He said nothing to the others, and allowed Cherry to assume his rightful leadership role as captain of the aircraft, but already concluded that sooner or later, he would most likely have to take the reins of command.

The eight lapsed into a long silence and fitful rest. "The wisecracks and the small talk," recalled Rickenbacker, "which sounded pretty silly in the immensity of the night, petered out and we were beginning to realize that we were in for hard times."[27]

"WE'LL BE PICKED UP TODAY, I'M SURE"

That long first night ended when the sun glimmered over the eastern horizon, broke through the nighttime mist, and cleared the skies. While it took a few hours to warm the eight from the nocturnal chill which, according to Rickenbacker, "penetrated to the bone," the brightness and warmth of the sun was a welcome gift. "Anyway, it was delightful to see the sunrise after a night of misery," Bartek explained. However, while the daytime might be less frightening, "Breakfast wasn't on the menu."[28]

Their main concern was whether they would be rescued that

day. They accepted that aircraft and ships had little time to locate them the previous afternoon, but now the Navy could use every minute of daylight. Each man carefully scanned the sky, hoping to be the first to spot an airplane and collect Rickenbacker's $100, and Cherry fired a flare in hopes that a pilot on dawn patrol might see it, but neither plane nor ship came into view. Rickenbacker sensed the disappointment and said loud enough for men in all three rafts to hear, "We'll be picked up today, I'm sure. They couldn't have missed hearing our SOS. And if they heard it, they got a cross bearing on our course. It's just a matter of time. The planes probably are taking off right now, and that $100 is still up."[29]

He advised the others to cover their heads with whatever articles of clothing they had, including undergarments, that they should restrict their movements to a minimum, and that they needed to be patient. Rickenbacker was not yet challenging Cherry for leadership of the group, but wanted to bolster their optimism about being swiftly rescued. "He was just giving us a good grown-up outlook on life," said De Angelis. "We were eight guys with the same objective—the idea of being rescued."[30]

The eight inventoried their possessions. They needed no more than a fast glance at their rafts to conclude that their oceangoing vehicles could do little more than provide the flimsiest of protection. The two larger rafts, built supposedly to accommodate five average-size men, were seven feet long by four feet wide on the outside, but due to the rubberized borders along the edges, the living space inside shrunk to five and a half feet by two and a half feet. Three fully grown men had to squeeze into a space equal to the size of a mattress for a single bed. The smaller raft barely offered enough room to house one person.

Specific colors on the rafts were designed to aid them. The blue-painted bottoms blended in with the ocean and, hopefully, lessened the chance that a shark or other fearsome creature would attack and puncture the underside. The sides, called gunwales or bulwarks, and the floor, or deck, had been painted bright yellow to provide an easy contrast to the ocean's blue surface for rescue aircraft searching from above. Eighteen inches thick and containing two inner tubes inside, those rubberized gunwales slowly leaked, forcing the men to use hand pumps to reinflate them each day. The decks consisted of three-ply rubberized canvas, one-eighth of an inch thick. The larger rafts had two inflatable seats of rubberized canvas that ran across the midsection, but since they were difficult to sit on during heavier seas, the occupants eventually decided they served no purpose and cut them out to make additional room.

The rafts offered poor quarters in which to brave the Pacific. Each swell nudged them together, then pulled them apart as it receded, jerking the rope and yanking the rafts in diverse directions. The confines provided adequate, if uncomfortable, safety from the sharks and barracudas lingering below and on the other side of the gunwales, but the ocean, despite its beauty and magnificence, could turn beastly at any moment, with fierce winds creating towering swells that drenched them in salt water.

The rafts contained emergency equipment, including two hand pumps to keep the rafts inflated and to help bail them out,

To promote war rationing, three military personnel display two of the three rafts into which the eight men squeezed during the twenty-four days adrift on the Pacific Ocean. Words accompanying the photograph emphasized that one worn-out rubber tire was sufficient to make one three-man raft similar to those that saved the Rickenbacker party.

a flare gun with eighteen flares, two jungle knives, two collapsible rubber bailing buckets, one pair of pliers, a set of patching gear in each raft, two collapsible aluminum oars, and a first aid kit with a bottle of iodine and salve for gasoline burns. In addition, the men carried out of the plane two handguns belonging to Cherry and Adamson, several pencils, Whittaker's diary, some coins and bills, Rickenbacker's map of the Pacific, and a small pocket compass. A few had also brought cigarettes, but tossed them away once the seawater had ruined them.

De Angelis had found two fishhooks and a piece of line zippered into the parachutes' cushions, but other items meant to be there, such as knives, hard biscuits, and chocolate, were missing from every parachute aboard the plane, supposedly pilfered by a mechanic in Hawaii or some other base. Without bait to lure fish, the hooks and line were all but useless for catching anything.

That morning the men turned to the map and compass to see if they could determine a rough approximation of their location. Rickenbacker believed they floated west of Canton Island, about 400 miles north of the Fiji Islands (Rickenbacker underestimated the actual distance to the Fijis by more than half), that they were drifting either to the west or to the south-southwest, and that if they were not rescued, with any sort of luck they should reach the Fiji Islands within a month. He and Cherry concluded that if they continued in a westerly direction rather than to the southwest, they would drift into the Japanese-controlled sector of the Pacific, making their seizure by the enemy more likely, a specter that Rickenbacker said "became a second nightmare to all of us."[31] Their nightmare was already a reality, as the location of their ditching, by all best guesses, was approximately 1° S and 178° W, putting them perilously close to enemy lines from the beginning.

They agreed that in the unlikely chance that a rescue craft failed to locate them, that if they came upon an island during the day without knowing who controlled it, they would remain at sea until nightfall. Shrouded by darkness, they would then paddle the rafts to shore, hide them in nearby trees and vegetation, and inspect the island to determine whether it was in friendly or enemy hands.

None of the eight knew that the plane had landed in one of the Pacific's open, sparsely traversed gaps, with shipping lanes connecting the United States and Australia swinging a distant 500 miles to the east and southeast. Aircraft operating out of Canton Island would thus be patrolling closer to those lanes instead of targeting the desolate stretch into which Cherry had ditched the bomber.

Their secure worlds had shifted from the bomb bay of a B-17 to the diminutive realm of rubber rafts, which were now their oceangoing habitats until rescue, imprisonment, or death arrived.

CHAPTER 5

"Rickenbacker Flight Down at Sea"
End of the First Week Adrift, October 23–27

WHILE THE EIGHT men drifted, Army and Navy aviators at Canton and elsewhere jumped into action to locate Eddie Rickenbacker and his companions. The first indication that something was amiss occurred at 1:30 a.m. on October 22, when the commanding officer at Canton, Lieutenant Clifford L. Ellsworth, radioed his superior in Hawaii, Lieutenant General Delos C. Emmons, a message that sent shock waves throughout the military command. "RICKENBACKER FLIGHT DOWN AT SEA," Ellsworth informed Emmons. "NOTIFY CINCPAC [Commander in Chief, Pacific, Admiral Chester W. Nimitz, stationed at Pearl Harbor] TO HAVE IMMEDIATE AIR SEARCH STARTED FROM ELLICE ISLANDS." Twenty minutes later, the Canton Island radio station contacted Palmyra Island with the request to begin an air search immediately. "PLANE DOWN AT SEA. PARTY INCLUDED CAPT EDDIE RICKENBACKER."

Two hours later, Ellsworth broadened the alert, informing all

Pacific commands that Eddie Rickenbacker was missing at sea. "SAD NEWS," Ellsworth radioed, "ALL PLANES AND SHIPS TO KEEP SHARP LOOKOUT FOR LIFE RAFTS FROM BAKER SEVENTEEN [designation for a B-17] PLANE DOWN AT SEA." He added that the "PARTY INCLUDED CAPTAIN EDDIE RICKENBACKER PERSONAL REPRESENTATIVE OF SECRETARY OF WAR. GOOD LUCK."

A little more than three hours later, Emmons in Hawaii sent a cautionary message to Ellsworth at Canton. "HOPE FOR BEST," Emmons radioed. He then added that Ellsworth should refrain from mentioning the World War I hero by name. "OMIT IN FUTURE RADIOS ANY REFERENCE BY NAME TO PASSENGERS ON BAKER SEVENTEEN THAT IS DOWN AT SEA. SEC'Y WAR [Henry L. Stimson in Washington, DC] DIRECTS NO PUBLICITY RELEASED REGARDING THIS MISSION."[1]

By early afternoon on October 22, the day after Rickenbacker and his party ditched at sea, Lieutenant Ellsworth had scrambled every available aircraft from Canton. Twenty-one Douglas C-47 transport planes, normally used to ferry troops and supplies to fighting forces in the Pacific, searched designated areas in every direction from Canton, including routes toward the Ellice Islands. Aircraft from other bases joined the operation.

With Canton lying in the middle as a hub, the four-man crews of each plane searched their sectors before returning to the island along a different route, all the while maintaining a close watch for anything unusual floating on the surface. They planned to conduct similar searches each day until they either located the eight men or received orders to halt the operation.

Ira Southern, a member of the 19th Troop Carrier Squadron

based at Palmyra Island, said that in hopes of finding the survivors, he "used binoculars during the search until my eyebrows and facial surfaces became sore from the continued contact."[2] Understanding what Rickenbacker meant to the people back home, who had already absorbed more than their share of disappointing war news in the past year, no one wanted to be responsible for missing a national hero whose exploits through the decades had given hope and joy to millions. However, since the aircraft hugged the normal supply routes far from Rickenbacker's location, they returned to their bases empty-handed.

"NO SHIP LOOMED ON THE MOONLIT HORIZON"

With naval aircraft focusing their search for the rafts to the east and south of the survivors' location, the eight men turned to their most immediate needs—obtaining fresh drinking water and food. They had gone almost a day without either, and their thirst would grow more severe each hour. Only salt water—lethal if consumed in sufficient quantities—stood within reach.

The four oranges provided temporary nourishment and eased their parched mouths. The group agreed to divide and eat one orange every other day, and to ensure that everyone received the same-sized portion, in the first subtle step in recognizing that Captain Eddie, the solver of previous dilemmas, was their naturally appointed leader, they asked him to slice the fruit in equal portions. Eddie Rickenbacker was slowly, almost imperceptibly, becoming the actual leader instead of the nominal commander, Captain Cherry.

The men clustered the rafts to receive their portions. With seven hungry men closely observing his every move, Rickenbacker carefully divided the orange in half, then into quarters, and finally into eighths. He handed each man his slice before taking one for himself. Some immediately devoured the fruit, while others sucked out the juices before eating pulp and peel. When one man wondered if it was safe to eat the peel, Bartek answered that while he had never heard of anyone dying from consuming an orange peel, he had certainly heard of people perishing from starvation. The orange morsel infused a welcome vitality into bodies already craving food, while Rickenbacker and Cherry, thinking to the future, saved a tiny section of their orange slices in hopes they might be useful as bait for fish.

They needed every ounce of strength to face the day ahead. As morning yielded to afternoon, clear, bright skies and a gentle breeze masked a calm, mirrorlike ocean, but the sun's unrelenting rays bore down on them, scorching heads, arms, necks, and legs. Exposed on tiny rafts, they had nothing to make a canopy for shade, and as the sun climbed higher and higher, it seemed to scald completely through them, stinging their eyes and plunging the men into a lethargic stupor.

To gain some relief, the men covered their heads with undershirts and shorts, then dipped them in the ocean and draped the wet clothing over their bodies. The salt water tempered their distress, but as the water evaporated, leaving the salt behind, an irritating, crispy coating covered their tender skin.

The sun dried the blood on Reynolds's face into such a revolting crust that it became difficult for his companions to look at him. Until scabs covered the wounds a few days later, Bartek splashed salt water onto his hideously sliced fingers, wincing in pain each time the liquid hit.

Rickenbacker had wisely retained his clothing to shield him from the sun. He wore his leather jacket, a new blue business suit, necktie, pocket handkerchief, vest, and his comfortable old gray hat. He even kept his shoes in hopes they would protect his oft-injured feet from further discomfort. Adamson sported his uniform and cap, Bartek wore a one-piece jumper, and Cherry and Whittaker kept their leather jackets, but Reynolds, who had stripped to his shorts, suffered from red, blistered legs. The darker-skinned Whittaker and De Angelis tanned rather than burned, but when the blisters on the others broke, salt water drenching the festering sores inflicted excruciating pain.

When the wind strengthened later in the day, waves pounded the rafts and bounced men into one another, further irritating their burns. Trapped inside the small rafts, men complained until Cherry angrily ordered them to pipe down. He ripped off his undershirt to fashion a small sail, affixed it to two oars serving as masts, and propped his back to his raft's side while holding the oars upright. This temporary measure nudged his raft ahead of the others, strung out the three rafts, and produced a smoother ride for everyone.

A BRILLIANT SUNSET painted the evening sky with a panorama of colors. Fierce winds at dusk crashed large swells onto the rafts, but more surprising again was the sudden drop in temperature, which defied logic to men drifting in waters bordering the globe's equator. In the daylight hours, they squirmed and blinked in the torrid heat, but in the darkness, the shivering men huddled together to escape the cold.

The roiling seas again prevented anyone from enjoying much sleep. They lurched from side to side and collided with one another as waves buffeted them. They rose with the rafts to the crest of one wave before suddenly plunging into a trough that inevitably preceded the arrival of yet another wave. They would have lost the contents of their stomachs if they had any, and they silently prayed for dawn and calmer seas to end their nocturnal discomfort.

The men in Cherry's raft fired another flare, but it proved to be a dud. After waiting until midnight, the captain expended the third of their eighteen flares, which erupted in a ninety-second burst of light as it dangled from a parachute and slowly descended to the surface. The men watched, mouths agape, as the flare bathed the rafts in a luminous red light that convinced Rickenbacker that any ship or plane in the area would easily spot it. "When it finally went out," he wrote, "leaving us in a night that was blacker than it had been before, we could not help hoping that keen eyes had spotted the flare and had marked its course—and that rescue was on the way. Our spirits were higher, our conversation enthusiastic, even gay. But as night went on and no plane was heard overhead, no ship loomed on the moonlit horizon, our spirits dropped again."[3]

Once more entombed in darkness, some tried to determine their location by studying the stars. When Cherry guessed that they had ditched in an area likely to be skipped by aircraft until the sectors closer to the air and shipping routes had been checked, Bartek gloomily concluded that few aircraft and ships would pass their way.

Frustrated, Bartek recalled his mother's admonitions about the importance of religion and began reading the New Testament given to him by the First Baptist Church in Freehold earlier that year. Whittaker, the lifelong atheist, first thought of teasing the private, but stopped, as Bartek had as much right to believe in God and the Bible as Whittaker had in rejecting them. Besides, the others appeared to be comforted by watching the young man turning to his Bible.

Disappointed that they had not yet been located, after that first full day on the Pacific, the men remained optimistic that within a day or two, rescue craft would arrive. They realized that they floated at the whim of an unpredictable ocean, but no one yet concluded that death was their ultimate fate.

THE SAME PAINFUL pattern emerged during their second full day adrift. Exposed in open rafts and already sunburned from the previous day, the eight could not evade the suffocating heat and the rays that reflected from the ocean surface.

They devoured the second orange on October 24, their third full day at sea, but figured they could not long subsist on only one-eighth of an orange every other day. The swarms of fish that darted and squirmed in the clear waters about the rafts teased them, but without bait for the hook and lines, the food source may as well have been miles distant. They considered killing one of the smaller sharks by stabbing it with a sharpened end of an oar, but feared the scent of blood might provoke other sharks to attack. Rickenbacker and Cherry wedged orange peels on hooks as bait and tried to snare a few of the smaller fish that lurked only feet below the surface, and while the fish darted about the peels for a few seconds, they left without even so much as a nibble.

Lack of food and water became a mounting concern, but the men still believed that rescue was only a matter of when, not if. Since Reynolds had spread a stream of distress signals across the Pacific as the Flying Fortress descended, they were convinced that someone in one of the island bases in the region must have picked up one.

Cherry fired another flare that night. It rose barely fifty feet before partially igniting, arcing back to the surface, and with smoke and sparks flying, heading straight toward the cluster of rubberized rafts. Fortunately, the flare splashed between them and disappeared. The flare could easily have harmed someone or, worse, have sliced through a raft as if it were butter, sending it to the bottom, and casting its occupants into the ocean.

"DANGER AND DEATH HAVE ALWAYS BEEN YOUR MATES"

Thousands of miles to the east, in the United States, the families of the eight men remained oblivious to the drama unfolding in the Pacific. For two days the government had purposely clamped a lid on the news to give rescue forces time to locate the

Rickenbacker party or, if that failed, to enable the proper authorities to compile the relevant information.

After forty-eight hours had elapsed without result, Hap Arnold, in what he later described as "one of the most difficult tasks I have ever been called upon to perform," telephoned Adelaide Rickenbacker prior to releasing the news to the press. He informed her that her husband's plane was missing in the Pacific but emphasized that he remained hopeful, because the Flying Fortress had life jackets for each person aboard and emergency rubber boats. He told her that he had ordered a widespread search for her husband and his companions, promised to keep looking for the survivors until hope for their rescue was gone, and asked her to maintain a positive attitude.

"You may depend upon it that no effort will be spared to discover their whereabouts and to afford a prompt release from what I hope is nothing more than an uncomfortable situation," he assured Adelaide. "I will keep you notified of every development."

Though stunned by the news, Mrs. Rickenbacker had gone through similar instances before and expected that this occasion would be no different. She told a reporter a few days later that since Arnold's call, "I've just been sitting here, hoping he will call again to tell me all is well."[4]

The news of Rickenbacker's disappearance, announced by the War Department two days after his plane went down, dominated newspaper front pages on October 24. RICKENBACKER LOST AT SEA! screamed a *Chicago Tribune* headline that stretched across page one. The *New York Times* broke the news with "Rickenbacker Missing in Pacific on Flight Southwest of Hawaii," while on the other coast, the *Los Angeles Times* greeted readers with "Rickenbacker Plane Missing in Pacific." The *New York Daily News*'s banner used up two-thirds of its front page to inform the public that RICKENBACKER MISSING ON OCEAN FLIGHT.[5]

This October 24, 1942, headline from Chicago was typical of the home front reaction to the news that one of the nation's idols, Eddie Rickenbacker, was missing in the Pacific.

FROM THE AUTHOR'S COLLECTION

Over the next few days, the startling news nudged other war stories farther down page one. "Captain E. V. Rickenbacker, confidential adviser to the Secretary of War on aircraft, and nationally known aviation expert, is overdue on a flight between Oahu and another island in the Pacific," began the official War Department announcement issued on October 23. "Captain Rickenbacker is on an inspection trip, acting for Lieut. Gen. H. H. Arnold, commanding general Army Air Forces." The announcement added that "Captain Rickenbacker's plane was in radio contact with an island southwest of Honolulu during the afternoon of Oct. 21, 1942, and was last heard from early that evening, when he reported that he had slightly more than one hour's supply of gasoline. No contact has been made since that time. Search is being made by all available air and sea forces."[6]

The War Department seconded Hap Arnold's promise to Adelaide by underscoring that although the plane was two days overdue, "All available army and navy air and sea forces for the southwest Hawaiian Islands are searching for Capt. Eddie Rickenbacker and the crew of a heavy military plane, missing in a Pacific flight." An article in the *New York Daily News* added that while officials expressed optimism in their public comments, they "admitted privately that the outlook was 'pretty gloomy,' but hope has not been abandoned that the famous airman and members of his crew—probably as many as nine—may have landed on some remote island or are still afloat somewhere on the vast Pacific."[7] In the eleven months since the United States entered the war, other rescued military aviators had floated in rubber rafts after being shot down over the Pacific, and possibly the same would occur with the Rickenbacker party.

Numerous island atolls existed in other sectors of the Pacific, but relatively few stood in the area of the ocean southwest of Pearl Harbor into which Rickenbacker's plane had flown. While the articles provided a general sense of where Rickenbacker's plane might have ditched, each added that the last message picked up from the bomber was that they had no more than one hour of fuel remaining, and "it was in that area that the search for Miss Earhart and her navigator centered after her last message that she was over the Pacific with no sight of land."[8] Reporters were optimistic that while the War Department announcement said that Rickenbacker was overdue, it had not added that the hero was presumed lost, a phrase that had often accompanied announcements about men missing at sea.

Rickenbacker's family reflected the same optimism with which their famous relative had approached every other calamity in his life. Adelaide told reporters after the news broke that "Eddie will turn up. He's too old a hand to get lost in any airplane now. I'm used to waiting for news that Eddie has arrived." She added that "he always has said that he's 'the darling of lady luck.'"[9]

Rickenbacker's brother Dewey brushed off the nation's concern. "This just isn't Eddie's time," he said. "If his plane escaped damage in a forced landing he'll show up sooner or later. After all, this isn't the first time he's been in a tight spot."[10]

The nation needed to believe those optimistic statements. For more than three decades, Americans had gained inspiration from his death-defying feats, his speed records, and his devil-may-care approach to danger. Now, in the midst of the first year of a ruinous war, the public hungered for that heroic inspiration more than ever. The disastrous attack on Pearl Harbor had produced an array of questions about the professionalism and readiness of the US armed forces and about the military might of Japan, a nation most had previously written off as an inconsequential threat to the mighty United States. Citizens were still reeling from the Hawaiian debacle when reports of Japanese victories over the United States and other Allied nations throughout the Pacific—including the losses of Wake Island, Bataan, Corregidor, and Malaya—administered further blows. By October

*The disastrous December 7, 1941, Japanese attack on the US Navy's
bastion at Pearl Harbor administered a titanic shock to Americans on
the home front. Here you see the battleship USS* West Virginia
(BB-48) billowing smoke and fire after being hit by torpedoes.

NATIONAL ARCHIVES PHOTO #NH-97398

1942, the United States had yet to mount a major assault against
Hitler in Europe, and the first Pacific land operation, at Guadalcanal, one of the Solomon Islands, was teetering in the balance
at the time that Rickenbacker's plane disappeared. The nation
longed for good news, but after eleven months of sour tidings,
people awoke to the shocking revelation that Eddie Rickenbacker, their hero, had vanished in the Pacific.

People remained optimistic because the alternative was too
dreadful to ponder, but a handful of newspaper columnists and
reporters tried to prepare their readers for what might unfold.

Americans sustained a second blow with news that the Japanese had overrun American forces at Wake Island and other bases throughout the Pacific. These wrecked Grumman F4F-3 Wildcat fighters of Marine Fighting Squadron 211 attest to the damage inflicted by the Japanese military.

NATIONAL ARCHIVES PHOTO #80-G-179006

An article in the *New York Daily News* included a photograph of Rickenbacker with Amelia Earhart at an air show, a troubling image for those who sought a positive spin, and the reporter's words emphasized that much as all might hope, the nation had possibly seen the last of its hero. "It is believed the thing Capt. Eddie Rickenbacker loved most killed him—the airplane. A former automobile racing champion and America's most famous World War ace, he was that rarity among mortals—the romantic and romanticized daredevil who successfully managed the evolution into the solid man of affairs."[11]

Popular sportswriter and close Rickenbacker friend Grantland

Rice feared the end had come for his associate. In an October 24 poem he simply titled "Rick," Rice, who frequented New York's taverns with the aviator, wrote:

> *Danger and Death have always been your mates,*
> *The pals you loved—above all else in life . . .*
> *You never bothered much—about the ride,*
> *As long as your two pals were at your side.*

Much as he hoped for Rickenbacker's safe return, Rice ended his tribute with:

> *Here at the Inn tonight we lift a glass : . .[12]*

The nation was not yet ready to face that outcome. People required a happy result, the return of a man who had often been smacked down but always regrouped and rose to fight again, and to serve as a foreshadow that if the nation did the same, all would be well against Germany and Japan.

The coming days would test that Pollyanna-style viewpoint.

"A SLOW ROTTING AWAY"

The optimism that prevailed back home was not matched by the men adrift on the Pacific. As one blistering day turned into another, without relief from the sun, the sea, hunger, and thirst, they resorted to measures they might never have previously considered in hopes of enduring an oceanic gauntlet that tested their strength, their belief in themselves and in one another, and their faith in a higher power.

Each morning, the sun heralded another scathing day afloat. The absence of strong breezes calmed the ocean surface, which made for a smoother ride, but it also turned the Pacific into an aquatic mirror that reflected the sun's rays and ravaged the men even further. They squirmed in the confines of their rafts, but they had no option other than to wilt in the heat. Abscesses covered mouths parched by thirst, and each droplet of sweat coursing down their faces stole more of the body fluids they needed to stay alive. Rickenbacker at times reached over the raft's side to fill his hat with ocean water and jam it down to his ears to gain some relief, but the salty coating left behind itched his face day and night.

Rickenbacker guessed that the sun heated the water temperature to 78 to 80 degrees, but each time a wave broke over the side of his raft, he felt as if a wall of ice water had been dumped on him. The cold water splashed onto his blistered hands, and when the blisters broke, salt water seeped onto the raw skin and stung his hands which, he decided, looked more and more like beefsteaks.

Rickenbacker thought of the tribulations he had experienced in his life and concluded that even though he had stared down death many times before, "These first five or six days [adrift on the Pacific] were the worst I have ever known." The combination of the heat, thirst, hunger, and uncertainty about survival contributed to "a slow rotting away,"[13] and unlike many of his prior incidents, he now had less control over his fate.

Burns covered every exposed inch of the men's skin, and even the soles of the feet of the men who had discarded their shoes upon abandoning the aircraft were burned raw. Each time ocean swells jostled the rafts, men stifled groans from the pain caused when their sunburned bodies smacked into another companion or against the rafts' sides. Without pants Reynolds's legs slowly turned into "a sodden red mass of hurt."[14] To shield as much of their faces as possible, the men took the handkerchiefs that Rickenbacker had earlier handed out and tied them bandit-style across their faces, which had the unintended effect of making the group resemble a gang of Western outlaws.

With little room for movement, the eight were forced to lie still, day and night. They could alleviate their discomfort by standing and stretching, but doing so could easily tip the unsteady rafts, plunging the men into shark-infested water. Instead, to gain any relief, no matter how temporary, they devised a wormlike motion and wriggled on the raft's bottom. Whenever one man turned or twisted, he forced the others to do the same, and tempers quickly flared each time anyone bumped into the man next to him and irritated his raw flesh.

Recovery from his Atlanta injuries proved difficult enough in his New York residence, where Rickenbacker could turn over in bed every hour to relieve the pain from lack of circulation, and where he benefited from regular diathermy and physiotherapy treatments. On the ocean, because he had to lie still in the crowded raft, he was unable to exercise his hips, legs, or feet. Rickenbacker's body tightened, which induced painful muscle cramping and spasming throughout his frame. He had to quietly accept his discomfort and remain in one position for much of the day and night, a tribulation he later claimed was the hardest for him to endure.

They lay in the sun by day and in the coolness at night and checked their impulses to complain. They were grateful that the B-17 carried these emergency rafts, for as small as they were, they were the sole items keeping the sharks at bay and preventing them from drowning, but at the same time, they detested the designers who had placed them in tight quarters better suited to small children than to adults. The six men in the two larger rafts felt especially sorry for Kaczmarczyk and De Angelis, whose raft was no larger than a bathtub.

For the indeterminate future, these rafts were their homes and all that stood between them and death. In the United States, they existed in secure regions, relatively free from dangers, but in one terrifying moment, those safe realms had shriveled to rubbery worlds no larger than a bed mattress. Inside that tiny area, the eight would now have to withstand sharks and storms, hunger and thirst, fears and doubts. Their security, and with it their futures, existed only inside the tiny rafts; outside lurked nothing but danger and death.

In the handful of calm, clear nights during that first week, when the stars shone brightly and rendered an exquisite spectacle for the eight to observe, Rickenbacker liked to lean back, gaze skyward, and let his mind wander. He stared at the clouds until they formed elephants parading through the heavens, eagles majestically soaring, knights galloping into battle, and beautiful women casting furtive glances his way. He at first wondered if he was hallucinating, but others told him that they, too, experienced the same. Bartek believed that the images had been sent by God, as a way to take everyone's mind off their hunger and thirst. He saw exotic animals, pretty females, and a mother nursing a child in her lap, and in those few moments, Bartek forgot his woes and appreciated nature's gift.

Colonel Adamson helped pass the time at night by lecturing about astronomical matters, often pointing out constellations and explaining the origins of their names. But soon, a more uplifting pastime emerged when, after a handful of days adrift, the comfort of prayer and Johnny Bartek's Bible emerged.

"DELIVER ME"

Turning to his New Testament for guidance, Johnny Bartek whispered a brief prayer, then randomly opened the book to the four verses of Matthew 6:31–34, in which the supplicant asks God, "What shall we eat? or, What shall we drink? or, Wherewithal shall we be clothed?" After stating that "your heavenly Father knoweth that ye have need of all these things," the verses urge the reader to "seek ye first the kingdom of God, and his righteousness; and all these things shall be added unto you." Bartek had read those words as a youth, but back then his interests lay more with sports and girls. Those same phrases now offered hope rather than boredom, especially with the message "Take therefore no thought for the morrow, for the morrow shall take thought for the things of itself."[15]

Buttressed with the reassuring notion that God would provide, Bartek continued to flip through the pages, gaining solace from reading the four gospels, the letters of St. Paul, and assorted Old Testament psalms in the appendix. The gift from his hometown church, bound in khaki, zippered, and waterproof, became a welcome partner.

Huddled in the same raft, Rickenbacker and Adamson noticed Bartek reading the good book. Soon men in the other rafts also observed him and began wondering if the Bible might prove valuable to them. Rickenbacker claimed that he suggested the idea to gather the rafts in a cluster and conduct prayer meetings, and that he insisted that Whittaker, an atheist, and Adamson, the agnostic, participate, but others credited Cherry. Which individual conceived of the gatherings, though relatively unimportant, added to the tension that had begun to foment between Rickenbacker and Cherry. Before the first week at sea had ended, the captain sensed that he had twice been upstaged by his famous passenger, first with the division of the oranges and now with the organization and implementation of a religious service.

The eight pulled the rafts together for prayer and meditation, at first in the morning and again in the evening, during which they passed Bartek's New Testament from man to man, with each reading a passage and leading a discussion about its relevance to their situation. They next shared a prayer, most often the Lord's Prayer or "Now I Lay Me Down to Sleep, I Pray the Lord My Soul to Keep," and ended with a song, usually "Onward Christian Soldiers," but soon dropped that portion because most of the group knew only a handful of Christian hymns. Above all, they beseeched God for food and fresh water. Bartek figured that some of his companions, especially Adamson and Whittaker, questioned the value of the meetings, but he concluded it could do no harm to seek help from above.

Captain Cherry usually addressed God as "Old Master," as if he were casually discussing an important issue with a friend, before moving to his entreaty, which most often consisted of a plea that he return to his wife and young daughter. Rickenbacker's prayers, on the other hand, were more demands than requests. He insisted on knowing whether God was coming to their aid, and wondered how God could ignore a group of believers who now begged for His assistance.

The agnostic Adamson took his turn, but Whittaker, who scoffed at the notion of a higher power, declined. He listened to the words uttered during the services but refused to accept that there was a God who could save them. If such a Supreme Being existed, why had He not provided proof in the form of food, fresh water, or rescue craft?

In the coming days they read the words of Psalm 71, which reflected the optimism during that first week adrift. "In thee, O Lord, do I put my trust: let me never be put to confusion," and "Deliver me in thy righteousness, and cause me to escape. Incline thine ear unto me, and save me; for thou art my rock and my fortress."

In reading Psalm 119, they begged God to listen to their pleas. "Let my cry come near before thee, O Lord. Give me understanding according to thy word," and in Psalm 120 they prayed, "In my distress I cried unto the Lord, and he heard me. Deliver my soul, O Lord." Turning to the Gospel of St. Matthew, they read, "Ask, and it shall be given you; seek, and ye shall find; knock, and it shall be opened unto you," and "Behold the fowls of the air, for they sow not, neither do they reap, nor gather into barns, yet your heavenly Father feedeth them."[16] Could He not, they asked, consider the survivors the equals of a bird or a lamb?

Colonel Adamson, who neither accepted nor rejected the notion of God, believed that the prayer meetings boosted morale and would help the men withstand whatever dangers came in the next few days. He participated in the services, but for religious succor he preferred to lean on the medal of St. Joseph of Cupertino, the patron saint of aviators, which actress Rosalind Russell had insisted that he keep for the flight. He lay in his raft, hungry, thirsty, and in pain, constantly clutching the medal in his hands. Bartek noticed Adamson's clenched fists and wondered what the colonel held, but figured it was none of his business so he declined to ask Adamson about it.

Religion had never been a major influence in Rickenbacker's life. He had lived by the Golden Rule of treating others the way he wanted them to treat him, but had never considered himself an avid churchgoer. Yet he made an exception for the crucifix and medals in his breast pocket, including a St. Christopher medal, which he had securely inserted in an expensive leather pouch. The case had accompanied him into World War I aerial combat, during hours-long cross-country flights, and in that horrible night near Atlanta. The items had become a part of his morning routine when, after donning one of his tailor-made suits, he slipped them into his pocket along with his wallet, handkerchief, and other items. Though he gave infrequent thought to the medals throughout the day, their presence comforted him, and during the ditching, while he tossed out his luggage and other personal items, he made certain to retain that case.

"I am not a Catholic," he said, "and, aside from the sentiment connected with such things, I was certainly under no illusions as to what they could do for me. Yet after all the years, and the good fortune associated with them, I found myself believing, as men will when everything else is going to pieces, that my fate was somehow involved with them."[17]

"LIVE HORS D'OEUVRES"

Near the end of their first week at sea, malnourishment and lack of sleep had taken a toll. They had at first decided to consume one orange every other day, but after Rickenbacker divided the second on October 24, they shortened the interval to one day. Two days later, their fifth full day adrift, they split the final orange, but the shrunken, dry, rotting fruit hardly eased their hunger pains. As long as the oranges had lasted, the men had something to look forward to, but consuming that fourth orange meant that, unless they found a way to reel in some of those fish that darted temptingly close, the men would have to go without food.

Compounding matters was that by their fifth day at sea, chances of rescue diminished with each hour. The lack of ships or planes indicated that they must be drifting far from any American bases, and even though they still watched for aircraft, the optimism they had held on to at first had diminished.

With the final orange now gone, and lacking drinkable water, Rickenbacker knew that on the Pacific, nature, not man, often held the upper hand. Unless a storm delivered fresh water and they were able to snare a fish, he could see no path out of their dilemma.

The ocean teased the famished men. Dozens of mackerel and sea bass, as well as sharks and barracuda, swam mouthwateringly close to the rafts, but the men failed each time they tried to grab the slippery quarry with their hands.

At least by now, they had become accustomed to the sharks. The smaller ones seemed almost playful, and while the men watched with a mixture of fear and amazement, the sharks would charge toward the rafts and scoot under them, rubbing their backs on the undersides and jolting the men inside by smashing the rafts with a flip of their tails.

Wondering if the smaller sharks might yield a nourishing meal, the men tried to snatch a few, but the speedy creatures eluded their grasp. Cherry and Whittaker crafted a spear from one of the aluminum oars, but when they targeted one shark, its hide blunted the spear's point and the shark swam away. Cherry cradled a revolver in his lap to shoot any bird that flew nearby, but other than one albatross that he missed, none ventured within range. The pilot eventually tossed the gun into the ocean after salt water had corroded it.

Near week's end, Cherry finally managed to snatch a two-foot shark and, with Sergeant Reynolds's assistance, drag it into the raft. The shark squirmed and thrashed until Cherry plunged his knife into its head, in the process slicing a quarter-inch slit in

Following repeated attempts to capture food from the ocean, Captain William T. Cherry Jr. finally hauled in a two-foot shark. The famished men had eaten nothing but inadequate shares of the four oranges they had brought with them from the B-17, but despite their hunger, none could swallow the repulsive-tasting shark meat.

the raft's bottom. When he tried to mend the hole, Cherry found that the patching material was ineffective, as water had moistened the glue and prevented it from adhering to the rubbery surface. He put off repairing the hole so that he could carve and hand out the bounty to every raft, but not one man, even as hungry as they were, could stomach any of the tough, repulsive-tasting meat.

Nature offered a consolation gift later that day when a school of minnows scurried by the rafts. The famished men reached out burned hands to scoop them up, capturing enough so that each could consume three of the tiny creatures. Some swallowed the two-inch-long, tasteless minnows whole, while others suppressed their disgust and chewed the squirming fish, which were, they joked, "live hors d'oeuvres."[18]

By the end of the first week, all talk focused on water and food. People could linger for longer periods without food, but it was imperative that they soon have fresh water. On the ocean, that meant a rainstorm had to brew. If they continued to drift aimlessly on the Pacific under a blazing sun, they would perish, probably within a week.

In discussions about food, fruit juices—pineapple, orange, grapefruit, apple, and tomato—vied for top place. Most talked of how they would love to carve into a T-bone steak smothered in mushrooms, or dig into heaps of turkey and pork chops. Reynolds mentioned the soda pop he would quaff, Cherry spoke of chocolate ice cream as if it were a sacred item, and Rickenbacker and others boasted of the malted milkshakes they would guzzle once they returned to the Hickam Field Officers' Club. Captain Cherry promised that after their rescue, he would treat everyone to dinner at a famous San Francisco restaurant. One evening, he even pretended to be a waiter taking their orders as if they sat inside that restaurant.

They swapped stories about road stands where they had devoured unusually succulent hamburgers, and began a roundtable where each person described his favorite home-cooked meal. De Angelis invited everyone to his parents' home where they could feast on his mother's spaghetti and meatballs, and Sergeant Reynolds crowed of the sumptuous banquet he would host at the family ranch, replete with fried chicken, cakes, pies, and fruit juices.

The lively discussion suddenly took a morbid turn. Since the orange peels used as bait had failed to attract fish, Cherry wondered if they could instead substitute fingernail parings or something similar. Overhearing the remark, Bartek joked from his raft, "Naw, the only bait we've got is our own hides."[19] The group hushed upon hearing his words. Might a desperate move they would never consider back home be an answer to their prayers? Once Bartek opened the door, the others rushed in with suggestions, sheepishly mentioning different body parts that could serve as bait. Rickenbacker said they could use any fleshy part of the body, and Bartek thought that an earlobe, which he judged an unnecessary appendage anyway, might work. Whittaker offered that the ball of the little finger might best serve their needs, while Reynolds suggested that a slice of toe would suffice.

The macabre discussion would have shocked families back home, but as the eight drifted alone on an ocean, starved and parched, they were willing to consider all options, including the possibility that they might soon have to begin cutting into their own bodies for bait.

No one wanted to mention the unspoken thought on everyone's mind—without food or rescue, they could be dead before another week had passed.

PART III

Week 2—Ecstasy and Agony on the Pacific

THE BARTEK FAMILY COLLECTION

AUBURN UNIVERSITY, SPECIAL COLLECTIONS & ARCHIVES

CHAPTER 6

"We Were Alone. We Were Cold.
We Were Afraid."

Into the Second Week Adrift, October 28–29

LIEUTENANT WHITTAKER SURREPTITIOUSLY surveyed his companions and concluded that the strain had taken an alarming toll. In Rickenbacker's raft, the World War I hero appeared confident and composed, and Bartek seemed to be in decent shape, but Adamson, at age fifty-two the oldest along with Rickenbacker, looked haggard and appeared to have already accepted a cruel fate. In his own raft, both Cherry and Reynolds, while exhausted, were holding up well, but in the smaller raft trailing behind, De Angelis and Kaczmarczyk showed signs of the ordeal and huddled together for comfort.

Lieutenant De Angelis, the twenty-three-year-old from Pennsylvania, had all but abandoned hope for rescue. He conveyed nothing about his despair to the others, as he feared he might undermine their morale, but after the first three days, he concluded their chances for rescue were close to nil.

Reynolds said that the only thing that kept him going in

these early days was the hope that they would be found. A different thought motivated Bartek—he wanted to return home and comfort his mother, grieving after his sister's death. She had already suffered enough, and he worried that the loss of a second child would be more than she could bear. He had to stay alive, for her sake if not for his.

The lack of rescue planes supported the conclusion that they drifted outside the regular paths used by patrol planes and ships. Whittaker feared that they were floating "in one of those culs-de-sac of the Pacific that may go years without a visit from ship or plane,"[1] and that the feeble hopes he held on to were speedily vanishing.

While some began to lose faith, Rickenbacker seemed unshaken. Whittaker thought it remarkable that the aging flier could exude such serenity so soon after doctors had prepared to sign his death certificate the year before, but according to Rickenbacker, "There was no time that I lost faith in our ultimate rescue, but the others did not seem to share this state of mind fully with me."[2]

Frustration seeped into the evening service. Captain Cherry again read the passage about food and drink coming on the morrow, and once more talked to the Lord as if he were having a casual conversation. The pilot said that unless they soon received food and water, they would die, and added, "We're in an awful fix, as you know. We sure are counting on a little something by day after tomorrow at least. See what you can do for us, Old Master."

Whittaker once more rebuked his compatriots' belief in divine intervention. "Always tomorrow!" he thought. "What is this; a come-on game?" He said that "it appeared ridiculous to me that men as practical as we and as hardboiled—and some of us were pretty hardboiled—could expect a mumbling voice out on that waste of water to summon help for us."[3]

Discord crept in. Tension between Rickenbacker and Cherry simmered barely beneath the surface. One day Bartek overheard Rickenbacker bluntly ask Cherry that if one man had to determine a crucial matter for the group, who would it be? Cherry answered that as captain of the plane, he would make all major decisions until relieved of his duties. Rickenbacker, Bartek observed, stifled the urge to reply and said nothing.

Yet as conditions subsequently deteriorated in the days that followed, Rickenbacker would not hesitate from asserting himself. He had survived too much to allow a man he pegged as a Texas cowboy to determine his fate.

That attitude slowly spread. While the bomber crew remained loyal to Cherry, they increasingly recognized Eddie Rickenbacker's importance to their survival. The only combat veteran among them might be silent now, but unless their situation improved, it was only a matter of time before Rickenbacker stepped up and took control of a group increasingly willing to place their lives in his hands.

KACZMARCZYK'S FAILING HEALTH alarmed them more than a potential rift between Rickenbacker and Cherry. The sergeant had begun to surreptitiously drink ocean water, but secrets do not long remain hidden on small rafts. When De Angelis awoke one night to find him treading in the water and gulping the salty contents despite the sharks, he chided the younger man in an effort to instill fight into him, but Kaczmarczyk answered that he could not resist the urge to drink the seawater.

Rickenbacker doubted the young man would last much longer. Kaczmarczyk shook throughout the day, and Rickenbacker said that the sergeant "was really in a bad way. His mouth was dry and frothing; he cried continually for water. He was only a boy—barely 22—and thinking he was quitting, I pulled his raft in close and asked why the hell he couldn't take it? It was a brutal thing to do, yet I was determined to shock him back to his senses."[4]

Kaczmarczyk sank deeper into delirium, mumbling Catholic prayers or staring at a photo of Snooks and speaking to it for hours in both English and Polish. At night, men in the larger rafts often heard Kaczmarczyk loudly wail for his fiancée. "It was sort of a nightmare type of moan that seemed to come right out of the dark," said Rickenbacker. "It was quite noticeable, and quite loud."[5]

"THE END OF THE 'ROARING ROAD'?"

While Rickenbacker and his companions tried to fend off the mental and physical demons thrown at them by the ocean, the American public began digesting the information that the military's search had yielded no results. Rescue efforts continued as that first week ended, with American carrier aircraft and ships from Holland and Australia joining the operation. Planes flew out of Canton and Palmyra Islands, and twin-engine PBY Catalina flying boats from the Navy's VP-14 Squadron searched from their base in Hawaii. Earlier in the war, Captain Elton L. Knapp, the Hawaiian unit's commander, had twice overshot a cloud-covered Palmyra Island while on patrol, and knew all too well that if he could miss that land feature, his chances of locating a few men in three rafts were slim.

On October 24 and 25, Captain Knapp searched northwest of Canton for eleven hours each day but returned to base empty-handed. He worried that they had combed the wrong area and wrote in his diary on October 25, "If results are still negative and unless further information is available, consideration will be given to recommending abandonment of the search."[6]

The military did not release the names of the seven men with Rickenbacker for four days. In its October 26 edition, a *New York Times* article informed readers, "The War Department disclosed tonight [the night of October 25] the names of seven Army men who were on the plane carrying Captain Eddie Rickenbacker, foremost American flier in the First World War, which has disappeared somewhere in the Pacific."[7]

The paper, as well as every other prominent publication, provided sparse information about the seven individuals, but it included an update on the military's effort to locate Rickenbacker. "Three days of intensive search by all available Army and Navy air and sea forces," stated the *St. Louis Post-Dispatch*, "failed to uncover a trace tonight of Captain Eddie Rickenbacker, American war ace of the first world war, and the crew of a big Army plane that disappeared [in Pacific] waters."[8]

Different publications explained that no one had abandoned hope, as downed aviators had earlier in the war lasted in rafts for two to three weeks before rescue forces found them, but the current unsuccessful searches dimmed the earlier optimism. "Hope grew faint Monday for Capt. Eddie Rickenbacker and seven members of the Army Air Forces," announced Captain Cherry's hometown newspaper, the *Fort Worth Star-Telegram*. "While all available ships and planes still combed the vast body of water for some trace of the men, War Department officials said that no word has been received since the ship last reported Wednesday evening that its gas supply was running low."[9]

Private Bartek's mother, Mary, leaned on her deep faith to help her through the trying days while her son was lost on the ocean. However, his father, Charles, could not ignore the possibility that he and his wife might have to plan a second funeral so soon after burying their daughter.

<small>THE BARTEK FAMILY COLLECTION</small>

An October 25 letter from the adjutant general, informing the Barteks that John had been listed as missing, intensified the sense of dread in the Bartek home in New Jersey. Bartek's father, Charles, walked around in a daze, worried that he and his wife might have to plan another funeral so soon after they had said farewell to their daughter. Mary, buttressed by her deep faith, reassured her husband that their son would return to them. Fortunately, she could also lean on her kindly neighbors for support, particularly the woman who stopped by every day to see how Mary and the family were doing, and one of Johnny's childhood friends, who reassured the parents that while his longtime pal was missing, he would return. To emphasize his certainty, he vowed to punch anyone who said otherwise.

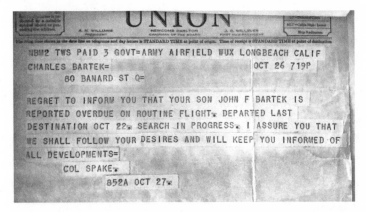

The October 26 telegram delivered to the Bartek family to inform them of Johnny's disappearance.

THE BARTEK FAMILY COLLECTION

Captain Cherry's wife of three years, Bobbie, who worked at the North American plant at Grand Prairie, Texas, waited for additional information at the Fort Worth home of friends with her two-year-old daughter, Paula. She had first learned that her husband was among those missing with Rickenbacker while driving back to nearby Arlington after visiting her parents, and a subsequent War Department wire confirmed the grim news. She had not seen her husband since March, when Captain

Cherry stopped on a flight to the West Coast, and had in the interim accepted a job with North American. Unaware that her husband was flying with the famous aviator, days earlier she had commiserated along with the rest of the nation at the news of Rickenbacker's disappearance. Now she had to wait, as did the families of the other men, for further information about her missing husband and hope all worked out for the best.

South of San Francisco, Lieutenant Whittaker's wife, Ann, told a reporter, "I haven't given up hope that they will find my husband and the others,"[10] and said that she was spending the anxious hours with their children, Shirley, age sixteen, and Thomas, nineteen.

In Winsted, Connecticut, northwest of Hartford, Sergeant Kaczmarczyk's fiancée, Coreen Bond, returned home on October 25 from her usual Sunday morning routine as a Sunday school teacher. Her afternoon crumbled when her mother met her at the door and asked, "How good a soldier are you?"[11] When Coreen asked what was wrong, her mother explained that a plane with Alex aboard had disappeared over the Pacific.

Distraught over the possible loss, and realizing that her future with the Army sergeant was suddenly in question, Coreen telephoned Adelaide Rickenbacker to see if the wife of the famous aviator possessed more knowledge than was handed out to the other seven families. Adelaide could provide nothing beyond what Coreen already knew.

Some of Alex's former teachers explained the incident to the current students and led them in prayer for Sergeant Kaczmarczyk who, not long ago, had sat in the same classrooms. His older brother, Henry, said he would return for Thanksgiving, and Adelaide even took time to write a letter to Coreen urging her "not to give up hope for one minute." She added she was confident that "my husband and the entire crew would be rescued."[12]

WHILE MOST OF the families attempted to acquire additional information about their lost loved ones, in the Pacific Colonel Adamson used paper torn from Whittaker's diary and wrote two letters to his wife, Lillian. He hoped that if he perished, somehow the letters would find their way to her. If he survived, he could hand them to her to show that in his last days he had thought only of her.

Despite his lack of nourishment, his injuries, and every other hardship he had faced, he wrote a surprisingly clear, emotion-laden note. "Darling," he began in a letter dated Tuesday, October 27, six days after they had ditched, "This afternoon we will have been adrift 144 hours. We do not know where we are nor where we are headed. We hope to stick it out until we find rescue, but so far we have seen no sign of anything other than sky and water."

"This has not been a pleasant trip," he added, "but you know that without my telling you." He thought it important for her to realize that, except for the military duties that swept him from home, she had been his inseparable companion. "If the end of this journey is the end of my journey through life itself, the end of 'our' journey, I want you to know that your shining eyes and tender smile were with me to the last." Adamson finished by requesting that if he failed to return, she was to seek future happiness with another man. "And don't grieve over me. Don't forget me, no; but find new happiness with some other man who may be even more able to appreciate your fineness than I have. If this is our final good-bye (my dear, I hate to say it, but believe me I say it as you would want me to), chin up and smile." He signed the letter with a simple "Hans."[13]

IN HOLLYWOOD, MEANWHILE, Rosalind Russell prayed for the safety of the lifelong agnostic whom she had asked to keep safe the religious medal of St. Joseph of Cupertino. By the fourth day of Adamson's disappearance, she said "most of my own personal hope had dwindled. By the end of the first week, I had given up all hope." Dejected at the presumed loss of their close friend, she turned to her husband, Freddie Brisson, for solace. He put his arms about her and, in a soothing voice, said Hans was fine. "He's alive. I know he is alive. He's getting strength from somewhere."[14] His comforting words caused the actress to wonder if that Catholic medal was helping their agnostic friend through his travails.

MOST OF THE nation's attention focused on Rickenbacker. New York City mayor Fiorello LaGuardia, a personal friend, broadcast a prayer for the aviator in his weekly radio broadcast in which he assured his listeners, "I have a hunch [Eddie] is still safe and will be found." Another New York personality, newspaper columnist Ed Sullivan, said that Rickenbacker's disappearance dominated discussions in the city's swank restaurants and clubs, which the flier often frequented. Sullivan wrote, "His friends still haven't given up on Rickenbacker; still believe that he'll turn up within a fortnight, because he looked death in the eye so often and made it back up."[15]

Ordinary citizens expressed their sympathies as well. The *Durham Sun* in North Carolina printed a poem titled "Hope," submitted by an anonymous writer. The poem stated that Rickenbacker

> *Is missing somewhere in the Pacific.*
> *America, accustomed as it has grown already,*
> *To the grim losses of war,*
> *Is stunned by the news.*
> *Not only has Rickenbacker been a war hero,*
> *But he has been one of our great heroes,*
> *Of peacetime, civil aviation.*

The poet wrote that he and the nation retained hope in the rescue of their hero, and pledged that

> *We shall hold fast to that,*
> *So long as we can.*[16]

Others were less optimistic. "Eddie has come out of some tight places heretofore," wrote one of Rickenbacker's closest friends, columnist C. B. Driscoll. "But, as this is written, it looks extremely improbable that he will return to us." He continued that "At 52, then, he gives his life in his country's service. Well, Eddie would undoubtedly say, 'How better could I die? I beat it in one war; how could I expect to beat it in another?'" Despite the pessimism, Driscoll could not completely concede hope for his friend. Reflecting on the hero's many escapes, Driscoll told his readers, "Against all reason, one cannot help hoping that Eddie will yet come through."[17]

Columnist Bill Corum, who had befriended Rickenbacker in Europe during World War I, wrote that "Rick was everything we had always thought a guy should be. An idol that had gone with us untarnished and unchanged for a quarter of a century, or since a long ago day in Neufchateau, France, when his path crossed ours for the first time."

Corum explained that Eddie "was born to be a leader, particularly in trouble." If anyone needed proof, "you only have to go back to that almost total wreck on his own Eastern Air Lines almost two years ago, when he lay battered and broken in the wreckage, saying to his fellow passengers, 'Don't light any matches, don't lose your heads; everything will be all right.'"

Corum admitted that after nearly a weeklong search without results, matters looked bleak, but stated that a friendship he had forged with the aviator a quarter century ago "will go on, no matter." He added that "All that matters is that the headline about 'Rick' being missing may prove to be, if not unfounded, premature. For he was the 'Captain Courageous,' the American Ace of Aces, the gamest, finest, and the first of America's soldiers." Pouring out his emotions, Corum continued, "Whatever happens—and we can always hope for the best until hope is gone—he was, and we are going to go on hoping is, the tops in everything that makes a man."

A cartoon of Eddie Rickenbacker accompanied Corum's column. The cartoon, with Rickenbacker drawn in the middle, pictured Eddie's many achievements positioned above a wrecked car on a speedway. Its title expressed the prevailing mood of the nation, a thought many had suppressed and dared not openly express—"The End of the 'Roaring Road'?"[18]

JOHNNY BARTEK SHARED the pessimism. Each day the men, from Sergeant Kaczmarczyk, the youngest, to Rickenbacker and Adamson, the oldest, had weakened under the strain and lack of food and water. Each man was familiar with the tales of other oceanic fliers who had ditched at sea and had never been heard from again, and if they did not soon acquire food and fresh water, they would most probably join the ranks of the lost.

If their troubles persisted, Bartek and his companions would need a miracle to last another few days.

"WE CHEWED IT SLOWLY, BONES AND ALL"

As their eighth day at sea dawned, Eddie Rickenbacker concluded that without food and water, some of them would die before the end of the week. Colonel Adamson and Sergeant Reynolds had already lost an alarming amount of weight and appeared the most critical, and he doubted Alexander Kaczmarczyk could hold on indefinitely. Unless events turned in their favor, one or more burials at sea loomed.

As it had during the first week, the sun continued to aggravate their conditions. "The sun beat down," said Rickenbacker. "We couldn't escape it. It burned the skins of the men red, then blistered them, and left them raw and bleeding."[19]

Severe sunburns plagued everyone but the darker-skinned De Angelis and Whittaker, and Rickenbacker bore scars on his hands and knuckles. "They swelled and blisters would raise, and then break,"[20] Rickenbacker explained. Salt water constantly irritated the cracked skin of both hands, which soon assumed the look of frayed leather.

Bartek sat on the bulwark and dipped his feet into the cooling water, but the sun's reflection bounced from the ocean surface and burned his tender, exposed neck and chin. At least he no longer worried about the sharks that accompanied their rafts, as some of the men had already jumped into the water for refreshing swims. Whittaker started it by suddenly blurting, "Oh, what the hell,"[21] and slipped into the water. As the others watched in dread over their companion's fate, he swam unbothered by the beasts.

Salt water corroded watches, discolored silver coins, blurred the words on the secret orders Secretary Stimson handed Rickenbacker, and faded the colors on Rickenbacker's map. It splashed into their eyes and temporarily blinded them with its sting, but lacking fresh water to rinse them out, the men had to endure the discomfort.

Salt from the ocean's spray created rashes that developed into painful ulcers, which repeatedly broke open and oozed foul pus. "This was particularly true of legs and hips," said Whittaker, "the parts of the body which were almost always wet with salt water. The rashes had grown red and sore through rubbing against the sides and bottoms of the rafts. They had been aggravated, too, by the scalding heat and merciless sun rays."[22] Men winced whenever they grated their skin against the raft's sides or against one another, sparking angry rebukes from men who were already short-tempered from their first week on the ocean.

EXHAUSTED AFTER BATTLING the heat, the men said little to one another in the dark. They drifted with the currents and bobbed with the waves, and while they sometimes gushed over meteors and falling stars, they mostly retreated to thoughts of home or tried to get a little sleep.

Rickenbacker hated the nights more than daylight hours because, with a cold, thick mist shrouding them in the dark, he often lost sight of the other rafts. Groans or prayers emanating from one of the other two rafts irritated him, and because the mist further soaked their clothes, he usually had to huddle closer to Adamson and Bartek for warmth. Whenever he awoke from a brief slumber Rickenbacker, concerned that the men in the other rafts might have cut away and drifted out on their own, tugged on the line connecting the trio to make sure he had not been abandoned. Even though they sometimes pulled the rafts together and listened to Colonel Adamson lecture about the heavens, most nights "we were alone," he said. "We were cold. We were afraid."[23]

WEDNESDAY, OCTOBER 28, presaged the arrival of their second week on the Pacific. They had consumed their final morsel of orange two days earlier. The elusive mackerel that swam so close only increased their misery, almost as if the creatures purposely taunted the ravenous men. Even the birds joined in. One that the survivors called a gull, but which was most likely a tern, returned each day and descended as if it were about to alight on one of the rafts, only to pull up at the last moment and fly away, leaving the famished survivors to watch it disappear in the distance.

Each day the men had watched as terns swooped down to snatch fish from the water. They hoped that just one bird might accidentally drop its prey into one of the rafts, but the skillfulness of the ocean hunters left them disappointed. Their need for food intensified, but the potential source of nourishment continued to elude them.

Bartek again turned to the faith his mother had tried imparting to him and began a prayer. He slowly reached into his pocket, unzipped his khaki-covered New Testament, opened to the familiar section in Matthew, and again began reading to the group about the supplicant asking God for food and water. He had muttered only a few sentences when an astonishing moment occurred. One of the terns that had been clawing fish from the ocean now circled the rafts and alighted on Rickenbacker's

With the ever-present sharks slicing through the waters near the three rafts, the famished group prayed that God would send them food and water. Each man understood that without those basic necessities, they could not long last under the Pacific's equatorial sun.

DRAWING COURTESY OF DUTTON

timeworn, waterlogged hat. The men fell silent. Rickenbacker sat as still as a corpse, the bird perched atop his head.

With the starving men watching, Rickenbacker inched his right hand upward toward the tern. His raft companions, Bartek and Adamson, sat deathly still, fearing that even the minutest movement might startle the tern into flight, and the other five men fell hushed. Only Bill Cherry in the second raft dared utter a sound, whispering to Rickenbacker to "take it easy, take it easy, come on up."[24]

As his seven hushed companions watched his every move, Eddie Rickenbacker slowly raised his right hand upward toward the tern that had astonishingly landed on his hat. When the famous aviator clutched the bird and wrung its neck, the men stared at their first meal, however meager, in more than a week.

DRAWING COURTESY OF DUTTON

From behind, slowly, almost imperceptibly, Rickenbacker's right hand rose toward the bird, its tiny head facing away toward the ocean. His hand passed by his chin, then his nose and eyebrows, until with a rapid thrust, he clenched one leg and held on while the tern squawked and flapped its wings in a vain attempt to escape his grip. Tightly clutching onto the tern, Eddie then brought the bird down and, with both hands, wrung its neck.

Rickenbacker and Adamson plucked the feathers before the aviator sliced it into eight equal portions. Retaining only the intestines to use as bait, Rickenbacker distributed three pieces to

Cherry's raft and two to the end raft holding De Angelis and Kaczmarczyk. Even though the bird's muscles reminded Whittaker of iron wires, after more than a week without food, they avidly devoured what they considered a feast fit for a king. "The raw meat was dark, sinewy, tough, fishy—and delicious," said Rickenbacker. "We chewed it slowly, bones and all."[25]

The men had no sooner finished their meal when Rickenbacker baited one of the hooks and handed the line to Cherry, then did the same for himself with the second line. Whittaker gave his ring to Cherry to use as a weight, and in seconds both lines plopped over the sides, with the tern's intestines a tempting lure for the swarms of fish below.

Cherry's line had hardly settled before a footlong mackerel lunged toward it, and moments later a small sea bass latched on to Rickenbacker's bait. With six men cheering in the background, both yanked the catches into their rafts before handing them to Adamson, who divided each fish into equal portions per man, with one to be consumed immediately and the other the following day. "Never was a man so closely watched," said Whittaker as Adamson carved into the fish. "Each of us received a fish steak about an inch square and a half an inch thick."[26]

The men chewed the bones and fins to gain added nourishment. Some balked at biting into the soft eyes, but hunger overcame their hesitancy, and four tossed the morsels into their mouths. Rickenbacker reminded them that as water comprised forty percent of each fish, they should thoroughly chew their meal to reap its full benefit.

"All this food in the space of a few minutes bolstered us

beyond words," said Rickenbacker. Men regained some of their strength, and even the sickest, Adamson and Kaczmarczyk, felt slightly invigorated.

The tern and fish did more than nourish their bodies. The dramatic, and timely, arrival of food seemed to have diminished doubts about religion's value. Whittaker had openly scoffed at religion's ability to aid them, and Adamson could not be certain of God's existence. But now Rickenbacker noticed that everyone seemed "aware of the fact that our gull had appeared just after we had finished our prayer service." He attributed it to more than coincidence and labeled the arrival of food "a gift from heaven." Back home, religion had played a peripheral role in Bartek's life, but on the Pacific, when one of God's creatures alighted on Rickenbacker's hat, "That's when we had all the faith and we started believing because we knew there was something to it."[27] They could not ignore what had unfolded before their eyes—they had prayed for food, and a tern and two fish fell into their laps.

Their bounty solved only half the problem, however. Without fresh water, the birds and fish could not prevent the inevitable fate that awaited—a slow, agonizing death from dehydration beneath a sweltering sun.

"IF WE'VE LOST RICKENBACKER, WE'VE LOST ONE OF OUR BEST MEN"

As the group feasted, back home hope for their rescue flickered. Secretary of War Stimson reminded the public that Eddie might "still turn up. You know, he is an exception to cut and dried rules,"[28] but added somberly that the widespread search had failed to uncover any trace of the group.

A dwindling number, including Adelaide, remained optimistic. The striking, gray-haired woman had been down this road and reminded people that her husband had eluded perilous situations before. "He's not reckless, and he knows the air," she said from their residence in Manhattan. "He always said he was the darling of Lady Luck."[29]

In his offices at Eastern Air Lines in New York, Eddie's personal secretary, Marguerite Shepherd, made certain each morning that, as had long been customary, one of her assistants replenished her boss's water container with fresh water. Marguerite, as usual, placed sharpened pencils and a fresh notepad on Eddie's desk and reminded others, "Don't give up on Captain. He may surprise you."[30]

Each day for as long as anyone could remember, the staff of the Café Louis XIV, a popular restaurant across the street from Rickenbacker's Eastern Air Lines office frequented by Eddie, put out fresh linen, glassware, and a carnation on a table near the top of the stairway leading to the second floor. Longtime customers knew it was Eddie's table, as he loved the high vantage point that allowed him to see who entered or left the restaurant. The staff continued to prepare his table as if they expected the famous customer to stroll in as usual and order a meal. "He'll come up that stairway. You wait and see,"[31] said the balcony waiter, a man named Joseph.

A burgeoning number of people, however, tempered their earlier hopefulness with a realistic assessment of the situation.

While newspaper editorials and a large portion of the public began losing hope as the days dragged on without word of Eddie Rickenbacker, his wife, Adelaide, reminded them that her husband had often eluded death and that he would return from this latest mishap as well.

National publications hinted that some who a few days earlier had held high expectations for Rickenbacker's safe return now feared the worst. Rickenbacker's friend, sports columnist John Kieran, said he had trouble focusing on his work because of his concern for the aviator. In an article titled "Good-By [*sic*] Rickenbacker?" the *New York Daily News* wondered if the end had come for the national hero, a man whose vibrant presence was so badly needed. The nation had already suffered hard knocks at Pearl Harbor and in the Philippines, and while the loss of Eddie Rickenbacker would be a minor matter compared to those titanic clashes, the public required as many heroes as possible to keep optimism afloat at a time when American naval and marine forces slugged it out with the Japanese in the crucial battle to control Guadalcanal. The newspaper claimed that "Rickenbacker always was a durable guy, so there is ground for hoping he may yet turn up alive in a rubber boat somewhere, but that hope grows dimmer each day. He was (or is) quite a fellow." It added in somber tones that, "If we've lost Rickenbacker, we've lost one of our best flying men and one of our best men."[32]

Columnist Henry McLemore, a close Rickenbacker friend, wrote an expansive column that sounded more like an attempt to lift sagging spirits than an elegy. "Somewhere out in the Pacific, dead or alive, is a man," wrote McLemore. "And when I say 'a man' you can spell it with a capital M, a capital A and a capital N. A MAN." McLemore admitted he had not given up on his friend, for "If the Fates gave him time to get in a rubber boat, or a wing to hang onto, he'll get home. He's that sort of gent. He may not have ever rigged a sail, but he'll learn how."

Eerily mentioning an action Rickenbacker had conducted only hours before McLemore's column was published, the newspaperman wrote that his friend "may have never caught a gull or knifed a shark, but he'll do it. His friends share with his wife the conviction that Rick, if given 1 chance in 100, will make it to port."

McLemore knew that should events turn against his friend, Rickenbacker would face it man to man. "If the Fates didn't give him any time—if they just told him, right quick, that his time was up, and that he would never have another tomorrow, I can tell you how he took the news. He took it with a little grin. He looked Mr. Death right square in the eyes and said, 'Okay, brother, you're in charge.' But you can always know that before Mr. Death had time to take complete charge, Rick did his best to see that the members of his crew had a chance to beat the final rap."[33]

"NOTHING HAS EVER TASTED SO GOOD, BEFORE OR SINCE"

The tern and the fish had lifted their spirits, but the men still needed fresh water. James Whittaker felt as if every drop of moisture in his body had evaporated over the past week, while Hans Adamson was so thirsty that at night, instead of fantasizing about beautiful women or thick steaks, he now dreamed of cutting into an ice water pie.

As the sun rose on October 29, their eighth full day at sea, Whittaker sensed that "the opinion was pretty general among our eight men that we all would die in our rubber rafts." He and Rickenbacker appeared to be the only exceptions, as both men "had been in some pretty tight places during our knocking around. I think you can tell whether it's your turn or not. I didn't think it was mine, and I was glad Rick was with us because he always comes back. I figured that if Rick was coming out alive, I was too."[34]

When the group assembled for the evening prayer service, Whittaker still denied the existence of God, but the arrival of the tern so soon after their previous day's prayers perplexed him. The lieutenant listened more attentively during the service, but he required more if he were to make a huge leap of faith and accept that there must be a higher power. As the group began to pray, something unexpected again occurred that permanently affected his disdain for religion.

After reciting the Lord's Prayer together, Captain Cherry looked to the heavens and pled, "Old Master, we called on You for food and You delivered. We ask You now for water. We've done the best we could. If You don't make up Your mind to help us pretty soon, I guess that's just about all there'll be to it. It looks like the next move is up to You, Old Master." Whittaker had no idea if Cherry's words would be effective, but he was willing to at least consider the possibility. "Let's not overlook any bets,"[35] he thought.

Once the service ended, Cherry hoisted his makeshift sail, and the wind once again nudged the three rafts into position, with the pilot, Whittaker, and Reynolds in the van. Shortly after the sun settled below the horizon, clouds began gathering, the temperature plunged, and a hint of wind picked up. For the first time in more than a week, Rickenbacker sensed that a storm, and with it fresh water, might be forming. He said nothing to his companions before drifting off to sleep, however, because he did not want to raise any false hopes.

He was not alone. With the wind nudging the rafts up gentle waves and lowering them into small troughs, Lieutenant Whittaker, much to his astonishment, concluded that a storm might be brewing. If a deluge engulfed them at this desperate moment and provided them with sorely needed fresh water, possibly, Whittaker conceded, there might be a God, and prayer might be effective.

Around 3:00 a.m. Whittaker looked to his left and observed that the fleecy white clouds that had been lazily drifting in the sky had coalesced into a darkening cloud mass. Suddenly "a bluish curtain unrolled from the cloud to the sea. It was rain—and moving toward us!" Captain Cherry watched the same formation and, convinced that a storm approached, thought of the conversation he had shared with God a few hours earlier. Upon witnessing his prayer materialize, he yelled to the others, "Here she is! Thanks, Old Master!"[36]

Johnny Bartek prayed that the storm would veer their way,

and Rickenbacker awoke from his slumber when gusts of wind pitched the raft up and down. A second or two later, someone shouted, "Rain!" and a few welcome drops splashed against the aviator's sunburned face. "I leaned my head back, opened my mouth, and let the cool, sweet water land on my face, my lips, my tongue. Nothing has ever tasted so good, before or since."[37] The drops halted almost immediately and came from the outer reaches of the storm, but Rickenbacker spied the unmistakable signs of a more severe squall gathering not far away.

With lightning bolts slicing through the darkness, the men frantically paddled toward the storm. The heavy swells slowed their pace, but the desire for fresh water infused strength into the men, who soon began closing the distance separating them from the deluge of fresh water that nature had accommodatingly placed close by. Their progress stalled when the smaller raft broke loose and spun De Angelis and Kaczmarczyk away, but De Angelis's cries in the dark helped them locate the raft outlined against a white wave. The six paddled over, mended the line connecting the trio of rafts, and resumed their journey to the storm.

The squall drew tantalizingly near. Everyone grabbed bailing buckets or empty canvas covers from the flare cartridges to use as receptacles in which to store the rainwater. Men removed and stretched their shirts to collect the water, and rested handkerchiefs on the rafts to absorb more. Colonel Adamson even removed his shorts so he could wring water from them into the containers.

"It was one hell of a night," said Rickenbacker, "all wind,

waves, noise, lightning and big black shadows." With their muscles straining to the point where Reynolds felt they would snap in half, the eight caught up to the storm and plunged into the welcome deluge. "Rain fell as from a waterfall,"[38] recounted a grateful Rickenbacker.

Giant drops cascaded down in sheets of drenching, cooling water. It washed away the encrusted salt on their skin, eased their sores and wounds, and splashed welcome liquid into their parched mouths. Men cupped their hands and gulped down handfuls of precious, life-saving water.

With an efficiency that rivaled an automotive assembly line, six men handed soaked garments to Rickenbacker and Cherry, who wrung them out into bailing buckets. The pair twisted the rainwater out of the garments until the clothing no longer tasted of salt, and then commenced wringing fresh water into receptacles, which they had earlier cleansed of any traces of salt. Rickenbacker squeezed the clothing with such vigor that he cracked open blisters and opened bleeding on his sunburned and blistered skin.

Unfortunately, the storm brought with it fifty-mile-per-hour winds that churned up the waves until they towered above the small rafts. One massive surge capsized Cherry's raft, dumping the three men, their flare pistols, and four flares into the ocean. In the raft behind Cherry's, Rickenbacker felt a sharp yank twist his raft about, giving him a clear view of Cherry's overturned raft and the three occupants flailing in the swells. With lightning flashes illuminating the scene, the trio dog-paddled back to their raft and grasped the line around its side. Cherry and

Whittaker, gasping for breath and coughing ocean water, flipped the raft right side up while Rickenbacker and De Angelis maneuvered their rafts beside Cherry's to hold it steady while the exhausted trio climbed back in. "I shall never stop marveling at the hidden resources of men whose minds never give up,"[39] Rickenbacker said of the three. If each man could maintain the same spirit exhibited by Cherry, Whittaker, and Reynolds, Rickenbacker felt certain that the chances of everyone pulling through were good.

After thirty minutes of pelting the eight survivors with fresh water, the wind abated and the rain ceased, but the storm lasted long enough for the group to capture sufficient water for their immediate needs. When the bailing buckets filled, Rickenbacker and Cherry pulled inner tubes from the Mae Wests, forced the air out, and expelled mouthfuls of water inside through the bicycle-tire-type valves. They later spit water into the shell casings from the flare guns.

Rickenbacker and Cherry estimated they had collected between two and three quarts of water, which they figured should tide them over for a few days until another squall dumped more rain on them. They were now certain that if they could rely on a steady diet of fish and fresh water, they could last for as long as it took for rescue forces to locate them or until they reached an island.

The eight pulled the rafts together to discuss how to portion out the water. Some contended that more storms were certain to come their way and argued for larger daily portions, while others took a conservative approach and countered that they should settle for smaller amounts to stretch out the number of days in case nature failed to cooperate. Rickenbacker's cautious outlook regarding food and water convinced the doubters, and the group decided that each day, everyone would receive a half jigger, or about three-quarters of an ounce of water. Once that issue had been settled, Rickenbacker poured the liquid into an empty flare cartridge case and passed it to the other seven. One by one, each man enjoyed what Rickenbacker described as "the sweetest water we have ever tasted."[40]

The men gained more than a satisfying sip of water. Because their bodies soaked up the excess fresh water during the storm, the squall restored badly needed fluids. The rain also rinsed salt from their bodies and cleansed their lesions, making the men feel almost normal for the first time in eight days. Refreshed, they celebrated by consuming the second mackerel.

The tern and rain squall combined to temporarily restore their hopes for survival. They concluded that the fresh water should, with proper rationing, last for at least three days, and buttressed with bait from the fish intestines, they should be able to hook additional meals from the ocean.

DESPITE THEIR BOUNTY, however, the eight men teetered on a perilous edge between life and death. After eight days adrift, they had yet to spot an airplane or seagoing vessel. Should rescue fail, and if they could not obtain a reliable source of fresh water, either from the skies or from an island, they might as well start counting down their final days on earth. The next ten to fourteen days, they figured, would decide whether they returned to loved ones or suffered a slow, agonizing death.

Only a determined man possessing an iron will could extricate them from their quandary, someone with the willingness to badger those who might be thinking of yielding to the elements. He had to be a person who refused to abandon hope and who believed that they would emerge whole from their ocean ordeal.

Fortunately for the group, that man sat in the second raft with Colonel Adamson and Private Bartek.

CHAPTER 7

"It Was Then That Rick Took Over"

Second Week Adrift, October 30–November 4

MIDWAY THROUGH THEIR second week on the ocean, the eight men had received a new lease on life with the sudden arrival of food and fresh water, but a morsel of a small bird and a few ounces of water would not suffice for long. When the next few days passed without a storm to replenish their water, someone had to step forward to keep their hopes alive. While morale plunged for most in the group, Rickenbacker refused to despair. In the first ten days, he had suppressed his instinct to assume command out of deference to Captain Cherry, but as the days lapsed without relief, the man who had so often slipped from death's grasp muscled his way to the forefront.

"AS LONG AS EDDIE WAS THERE I FELT CONFIDENT"

The gradual shift to Rickenbacker started imperceptibly. The crew acknowledged that Rickenbacker and Adamson, even though both had risen to the rank of colonel, were civilians and as such had no authority during this flight, but no one could deny Rickenbacker's credentials. Displaying audacity and clarity of purpose, he had catapulted to the highest ranks of international racing and to the number one spot among World War I American aces, receiving a Medal of Honor in the process. Relying on a disciplined, autocratic style of executive leadership, he had transformed the Indianapolis Speedway into a profitable enterprise and lifted Eastern Air Lines out of its financial woes. Boasting such a stellar resume, little chance existed that a man with Rickenbacker's traits would yield command to anyone, let alone to a goateed man who, in his opinion, bore little resemblance to a military commander and had never been tested with similar adversity.

Private Bartek, as did all five of the Army crew members, respected Captain Cherry, yet he could not ignore the vast shadow cast by the national hero. Cherry commanded the group, but as Rickenbacker had more experience with critical situations, the men gradually shifted their attention to what he suggested.

An incident involving his friend Colonel Adamson proved to be the spark that incited Rickenbacker to grab command. Because of the colonel's painful back and horrible burns caused by the sun's rays reaching through his rotting uniform, he often lapsed into semiconsciousness, and when awake, he babbled incoherently, as if he were unaware of where he was or in what physical state he lay. Adamson's cap, abetted by the handkerchief Rickenbacker had given him, helped block some of the sun, but enough rays pierced through to burn his feet, legs, arms, wrists, and face to a red pulp. The festering sores, aggravated by the salt water, ravaged Adamson's fair skin more than it did the others, and the raft's twists and turns further irritated his abscesses.

Adamson teetered on the precipice of a complete physical and mental breakdown. Lying awkwardly in his tight space, he retreated into a melancholy that, at times, caused Rickenbacker to worry that his friend would soon succumb. The aviator kept a close watch on Adamson, who peered back through swollen, bloodshot eyes. "It was during this terrible calm with the burning sun in the daytime and the cold nights, that he seemed to become more affected than he should have, in my opinion," said Rickenbacker. "He would become irritable and impatient." The aviator sensed a deeper malaise had set in. "He would at times seem to be in a stupor, and then there were times when he was rather violent in his denunciation of some of us."[1]

In mid-afternoon of October 30, their ninth full day at sea, Adamson suddenly lifted himself up over the raft's side and toppled into the water. Rickenbacker, a few feet from Adamson when his friend rolled into the ocean, at first thought that a shark had jarred the raft. When he noticed the colonel's absence, Rickenbacker shifted to the side, grabbed him by the collar, and began pulling him back, while Bartek moved to the raft's other end to prevent it from capsizing from the combined weight of the other two. Cherry, in the raft ahead, heard the commotion and steered next to Rickenbacker's, where he and Whittaker helped Captain Eddie lift Adamson out of the water and into the raft.

Adamson may have been trying to kill himself to be free from the pain, or he may have wanted to help his eight companions by subtracting one mouth and thereby increasing their portions of fish, but Rickenbacker, irate at his friend for attempting suicide, refused to listen to any explanation. For the remainder of the day, he lay in the raft without speaking another word to the colonel.

His anger had not subsided the next morning. When Adamson reached out his hand to apologize, Rickenbacker unleashed a stunning torrent of profanity that shocked Bartek and everyone else. In between the swear words, Rickenbacker scolded his friend, "If you want to shake hands, you've got to prove yourself first,"[2] and admonished Adamson that he had let everyone else down by trying to kill himself. He said if they wanted to survive, they had to stick together and work as a unit, not as a collection of individuals, and added that Adamson's desperate move had weakened the team. Not even trying to control his anger, Rickenbacker asserted that he had won automobile competitions on racetracks and returned home safely from the first world conflict because he had cooperated with others.

"I don't want you to try that again," Rickenbacker reproached the colonel. "We've been friends a long time," and added that "I don't want to lose my best friend."[3] Rickenbacker, growing angrier by the word, said that as he had outlasted rough times before, he knew how to get the men home safely, and if they followed his advice, they would return to their families.

Rickenbacker's harsh words restored Adamson's will to live, but they also benefited the others. Listening at the other end of the raft, Bartek was heartened by Rickenbacker's assurance that they would survive, and told himself if an aging Rickenbacker could continue to fight, so could he. "That gave me the confidence to go on. As long as Eddie was there, I felt confident."[4]

Rickenbacker purposely employed a severe tone with his friend to restore his will to live, but he also hoped his strong words would make the others think twice before trying the same. "It does us no dishonor to say that we were all becoming a little unhinged,"[5] he mentioned, but nonetheless, he feared that the others might allow despair to seep in and follow Adamson's example. He hoped his harsh words to Adamson would prevent another such occurrence.

"It was then that Rick took over,"[6] said Whittaker. The aviator figured that Captain Cherry might object, but Rickenbacker had closely studied the words and actions of the group and had sensed that in the nearly two weeks since they had ditched, they had increasingly looked to him as their leader. Now, in one of the darkest moments of their ordeal, when everyone's survival depended on taking the proper course of action, they needed Eddie's steely will and his conviction that they would emerge from their nightmare.

From that moment on, Rickenbacker refused to allow pessimistic comments. If someone seemed ready to give up, he tore into that man as he had just done with Adamson. He labeled them quitters, dared them to stand up for themselves and for their loved ones, and challenged them to be men, not crybabies. He reminded his companions that he had survived a near-catastrophic crash in Georgia, partly because he never doubted

Going back to his racing days and combat action in World War I, Eddie Rickenbacker had evaded death and dealt with dangers more times than almost any contemporary. As this photograph from the first war shows, he exuded toughness and confidence. On the Pacific Ocean in 1942, he was not about to allow anyone else to decide his fate.

US Air Force photo courtesy of the National Museum of the United States Air Force

that rescue would arrive. He employed every critical word in his vocabulary to bolster their spirits.

Blind hero worship for a World War I ace did not alone dictate their acceptance. A military man himself, Adamson concluded that while Captain Cherry had been the boss in the air, the logical course now would be to accept Rickenbacker, the Medal of Honor recipient, trophy-winning race car driver, and successful businessman, as their leader in an emergency on the water. He exuded confidence with his words and actions, and possessed a mental toughness that none of the others could match.

Adamson later appreciated what his friend had done, not merely for him but also for the group. He believed that the aviator assumed control because that was what the man had always done in challenging moments, but also contended that another reason Rickenbacker stepped up was because he blamed himself for their predicament, since they would never have been flying over the Pacific if he had not required a flight to carry out Stimson's request to see MacArthur, and if he had not resisted the idea of checking the safety of the plane and its navigational equipment.

Rickenbacker believed he had no choice, for their survival as well as his own, but to take command. He later said that with "most of them so young, they needed the strength and understanding of a man who had been down in the valley of the shadow, who had suffered and made sense out of his suffering. To those men I was able to bring the essence of the religion and philosophy I had distilled in the hospital at Atlanta."[7]

"I HAVE, I BELIEVE, MADE MY PEACE WITH GOD"

Rickenbacker stepped in at the appropriate moment. As the prospects for rescue dimmed, the likelihood rose that they would vanish from the earth and leave their families without clues as to their demise. Men sat in silence for longer stretches, not so much because Rickenbacker had suggested they do so as a way to conserve their strength and avoid drying their mouths, but because the weakened men escaped their problems by fleeing into their thoughts.

Private Bartek thought of being home in New Jersey, having fun with his friends and enjoying his mother's cooking instead of languishing on the ocean. His mother, especially, captured his attention. "Well, it's sort of funny," he said, "you sit there, and you don't think of anything, you just sit and bob with the waves, and get a crack on the bottom from a shark once in a while. You get thinking to yourself of a milkshake or something, then you get thinking of your parents at home." After a moment of reflection, he added, "You mostly think of your mother."[8]

The distress that their parents or loved ones must be going through troubled every man in the rafts. Since they had not had the opportunity to inform their families that they were aboard the ditched aircraft with the national hero, they prayed that the government would not release their names to save their parents the agony of knowing their sons or husbands had disappeared. They had no way of realizing that newspapers across the nation had already printed their names before their first week on the Pacific had ended.

Colonel Adamson had already written one letter to Helen on paper retrieved from Lieutenant Whittaker, and even though he feared she might never receive them, he now added a second. "We are still hanging on. Still hoping," the colonel began. He wrote that the rain "gave us a quart to divide among us, and it should last three days. Alex and I got extra rations" because both had been weakened from the time at sea, but he expressed his concern that Kaczmarczyk might not last much longer. "Poor Alex! He is heading out. All he talks about is his girl. But that is what all of us talk about, and think about, just our love. We seem to have no thought of anything but Home and Love."

Adamson ended by addressing the dilemma he faced. "Oh, my dear, I don't know why I write this! You will never see it anyway. What bothers me most is that this is not a nice fixed way out but one of uncertainty and worry for you at home as to what really happened to us. I have, I believe, made my peace with God and look forward with frank eyes."[9]

Sergeant Reynolds thought of the marriage ceremony he had planned and how, instead of enjoying a wedding night with his bride, he suffered in a cramped raft with Captain Cherry and Lieutenant Whittaker. At night, alone with his thoughts, Cherry mostly thought of his wife, Bobbie, and his two-year-old daughter.

The men found small amounts of humor. Bartek figured that as he and the other military personnel were entitled to receive six dollars to cover expenses for each day they served away from their home base, they would pocket a hefty amount once they returned. Each day, the private reminded his military companions that they had earned another six dollars.

The group occasionally queried Rickenbacker about his racing days, what aerial combat had been like back during the last war, his opinions of the famous people he had met, and other facets of his extraordinary life. Rickenbacker enjoyed the inquisitions into his personal life, for he recognized it as a way to take their minds off the ever-present anxiety that simmered barely beneath the surface and the fear that they might not return to loved ones. Those feelings emerged each time one man berated another or exchanged angry words over trivial matters. They expressed irritation even during evening prayer services, when some men heatedly questioned God why they had not been rescued.

To prevent arguments from hampering morale, and to keep the group united, Eddie turned to the tactic that had always brought him success, in and out of war—tough, no-nonsense, autocratic leadership. His tyrannical methods caused some to mutter under their breath, but Rickenbacker was willing to incur their anger if his management increased their chances of returning to loved ones.

———

NEAR THE END of the second week, Bartek noticed that the men now prayed with increasing fervor. Rescue in the early days had seemed inevitable, but as they approached the beginning of their third week adrift, that initial optimism had faded. Desperate and fearing for their lives, the men "all wanted something to help, so they all joined in," and "as we went on we all began to believe in the Bible and God and prayer."[10]

They listened when Bartek read from Psalm 38, in which a supplicant begged, "Forsake me not, O Lord. O my God, be not far from me. Make haste to help me, O Lord my salvation." They gained succor from Psalm 121, which promised that "The Lord is thy keeper," and that "The Lord shall preserve thee from all evil. He shall preserve thy soul."

They heard the words in St. Matthew, Chapter 8, when Jesus provided reassurance to his disciples, who were apprehensive over being tossed into the sea during a storm. "And behold, there arose a great tempest in the sea," read the Scripture verse, "insomuch that the ship was covered with the waves, but he was asleep. And his disciples came to him, and awoke him, saying, 'Lord, save us, we perish.' And he saith unto them, 'Why are ye fearful, O ye of little faith?'"

Above all, the Beatitudes, the central message of Jesus's teachings delivered in his Sermon on the Mount, shed light on how they should live their remaining years and offered hope in the midst of their nightmare. "Blessed are the poor in spirit, for theirs is the kingdom of heaven," promised one Beatitude, while another added, "Blessed are they that mourn, for they shall be comforted." The men heard that if they live according to Jesus's precepts, "they shall inherit the earth," if they seek a righteous path, "they shall be filled," and if they promote peace and love, "they shall be called the children of God."[11] Even Whittaker and Adamson, concluded Bartek, seemed to be paying closer attention.

Rickenbacker kept the prayers on a positive note. He had achieved success in his life by never giving in, never accepting defeat or allowing pessimism to shadow his endeavors, and now, when his life was once again on the line, he was not about to allow anyone to distract him from his mission. Similar to the message he conveyed to the 94th Aero Squadron in France during the first great conflict, they were in this together, and together they would endure.

As a result, Rickenbacker thought the prayer services infused sorely needed strength and hope into the group, but he rebuked one man who begged the Lord to kill him and end his sufferings. "Cut that out!" Rickenbacker instantly shouted. "If you want to pray, pray that the help that's coming will hurry up and get here. Don't bother Him with that whining. He answers MEN'S prayers, not that stuff!"

Whenever Rickenbacker took his turn to pray, he addressed God as Our Father, and always crafted positive requests. The aviator usually asked God to guide rescuers to their rafts, or pled for favorable wind and currents to whisk them to an island bearing plentiful food and fresh water. Sitting not far away, the more Whittaker listened to the hero's prayers, the more he started to believe that something good would soon occur.

They needed speedy answers if they were to survive the ensuing days.

"LORD, HOW THEY LEARNED TO HATE THAT MAN!"

The tern's arrival on October 28 and the violent storm the next night had led the men to believe that nature would deliver regular handouts, but instead, the skies calmed, and, as Rickenbacker stated, "the sun started to burn our guts out all over again."[12] Another forty-eight hours passed, and discouragement and despondency set in.

Rashes worsened when even the gentlest sway washed against their rafts and shoved arms, legs, and toes against the rubber sides, and saltwater ulcers, which Whittaker called "the scourge deep water men dread," became further inflamed. The unforgiving sun combined with the dehydrating effects of salt encrusted on their bodies to produce more boils, bringing "agony for a man to touch these eruptions."[13]

In rough seas, the raft in the middle with Rickenbacker, Adamson, and Bartek suffered the worst, as every wave yanked Cherry's raft in one direction and Kaczmarczyk's in another, trapping Rickenbacker's in a maddening swirl that made the three feel as if they were caught on a demented carnival ride. Bartek likened riding the larger, long swells to quick ascents up a ridge and speedier descents along the down slope.

The swells lifted and dropped the rafts endlessly, tossing tired, hungry men against the sides and into each other, drenching them all and forcing the men to constantly bail water. As often as they scooped water out, more splashed in, denying them sleep and any hope of getting dry.

While grouping the rafts would hopefully make it easier for rescue craft to spot the men, the arrangement posed problems in heavier seas, when they rose and fell individually rather than in unison, which strained the line and yanked them in diverse directions. The first aid kits, which some careless home-front designer attached to the floor, scraped lesions on their backs and made it difficult to sleep. Despite the discomforts, Rickenbacker still believed the potential outcome of staying together compensated for the distress, since in his experience men who worked as a unit had invariably increased the odds of success.

Even in calmer seas they could not avoid bumping into one another. "We were all in constant physical contact," recalled Rickenbacker. "The slightest move made by any of us rubbed a sore spot on another man, perhaps two other men."[14] The trio in Cherry's raft almost came to blows several times because one man accidentally rubbed up against another. Sergeant Reynolds cursed at Captain Cherry, his superior officer, and Whittaker had to mediate when Cherry vowed to slit Reynolds's throat if the radioman failed to stop slamming into him. Most of the fiery exchanges, words spoken in anger by men at the edge of their limits, ended quickly, but they indicated how brutal the past two weeks had been.

The men had not consumed enough food to have bowel movements, but they needed to urinate. Since they could not stand in the rafts without risking their stability, they adapted by using the only receptacle on hand—the same flare cartridges they had been

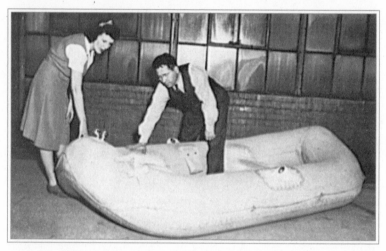

These photographs show the cramped conditions that the eight men had to endure in the rafts. Although theoretically designed for two and three men, the rafts offered far less space than that.

utilizing to store drinking water during storms. Each man washed out the cartridges with salt water whenever he urinated, but the method indicated the desperate lengths that a person in peril employed when necessary. The problem ended once they became bold enough to ignore the sharks and leave the rafts for a cooling dip, where they freely urinated in the ocean.

Thirst dwarfed hunger pains. Bartek wished he had only a fraction of the water that people back home wasted in the course of a normal day, where leaking faucets and washing automobiles consumed quantities he knew would easily take care of the men on an ocean. Lieutenant Whittaker's desire for water became nearly unbearable, and Colonel Adamson, who earlier had attempted suicide, wondered if any of the parched men might turn to the same method.

As Rickenbacker lost weight, the gums in his mouth receded and a dental bridge loosened, allowing saliva to seep underneath and develop into a cottony substance that produced a wheeze whenever he talked. To gain relief, he had to remove the bridge, rinse it in the ocean, swirl salt water in his mouth, and reinsert it.

No matter what it took, the fifty-two-year-old Rickenbacker would not permit any of his younger cohorts to quit. He shouted, cursed, and prodded the men to hold on to the will to live. If they objected, he strung together a louder litany of profanity and contended that they were simply experiencing one event similar to his many past escapades, which he related in detail to illustrate that determination can surmount anything. "I used every trick I knew on them," he explained. He mostly restrained his ire, but when necessary, "I rode them; I tore them to pieces; I struck at every raw nerve in their bodies."

He knew that most of them had never suffered beyond the normal mishaps of life, and that the aches of training camp or the pains of a broken heart were inadequate instructors for the miseries they now endured, but he would show them the way out. He called them quitters and asked what their families would think of them if they knew they had not fought to remain alive. He questioned their masculinity and pushed them to their breaking points, for he figured that if he could direct their anger toward him, they would, at least for a time, forget their troubles. He loved hearing someone call him a son-of-a-bitch, as it proved that the individual still retained the will to live. "If he could snarl back at me, he could snarl back at death."[15]

Colonel Adamson recognized his friend's methods, which purposely stirred a deep hatred of Rickenbacker, but his methods prodded the others to discover a reason to live. Adamson admired how the aviator altered tactics to suit each individual, whether he addressed young Private Bartek and Lieutenant De Angelis or the more experienced Captain Cherry and Lieutenant Whittaker. "He spoke softly and gently when soothing was in order; and he blasted out in thundering wrath when he thought a dose of anger was the best medicine. That the men were sometimes boiling-mad at him did not bother Rick in the least." He wanted the men to "fight their way out of approaching coma just because they were mad at him. Lord, how they learned to hate that man! There were times when they would gladly have thrown him into the sea, granted the strength."

At times even Adamson, who had known Rickenbacker for twenty-five years, cringed at his friend's words, but he always quickly forgave him. "Rick's sarcasm was bitter and acid, but the pulsing anger kept the sick men from slipping into listless indifference, the first step into the realm beyond." At the same time, he pointed out with admiration that he "loved Rick for a quarter of a century but hated him for twenty-four days."[16]

That intense determination to surmount all obstacles was one reason why, at the same time as Rickenbacker prodded his companions to defy the odds and survive, in Washington, DC, Henry Stimson could express optimism in a November 1 letter to Adelaide. Despite the failure to locate the national hero, the secretary of war expressed his confidence that Rickenbacker would return to them. "I cannot even yet bring myself to the belief that we shall not still find your husband alive. He was always so brave, so resourceful and so self-reliant"[17] that Stimson contended his friend's

Throughout the twenty-four-day ordeal, Lieutenant General Henry H. "Hap" Arnold offered cooperation and optimism to Adelaide Rickenbacker.

incredible strength of character would lift the group from their quandary.

The only man outside Rickenbacker's reach was Sergeant Kaczmarczyk. Listless and detached, the young man had retreated to an inner world. The group's concern heightened to the point where they handed an extra portion of water to the sergeant who, according to Whittaker, "was much weaker than the rest of us. Even Col. Adamson appeared robust in comparison— and he was far from well."[18]

"I CONSIGN YOUR BODY TO THE SEA AND YOUR SOUL TO THE LORD"

Near the end of their second week on the Pacific, Sergeant Kaczmarczyk's condition worried everyone. Weakened from the diseases that had required his hospital stay and further enfeebled from boils and sunburn, Kaczmarczyk frothed at the mouth. Sapped of energy, he continued to surreptitiously drink the ocean's salt water, which while providing momentary relief, affected his kidneys' ability to function properly. The group wanted to help, "But he was failing fast," said Rickenbacker. "We all felt so sorry for the poor, burned, shivering kid."[19]

Each man empathized with the ailing sergeant. Everyone felt the allure of avoiding further suffering by simply giving up, but a flicker of optimism spurred them on. As long as that lasted, they would fight. They did not fault Kaczmarczyk for an inability to fend off what appeared to be his imminent death, as they understood the damage his prior illnesses had done, but for now at least, they opted for a different path, one that while it might result in a similar fate, also held out hope that rescue craft would pluck them from their miseries and shuttle them back to loved ones.

De Angelis kept a constant watch on Kaczmarczyk to prevent him from rolling out of the raft and drinking more ocean water, but Alex had lost the will to live. Even Rickenbacker's admonishment about drinking from the ocean failed to put any fight into him. Whittaker noticed that the delirious Kaczmarczyk could barely recognize anyone and babbled incoherently.

De Angelis tried to shield the horribly burned sergeant from the sun, but on the open ocean, and with his own needs demanding attention, the navigator could not grant full care to his companion. A festering sore soon covered Kaczmarczyk's lips and part of his chest. Each night Rickenbacker witnessed Kaczmarczyk shaking uncontrollably, and wished he could do more for the unfortunate young man.

As a last resort, Rickenbacker told Bartek to switch places with Kaczmarczyk so that Rickenbacker could tend to him in a larger raft. Lifting the sergeant out of the smaller raft and into Rickenbacker's required the combined strength of three men—Rickenbacker, Bartek, and De Angelis. They gently placed Kaczmarczyk in the lee side, the side away from the wind, where Rickenbacker cuddled him like a mother holding a newborn so that his body warmth might ease the young man's shivering. Kaczmarczyk, in obvious pain, constantly moaned, and he mumbled incoherently about Snooks and his mother until he finally fell into a deep slumber. For most of the next two days, Rickenbacker cradled the man, trying to instill warmth and will into Kaczmarczyk.

Although Kaczmarczyk appeared to have slightly improved on the morning of Sunday, November 1, their eleventh full day at sea, he would not live to see another dawn. Perhaps sensing he had entered his final hours, after prayer services that evening, he asked Rickenbacker to return him to the smaller raft. The men joined the two rafts and gently lifted Kaczmarczyk into the smaller one with Bartek, while De Angelis moved in with Rickenbacker and Adamson. Bartek cautioned his companion to avoid drinking more salt water, but he doubted the dying man understood his words. "I knew he was incoherent," said Bartek. "When he started to lower his hand into the water, I grabbed it and laid it in his lap. Whether he understood or not, I didn't know, but he did calm down."[20]

When Bartek suggested that Kaczmarczyk try to sleep, the sergeant briefly spoke about Snooks, about his mother, and about dying. After putting his head down and praying for fifteen minutes, Kaczmarczyk suddenly regained his composure, stared at Bartek, and spoke about journeying to another world. Near 3:00 a.m. on November 2, Bartek heard the sergeant whisper another prayer, and then suddenly stop moving. Bartek inched over to feel the man's pulse, but found no signs of life.

Nearby, Rickenbacker thought he detected a deep sigh rise from the smaller raft, followed quickly by silence. A few seconds later, Bartek shouted that Kaczmarczyk had stopped breathing.

"Has he died?" Rickenbacker asked Johnny.

"I think so," the private replied.

"Our little sergeant was suffering no more,"[21] Rickenbacker wrote. He decided to wait for dawn, when he and Cherry could confirm that Kaczmarczyk had perished, before consigning their companion to the sea. For the next few hours, Bartek lay in the tiny raft intermingled with the deceased sergeant.

A gorgeous dawn contrasted with the grim mood in the rafts.

"The east flamed up in spectacular shafts of red, purple, and gold," noticed Whittaker. "The sun seemed to leap out of the sea into the sky." With the sunrise, the group pulled the rafts together so that Rickenbacker, Cherry, and Whittaker could examine Kaczmarczyk before letting the body drift away. Because the torrid sun would accelerate the decaying process, they could not keep the sergeant with them in hopes that a rescue might permit his remains to be returned to the family. The seven survivors hushed as Lieutenant De Angelis, the former Catholic altar boy

The seven survivors had no option but to bury Sergeant Alex Kaczmarczyk at sea. The former altar boy, Second Lieutenant John J. De Angelis, conducted the funeral service.

AUBURN UNIVERSITY, SPECIAL COLLECTIONS & ARCHIVES

who shared the same faith with Kaczmarczyk, improvised a burial service. After leading the group in the Lord's Prayer, he told God that Alex had been a good person, and asked that he be granted a speedy entrance into Heaven. Recalling as much as he could from the Catholic burial service, De Angelis sang two beautiful Latin hymns, *"Tantum Ergo Sacramentum"* and *"Panis Angelicus,"* and ended the service with the words, "I consign your body to the sea and your soul to the Lord."[22]

The men removed Kaczmarczyk's identification tags and wallet and handed them to Cherry for safekeeping. Hushed with emotion, they tenderly lifted the body to the gunwales and allowed it to gently slip into the Pacific. Kaczmarczyk drifted forty feet from the rafts before sharks pulled his body beneath the surface.

Rickenbacker had seen men die before, but the sergeant's death affected him in ways he had never experienced. Maybe it was that neither Kaczmarczyk's mother nor his girlfriend would gain closure from a death that occurred so far from home, under circumstances they could never truly understand. Or maybe it had been watching sharks pull the young man's body beneath the waves. Whatever the reason, Rickenbacker later termed this as one of the most wrenching moments in his life.

The sergeant's death impacted the others, who wondered if a similar fate awaited them. Rescue forces had not come in time to save Kaczmarczyk, so what chance did they have, especially if the military had called off their search? Colonel Adamson assumed that he would be the next to perish, while a downhearted De Angelis had figured that after Kaczmarczyk's death, the question now became when, not if, they would perish.

Rickenbacker was certain that he could last another week to ten days, but he doubted the others would. Adamson seemed the most likely to succumb next, followed in order by Sergeant Reynolds and Private Bartek, two of the youngest members. Lieutenant De Angelis and Captain Cherry might hold on longer than a week, and Lieutenant Whittaker, while he exhibited an admirable fighting spirit, would, too, eventually succumb. Rickenbacker intended to do what he could to keep the others fighting, but each man had limits to what he could endure.

A rendezvous with death appeared imminent for the seven surviving members.

PART IV

Week 3—Desperation and Rescue on the Pacific

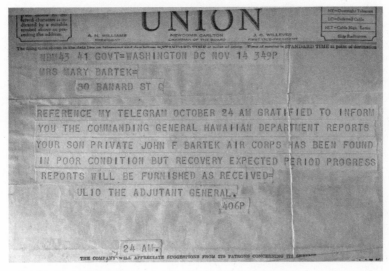

National Archives Photo #80-G-K-15960

CHAPTER 8

"We Will Help Ourselves, If You Give Us the Chance"

Desperation During the Third Week Adrift, November 5–9

THE MEN—NOW aligned with Cherry, Whittaker, and De Angelis occupying the lead raft; Rickenbacker, Reynolds, and Adamson following behind; and Bartek alone in the smallest raft—slowly drifted southwest toward the Ellice Island group and the international date line. Their movement suddenly halted, though, when the wind died and the ocean calmed, stilling the three rafts on a watery mirror. Lacking wind or an ocean current, the men were trapped motionless beneath an unpitying sun.

They had become entombed in the doldrums, a phenomenon that had instilled terror in sailors' hearts through the centuries. Known to oceanographers as the Inter-Tropical Convergence Zone (ITCZ), and called the doldrums by sailors after the despair that sets in after weeks without motion, the ITCZ is a region extending 5 degrees north and south of the equator. When the trade winds from the Northern Hemisphere blow to the southwest and collide with the counteracting trade winds from the Southern Hemisphere flowing northeast, the warm, moist air circulates upward into the atmosphere, taking both wind and rain with it and leaving little, if any, surface wind to aid sailing ships or, in this case, rafts. In the days before mechanized ocean-going vessels eliminated this concern, doldrums could hold ships captive for weeks at a time, producing severe depression among sailors unable to escape its clutches.

The blistering days and chilly nights on the equatorial Pacific numbed both body and mind. The worst period consisted of the hellish days trapped in the doldrums, which brought to mind the classic poem by Samuel Taylor Coleridge, The Rime of the Ancient Mariner, *which depicted some of the same hardships they now encountered.*

Seafaring novels depict the doldrums' horrors, and poets describe its terrors. Lieutenant Whittaker thought that "the ocean was glassy and glaring as far as we could see. Our eyes ached from the merciless, blinding light." The doldrums reminded him of the classic epic poem by Samuel Taylor Coleridge, *The Rime of the Ancient Mariner*, published in 1798, which vividly conveyed the experiences of a sailor who returned from a lengthy sea voyage. Whittaker especially recalled two verses that reflected his current dilemma of being stalled beneath the equatorial sun:

> *Day after day, day after day,*
> * We stuck, nor breath nor motion;*
> *As idle as a painted ship*
> * Upon a painted ocean.*
> *Water, water everywhere*
> * And all the boards did shrink;*
> *Water, water everywhere,*
> * Nor any drop to drink.*[1]

The appalling conditions that marked the first two weeks heightened in the third. The misery caused by the sun, thirst, and hunger intensified, leading some of the group to label this stretch the worst of their ordeal. Saltwater ulcers infested the legs and feet of six of the seven remaining men, and their raw bodies, already toasted by the sun, throbbed with pain each time the saltwater spray doused them. The small amount of drinkable water they swallowed each day provided meager succor for men who required a mass infusion of liquid. Clothes, tattered from the days adrift, disintegrated into strips of cloth hanging loosely off their skinny frames. Even the smallest efforts to scoop minnows or catch larger fish exhausted the men, and the salt air had so rotted the fishlines that sharks snapped them off and carried them away.

Everything—the ocean, the deprivation of food and water, the lack of sleep, the separation from family and friends—conspired against their survival. Hans Adamson noticed that the sporadic chatter of the first two weeks had dwindled, and "silence hung over all the rafts," only to be broken when one occupant bumped into the man next to him, who replied with a string of profanity that had all three men "shrilling hysterically."[2]

In Captain Cherry's raft, he, Whitaker, and De Angelis debated why they had so suddenly departed from Hawaii instead of waiting a few hours to carefully inspect the bomber. De Angelis contended that had they done so, they would not now be in their current predicament. Though they failed to resolve the issue, they quietly put the blame on Rickenbacker's desire to continue west as quickly as possible. Out of deference to their prominent passenger, though, they kept silent and let the matter fade for the time being.

If he were in New Jersey, Johnny Bartek could go to the hospital or see his family doctor to be treated for his painful ulcers, but on the ocean he could only suffer in silence. The sun's rays inflamed and pained his eyes as if hundreds of needles pierced through to his skull. Salt from the ocean water had crusted his eyes, making it difficult to see clearly or even to blink heavy lids stuck together by the salt. His badly sliced fingers refused to heal, and sores, aggravated each time he rubbed against the raft, had penetrated his skin and spread over much of his body. Water splashing around inside his raft softened his feet and made them more susceptible to cuts and bruises.

Everyone, even Rickenbacker, battled periods of delirium. "Our bodies, our minds, the few things we had with us were slowly rotting away,"[3] he said. His legs and hip throbbed, and as he lost weight, his gums constantly irritated him. Desperately thirsty, and losing the ability to think clearly, Reynolds and De Angelis undressed and dove ten feet beneath the surface searching for purer water they erroneously surmised might flow at that depth.

As always, the sun proved to be a harsh mistress, but now, with them ensnared in the doldrums, it beat on the men tenfold, stinging the salt water on their bodies and covering everyone in a white, grainy crust. They had been hot and thirsty before, but at least they had been moving with the currents, and with each mile traveled, they could hold on to the hope that land or a plane lay just over the horizon. By clutching them in a windless dungeon, the doldrums swiped that dream, however faint, from the ravaged group. No water swished by the raft to indicate motion; no breeze cooled their brows. They were cemented beneath a merciless sun, held in place for an indeterminate time, and blocked from journeying to an island and potential rescue beyond the horizon. At times the sun's oppressive heat caused De Angelis to think he smelled human flesh burning.

Rickenbacker often spotted squalls in the distance, but lacking the strength to paddle toward them, he knew the rain would always remain out of reach. His life had always centered around action, whether on the ground during a race or in the skies over France. It had invigorated him, but trapped in the windless doldrums, he could only sit in his raft and yield control of his fate to the ocean.

He recognized telltale signs that the other men had weakened in their resolve to live. Listless and inattentive, they spent hours lost in their thoughts. He worried that Adamson, Bartek, and Reynolds were near death, and "the rest of us were showing an accelerated decline in energy and alertness."[4]

To snap them out of their lethargy, he harangued his companions to hold on, and he cursed and admonished them to face their tribulations like men. He savaged anyone who lost hope and retaliated to every negative remark. "What's that? What's that? So you're off again, are you? And you call yourself a man! Why, you blankety blank blank quitter! When we get out of this, you'd better crawl home to the women where you belong." He harped that if they gave their complete effort to survive, when they returned home, they could look their loved ones straight in the eye and say they had battled to remain alive for them.

According to Whittaker, in the doldrums Rickenbacker swore nonstop, employing "some mighty powerful plain and fancy cussing" that would make anyone blush. "But I think Rick was using his vocabulary in a good cause. It certainly got results."[5] Rickenbacker stopped cursing only long enough to join the group's new prayers for a stout wind to free them from the doldrums.

Rickenbacker hated to adopt such a heartless manner, but he believed that under the circumstances, he had no alternative but to "brutalize anyone who seemed to show a weakness or a willingness to give up." He lashed out with a singular objective—to make the men so mad at him "that they swore they were going to live if for one devout purpose only, to bury me at sea. That was, of course, the reaction I was after, and the reason for my vitriolic attack on them."[6]

Since their first day on the ocean, sharks had been an unwelcome, constant presence, but now in their third week, and with hope dissipating, the weakened, bearded men lost their fear of them. They were too concerned about food and fresh water to care much about the predators, and consequently a few slipped into the water to cool off and swim about the rafts, especially Lieutenant De Angelis, who left his raft every day to dip below the surface and swallow small amounts of the salt water. Sharks swam within feet of the navigator or brushed against his legs, but De Angelis admitted that trapped in the doldrums during this third week, he almost hoped the sharks would free him from his suffering.

One night the men heard a loud splash. Looking over the sides, they saw in the dark zigzagging phosphorescent streaks slice toward the surface, followed by loud thumps as a school of mackerel rose out and smacked back into the water while trying to avoid pursuing sharks. Most disappeared beneath the surface, but a few landed in the rafts, providing welcome food for the group.

Early one morning soon after, hundreds of finger-length fish wiggled by the rafts. Men reached out and scooped them up by pinning the fish against the raft and sliding them inside, and while most of the slippery sardine-type fish eluded their grasp, they caught enough for a meal that they crunched and swallowed whole. Occasionally, small white crabs the size of a dime clung to the sides of rafts, giving them another source of nutrition. Unfortunately, these meals did not occur often enough to long sustain the men, who consumed the creatures in a robotic, trancelike fashion while sitting in their rafts.

THEIR HORRIFIC DAYS in the doldrums ended in the middle of the third week with what Lieutenant Whittaker described as the first of two miracles to "complete my redemption." Since Kaczmarczyk's burial, he had withdrawn into a darker mental space because he saw "in Alex's fate the precursor of my own."

His mood changed in midmorning when a squall toward the horizon blotted out the sun and a blue curtain of rain swept toward the rafts. The men held their breath, hoping that the precipitation would reach them, but the storm abruptly veered away with less than one quarter of a mile separating it from the group. Although downcast, "Somehow, my faith didn't die," said Whittaker. "I prayed with the rest—wholeheartedly, I believe, for the first time."

One man expressed anger that God had abandoned him by turning away the storm, but Whittaker simply talked to God as if he were visiting with a friend. "God, You know what that water means to us," he said loudly enough for the rest to hear. "The wind has blown it away. It is in Your power, God, to send back that rain. It's nothing to You, but it means life to us." Whittaker ended with a request. "God, the wind is Yours. You own it. Order it to blow back that rain to us who will die without it."

The first of what Lieutenant James C. Whittaker described as the two miracles that convinced him God existed occurred when a storm on the horizon, which was moving away from the group, suddenly reversed course and engulfed the rafts after the men begged God to change the winds and blow it to them.

DRAWING COURTESY OF DUTTON

The ensuing moments sparked the transformation of a man who had long denied the existence of a Supreme Being. Even though the wind continued to churn the surface, blowing the waves away from the rafts, the rainstorm inexplicably stopped, and "Then, ever so slowly, it began moving back toward us—against the wind!" Whittaker said that the squall "moved back with a majestic deliberation. It was as if a great and omnipotent hand moved it back across the waves." Within moments, the storm inundated the rafts, delivering sorely needed fresh water and allowing the men to luxuriate in the rain's cleansing effect. "Many of the boys had shed skin three or four times by now, and there were raw places where they had chafed against the sides of the rafts." He added "That rain was a Godsend—I use a capital G intentionally."[7]

The powerful winds nudged the rafts out of the brutal doldrums. Moving once again, hopes flickered that they might drift toward an island, and Whittaker had an opportunity to deepen his belief in a God that had apparently fashioned a miracle in their behalf.

"WE THOUGHT WE OUGHT TO COME CLEAN WITH HIM"

Johnny Bartek tried to pull off his own miracle a short time later. Occupying the small raft by himself at the end of the line, he had begun to mull the possibility of cutting the line and drifting off alone. The cluster of rafts had done nothing to resolve their crisis, he reasoned. He might catch a current that would whisk him to an island. At the very least, two separate sets of rafts increased the odds of an airplane or ship spotting one or the other, so the notion of splitting up seemed logical. The private knew how to catch rain and minnows, and figured that he still possessed enough strength to make the attempt, but if he lingered another day or two, he doubted he would be strong enough to carry out his plan.

Even if he died alone on the ocean, any rescue forces that subsequently discovered his raft would conclude that the other rafts had to be near. Bartek had no illusions about being a hero, and he had certainly not given up on life, but as far as the desperate youth was concerned, he faced a simple choice—make the attempt now or perish.

Bartek could not share his plan with Rickenbacker, who had insisted that the group stick together. Instead, he patiently waited until night provided cover, when he carefully untied the line connecting his raft to the others and floated away. To gain speed, Bartek removed his shirt, lifted his feet on the raft's side, and attached one end of the shirt to his oar and the other to his elevated feet to fashion an improvised sail. He drifted all night in that manner, sporadically assessing his progress by placing one hand in the water and feeling the ocean rush by.

Rickenbacker awoke the next morning and, as usual, checked Cherry's raft first before turning to his rear. To his surprise, he found the line connecting Bartek's raft with Rickenbacker's floating on the surface and Bartek's raft gone. Bartek awoke almost simultaneously, expecting to be far from his comrades, but a voice cut through the dawn shouting, "Johnny! Johnny!"[8] When the private turned in the direction from which it came, he saw two rafts riding the crest of a wave only half a mile away.

Bartek sheepishly paddled back to his companions to face a certain interrogation. When Rickenbacker asked him why he had attempted such a foolish step, Bartek offered no apology because he believed he was only trying to survive. However, he did agree that his separation from the group might not have been the wisest thing to do.

IN THE LEAD raft, Captain Cherry took a keen interest in Bartek's return. That the young man had taken a chance inspired him, and even though Bartek failed, Cherry thought that with his own expertise and strength, he might succeed. When the group debated the issue again the next day, Rickenbacker steadfastly argued that the seven should stay together. Cherry countered with the idea of splitting up, but Rickenbacker bristled and asserted that as a retired colonel, he outranked Cherry and had the right to direct the group. Cherry curtly replied that as captain of the airplane, he would remain in charge until rescue came.

The argument between the two men—one who expected the others to follow his wishes because of his high rank and his celebrated accomplishments, and the other who took offense at a civilian who questioned his rightful authority—grew more heated. When Rickenbacker noticed that Whittaker and De Angelis favored Cherry's view, he reluctantly conceded that one raft might have a slight chance of rowing against the current and paddling southeast toward the shipping and air routes. If luck favored them and they encountered a ship or an airplane, the three could direct rescue forces to the general area in which the other four men drifted.

Cherry, Whittaker, and De Angelis left in the early afternoon of November 4, but, like Bartek, made little progress against the currents. A few hours later, Rickenbacker could still see their raft on the horizon, and when dawn arrived the next morning, the three had only progressed one mile. Though his attempt had failed, the captain was convinced that with the right currents and a bit of luck, he could reach an island or be spotted by aircraft. Cherry decided to try again at the earliest opportunity, and if he made it, he could direct rescue forces to the other six men and prove to the Medal of Honor recipient that he had been right all along.

HAVING WITNESSED TWO failed attempts to defeat the currents, the men lapsed into long silences in which they began to examine the course of their lives. They wondered about choices they had made or not made, and posed questions they had not dared ask of themselves in years past.

When he was unable to sleep, Whittaker reflected on his newfound notions of God, religion, and the state of his soul. He had always dismissed the idea of a Supreme Being, but now, lost in the Pacific, drifting toward what was beginning to seem an inevitable death, he questioned those beliefs, especially in light of the unlikely good fortune they had received. "I was finding my God in those watery wastes and we were meeting as strangers," he recalled. "I don't deny that there was still a reluctance, somewhere deep within me. After 40 years and more of indifference and selfishness, it would have been strange indeed if I hadn't felt something of the sort." Yet his ordeal had forced the lieutenant to come to grips with a part of his life he had always avoided. "We might have remained strangers, had it not been for Him" and His benevolence toward the group, actions that "were to save my life and change the way of it about as completely as a life can be changed."[9]

The prayer services reflected the alterations overtaking the men. In their first week adrift, they had mainly asked for food, water, and deliverance. They had received answers for the first two, but that rescue forces had not arrived angered some in the group, who began cursing the Lord for His inaction in their behalf.

That resentment subsided as they entered the third week, when most of the seven survivors reluctantly accepted that the military, after devoting men and resources to find the group, had probably canceled the operation. If true, their only chance of survival now lay in drifting to an island. Confronted with that bleak outlook, rather than pray for food and water, in the third week the group utilized the prayer services to cleanse their souls and confess their shortcomings. "We thought we ought to come clean with Him,"[10] said Private Bartek of the confession-like tone of their prayers.

They gathered now as a group of penitents, willing to admit their sins to the only collection of men who could empathize with what they had gone through. No one led the services; each man spoke when he desired and talked without interruption for as long as he wanted. "We had plenty of time—what the hell. We'd let him talk until he got tired," said Bartek. The confessions cleansed their consciences and freed their minds so that they could better accept what only two weeks ago had been unthinkable—their deaths in a remote part of the world, far from home and loved ones. "There isn't a man living who has the innermost secrets of those youngsters who were with me that I have," explained Rickenbacker of the prayer services in that third week. "Thinking they were never going to be found, they confessed their indiscretions as they remembered them" as well as "the sins of omission and commission of all of them that can never be printed."[11]

Some vowed that if they survived, they would rid themselves of bad habits and live better lives. One man promised to improve as a husband and father, while another pledged to work harder to ensure that his family had everything they needed. They talked about how they had mistreated some people, spoke of the debts they had accumulated, and mentioned their concern that their loved ones would bear the responsibility for their payment. They discussed matters they would never broach with anyone at home, but believing their chances of surviving were slim, they felt free to admit to distasteful events, including two married men who disclosed that they had dated other women while overseas. Some joked that the group knew more about each other than their families did.

Captain Cherry, who often talked about his family, regretted the serious argument he had with his wife shortly before leaving Texas for the Pacific and pledged to make amends. He also expressed guilt that he had already missed too much of his young daughter's life and admitted that he now wanted nothing more than to sit in a chair with her and bounce her on his knee.

Lieutenant Whittaker spoke of the love he had for his wife, and Sergeant Reynolds doubted that he was good enough for the girl he planned to marry back in California. Lieutenant De Angelis thought he should have taken his newlywed wife to dances and movies more than he had, and vowed that if he returned, he would take her to nightclubs or the theater every night of the week. He expressed his wish that, if he died, his parents could somehow learn what had become of their son, and hoped that Heaven did exist, because he wanted the opportunity to explain to people he had once known what had unfolded on the ocean.

Rickenbacker took a different tack, telling the six men, "If I start confessing, I have so many sins I wouldn't know where to start." Instead, he offered a prayer that the group be granted the opportunity to reunite with their families, even if at this stage the odds seemed stacked against them. "You, Our Father, know we are not asking You to do it all," prayed the aviator. "We will help ourselves, if You will give us the chance."[12]

After the group finished confessing their shortcomings, they crafted final letters to loved ones in Whittaker's notebook on the slim chance that someone might come across the rafts after their deaths. They wrote of debts owed and instructed their wives how to settle them, and expressed their love for wives, sweethearts, and families.

The seagoing confessionals refreshed them spiritually and prepared them for what lay ahead. Whatever was about to unfold in the coming days, they had at least made their peace with God and with their loved ones.

"THIS IS DAVY JONES, JIM. COME ON DOWN, DOWN TO MY LOCKER"

Confession might be good for the soul, but the body still required relief from hunger, thirst, and the elements. Rickenbacker and Adamson could hardly move a muscle without pain, and Bartek's childhood idol spoke only when he had to. Adamson lay prone in the bottom of the raft, with a hat providing meager shade for his face and his hands across his chest, as if adopting a deathlike visage.

Bartek was not much better. Salt spray continued to crust his eyes, and without rain to wash it away, he felt a sharp, stinging pain each time he pried open his lids, making it all but impossible for him to read his Bible. "I was physically and emotionally drained; so thirsty and tired and on my last legs." When the private glanced at Cherry's raft, he most often saw the captain with his head resting on one of the sides, listless and displaying little of the energy he had always exhibited in a plane's cockpit. He said the seven were "again broiling in the hot sun, going around in circles in slow motion, slowly dying."[13]

Suffering from the searing heat, Whittaker noticed that most of his companions now displayed signs of delirium. They shouted without reason and talked as if family members sat beside them. "Nearly all of us were holding long and serious conversations with people who were not there," the lieutenant explained. "Water low. Hopes low," he scribbled in his makeshift diary. He noted that some men appeared on the brink of losing their minds, yelling madly and staring off into the distance. Only one man besides himself seemed to retain any optimism at all. "Rick never lost his confidence that we would be rescued, and I don't think I did. Hope was low, but I never told myself this was the end."[14]

Even Eddie Rickenbacker, however, had limits to what he could endure. "As the days wore on and our strength left us, we talked less and less," he wrote. "A drowsiness, which in the later stages amounted almost to coma, had taken possession of us. We would lie for hours in the intense heat of the sun without a single word being spoken. What I seem to remember most about the last days was the almost complete silence. If one man spoke there would be no response."[15]

Bartek held on by a slender thread. When they had left Hawaii, he was struck with the breathtaking beauty of the moon that basked the bomber in its glow. He had hoped to capture an image of it with his camera, but onboard duties prevented him from doing so. Now, motionless on a still, calm ocean, he doubted he would ever get the chance.

Men hallucinated, heard loved ones' voices, struggled to discern the real from the imaginary, and wondered if they were on the verge of madness. Bartek thought he heard a train or boat whistle, and other men swore they saw an island on the horizon offering a lush, sandy beach, coconut trees, and fresh water. Rickenbacker sometimes slipped into a stupor and stared straight ahead, lost in his thoughts. On one occasion, Adamson watched his friend blink his eyes, emerge from a trance, and mutter to the colonel that he had just telephoned Adelaide, who agreed to drive the car out and pick them up.

Rickenbacker experienced a recurring dream in which he landed on an island where a friend resided in a gorgeous house. The friend always offered Rickenbacker a soft bed for sleep, followed by a bountiful breakfast with a variety of fruit juices. After devouring the feast, Rickenbacker telephoned Secretary Stimson to request that he immediately dispatch a plane to pick him up. Sadly, each dawn ended the dream, and "I would awaken to find to my horror and amazement that I was still on the broad Pacific, with its gray mist and that everlasting rocking to and fro that goes on with the swells on any ocean."[16]

Lieutenant Whittaker's delusions featured the voice of Davy Jones, the mythical keeper of sailors' souls, whispering, "This is Davy Jones, Jim. Come on down, down to my locker. I want to see you." Each time, Whittaker would slip over the raft's side and descend through the warm water to the ocean floor and a waiting Davy Jones. "On the bottom I came face to face with Davy, a powerfully built man with a white mustache that curled down over the corners of his mouth." With his assistant, Jim Blood, standing at his side, Jones asked the lieutenant, "Are you ready to come down here for good?"

Whittaker always declined, prompting Jim Blood to join the conversation. "We're all ready for you, down here, Jim," he said affably. "You'd better stay. You don't belong on land, Jim. You belong with us. You've been a sailor, and all sailors should be

The wearying days and nights on the Pacific led every man to hallucinate and to hear sounds, such as a train whistle or a loved one's voice, that could not possibly exist on the open ocean. This drawing depicts the "conversations" Lieutenant James C. Whittaker conducted with Davy Jones, the mythical keeper of sailors' souls, who begged Whittaker to jump into the ocean and join him, and with Jones's assistant, Jim Blood, who tried to convince Whittaker he belonged in the ocean depths with them.

Drawing courtesy of Dutton

with us. How about it?"[17] After telling Blood that he was not yet prepared to join either Davy Jones or Jim Blood, in his delirium Whittaker returned to his raft.

Whittaker's nineteen-year-old son, Thomas, who was stationed in the Navy in San Francisco when the lieutenant left on the Rickenbacker flight, also materialized in his dream. When the father asked why he had left California to join him in the raft, Thomas replied, "I was sent to sea over two weeks ago, Dad. You see—we were sunk. And since I was out here I thought I'd drop in and see how you were getting along." In his saner moments, Whittaker worried that the hallucination indicated something bad had happened to his son, for "I had heard of persons recently dead appearing to near relatives or friends. And in my abject state on that 18th day adrift I would have believed anything."[18]

Johnny Bartek's dreams and hallucinations also involved family. In one dream his recently deceased sister, Ruth, stood behind a net separating the two. The seventeen-year-old spoke while standing amidst a picturesque garden of exquisite flowers, and promised her brother that he would survive his Pacific ordeal and would one day be reunited with her. "Well, Johnny, you're going to pull through this, but you're going to have a tough job after you get through with this raft," she said. "Over here, I am happy and I've got plenty of places to play, and I'm going to wait for you, but you've got a tough job to do, tougher than you think. You're going to run into a lot of trouble. Well, goodbye, Johnny, I'll see you again, it's going to be a long time."[19] Laughing as she turned, Ruth slowly walked away.

When he dreamed of his mother, Mary stood at the door and assured him that if he relied on God, he would return to the family. He would, though, she said, be altered by this experience. "Johnny," she calmly said to her son, "I told you you were going to get yourself in trouble sometime and you're going to have to depend on somebody higher to pull you out of it."

Through an endearing smile, she added, "Now that you're out there, you're going to be out there for quite a while, but you'll be back with your mind changed and a different type of fellow." She ended with a laugh, and as she closed the door she reminded her son, "I told you it was coming."[20]

Other nightmares cruelly teased the men. In one recurring delusion, Bartek sat in an ice cream parlor asking for an ice cream soda, or ordering a Coke and a hamburger at a road stand, but just as the waitress placed the food in front of him, Bartek received orders to report to duty and had to rush out before taking his first bite.

Captain Cherry so often conducted conversations with his fingers and toes that he wound up naming each one of them. Sergeant Reynolds claimed that Cherry and Lieutenant De Angelis had been sneaking to a nearby island to quaff fresh water and to search for oil. "I don't know whether I should tell you fellows or not," ranted Reynolds, "but they are drilling secretly for oil there. I saw the big condensers they use to get water from the sea." Rickenbacker heard the chatter and shouted, "Well, I'll be damned! If anybody has an island they're going to, damn it, they better take me!"

"The oil is a secret," Reynolds replied, "but I think Bill Cherry knows all about it." Although Cherry denied the allegations, Rickenbacker persisted in hopes of discovering that the island actually existed. Eddie later admitted that he was probably in a delirium of his own, "But I wasn't overlooking any bets that concerned islands with water condensers on them."[21]

Nightclubs or local inns frequented their hallucinations.

Whittaker once thought that he spotted an establishment offering food and dancing, and asked Cherry, "Bill, why didn't you stop at that big roadhouse with the neon signs?" De Angelis said that on other occasions, the hungry men dreamed about sitting at a large table holding a bounty of food, but each time Cherry would rise, order them to follow him, and lead them out before anyone had the chance to taste one mouthful. "Why in hell did you leave when we were going to get something to eat?"[22] one of the men angrily demanded.

BY THE MIDDLE of their third week adrift on the Pacific, the seven survivors had reached the limits of their endurance. Each man had so deteriorated, physically and mentally, that their demise seemed a matter of days, possibly hours, away.

As November 9 approached, it appeared that no one from the group would live to tell their stories.

CHAPTER 9

"I Hear an Engine! I Hear an Engine!"

The First Rescues, November 9–11

FLYING IN A Vought OS2U Kingfisher floatplane, Lieutenant (jg) Frederick E. Woodward and Radioman 2/c Lester H. Boutte arrived at Funafuti, the largest of nine atolls comprising the Ellice Islands, in early October, shortly before the Rickenbacker bomber disappeared. They joined other aviators operating four additional Kingfishers based at Funafuti's expansive lagoon, along with four PT boats and the PT boat tender USS *Hilo* (PG-58). Since October 2, Woodward and Boutte had conducted daily patrols, mostly routine flights searching the waters about Funafuti for the presence of enemy forces trying to threaten the vital supply routes from the United States to Australia, but on October 22 superiors added one more mission—find Eddie Rickenbacker.

Woodward and Boutte assumed they or one of the other Kingfisher teams would soon pick up the aviator, but as the days and weeks slipped by without result, it appeared that the military would call off the search and return the pair to their primary mission of protecting the Pacific supply routes. Neither Woodward nor Boutte would bet against Rickenbacker, but they conceded that his chances of surviving much longer on the open sea were slim. They would continue to look for a tiny rubber raft tucked into the Pacific's swells, but they might just as well search for Amelia Earhart as well.

ON THE OCEAN surface below, the seven men had just swallowed their evening ration for November 7. After another scorching day, they sat silently in their rafts, waiting for another tedious evening that preluded a long, shivering night. Suddenly Captain Cherry stood up, scanned the horizon, and shouted, "I hear an engine! I hear an engine! Hear it?"[1]

The men squinted into the distance, hoping that the captain was not hallucinating, and heard a deep roar. Within seconds, Rickenbacker and Cherry spotted a single-engine pontoon scout plane, similar to a Navy Kingfisher, silhouetted five miles out against a low cloud bank to the west. They could not determine whether it was American or Japanese, but by this stage, survival, not the nationality of the pilot who rescued them, mattered more. However, they realized that if American aircraft plucked them from the ocean, their worries would end, but if the rescuers were Japanese, the seven men would simply replace their oceanic penitentiary for a prisoner of war camp.

Bartek, once again in Rickenbacker's raft, rose, and while the aviator grabbed the private to hold him steady, the Freehold

The seven survivors madly wave and shout at the scout plane that flew in the distance. When the aircraft continued on without sighting the group, Eddie Rickenbacker chastised the demoralized men and told them that if one plane had come along, others would, too.

native waved and shouted with newfound energy. The other men joined from their rafts, hoping that somehow the pilot in that single plane would spot three tiny specks bobbing in the swells. They even waved their underwear, but the plane never drew closer than three miles to the excited group before disappearing. That outcome, according to Whittaker, "dealt us such crushing blows" that the men collapsed in their rafts. "If some of us didn't weep," he added, "it was only because there wasn't enough moisture left in us to form the tears. It was the worst blow we'd had."

Rickenbacker countered the negative reactions with a scolding that proved to Whittaker the national hero "was two jumps ahead of us." He berated each man for his pessimistic reaction, and reiterated that he would not allow them to give up. He pointed out that if one plane had materialized, either the same aircraft would return or others would appear, which meant that rescue had to be at hand. "I think the cussing Rick gave the gang that evening was the masterpiece of his career," said Lieutenant Whittaker. "In about a minute he had everyone roaring mad, then he got under their skins individually. He finished up with a broadside at the whole bunch. It was the most wonderful handling of profane language I ever have heard."

Whittaker categorized this moment, as well as earlier miraculous events in the rafts, as signs from God that He would save them. He claimed that "had it not been for the fortitude built up in hours of prayer since our crash landing at sea Oct. 21, I think we all would have given up. It was my new found faith in God that sustained me."[2]

Faith, plus the combative attitude of Eddie Rickenbacker. The man who had already triumphed on land with his racing victories and in the air during World War I was not about to allow the ocean to best him. Throughout the night, he exchanged thoughts across the rafts with Cherry and Whittaker about the possibilities that lay ahead. For the first time since the ditching, they had proof that outside help existed somewhere beyond the horizon. All they had to do was wait another day or two, and their watery nightmare might end. "Yet just to see that airplane was a terrific stimulus," wrote Rickenbacker. "It was the first outside sign of human life visible to us in two and a half weeks. Here at last was proof that land was close by, or at least a ship capable of catapulting such an airplane."[3]

Rickenbacker's task of buoying the men's spirits was not getting easier, though. They had already lost one man, and others were on the brink of collapsing. Reynolds moaned throughout the night, stomachs too long empty rumbled, and thirst made the normally simple chore of swallowing an exercise in agony.

During the morning of November 8, the men again prayed that a second aircraft would appear in the sky. Minutes ticked by, with only the noise of the ocean lapping against the rafts breaking the stillness. In the afternoon, they heard the faint sounds of airplane engines and spotted what looked like a Kingfisher in the distance, but it, too, flew on. Thirty minutes later, another scout plane raced by in the opposite direction to the first. Even though both times the men shouted and waved their arms, the pilots maintained their courses and disappeared, apparently on their way to an island base or back to a battleship or cruiser.

Sleep, always laborious, was torturous that night, but the next morning, as the rafts floated northwest of the Ellice Islands on the other side of the international date line, four more aircraft appeared. One pair flew to their north, while the second duo raced by to their south. Though none of the pilots detected the rafts, the mere sight of additional planes was a positive indicator that rescue might occur within the next few days.

When by the afternoon of November 9 no additional planes had appeared, the men panicked. What if they had drifted beyond the range of a nearby base and were headed into the open Pacific, where the prospect of rescue would be dim, at best? The disappointing results emphasized the difficulty those aviators and their crews faced from above in discerning three tiny rafts bobbing among hundreds of whitecaps and swells.

They had reason to worry. Should the currents take them beyond the Ellice Islands, nothing but 900 miles of ocean—more miles than they had drifted since ditching the plane almost three weeks earlier—stood between them and the Santa Cruz Islands, the next cluster of isles in their path. None of the eight possessed the stamina to withstand three more weeks on the ocean.

Rickenbacker forestalled any negative reaction with additional profanity-laden outbursts. "Each time it [a plane] appeared," said Whittaker, "we almost went out of our heads with excitement. Its pilot still failed to see us. And each time, before we could settle into black despond, Rickenbacker was right on the job, working the lads into such fury that the ship became a minor matter. This was one of the occasions when I was sure the fellows were going to live if only to spite Rick."[4]

Despite the disappointment, they had at least seen aircraft. The single-engine, single-pontoon planes must have been conducting routine patrols, which indicated that they flew out of some nearby base and that they would likely return. Somewhere beyond the horizon help awaited, and the survivors prayed that those forces would spot the tiny rafts hidden in the swells of a vast ocean.

"SO LONG, RICK"

Captain Cherry had been surprisingly quiet over the last few days, but later that evening, the pilot announced that he intended to take the small raft and split from the group. Encouraged that aircraft had finally entered their sector, he hated doing nothing but wait in a raft for a rescue that might not arrive.

When Rickenbacker asked why he wanted to risk the ocean on his own, Cherry replied that if the three rafts separated and spread out over a wider area, the chances of being spotted by aircraft would improve, and once search forces had located one raft, they would quickly conduct a more extensive search that was bound to find the other two. If he were not detected, he might still be able to locate an island from where help could be arranged. Cherry contended that his suggestion offered the best chance for survival, but he told Rickenbacker that he would not leave unless the aviator agreed with him.

The two argued for an hour, with Rickenbacker cautioning Cherry that he might be embarking on a journey to nowhere. Besides, Rickenbacker asked, if the planes over the last few days had failed to spot three rafts floating in unison, what chance would they have in locating Cherry alone in the smallest raft?

Colonel Adamson, as the senior military officer present, forbade Cherry from leaving, but the Texan had already made up his mind. He maneuvered his raft toward the smaller one and climbed in while De Angelis joined Whittaker and Reynolds in their larger raft. Adamson, irate that Cherry ignored his dictate, shouted, "I'm telling you not to go! That is an order. I am the senior officer here."

"That's true," replied Cherry, "but you're not the commanding officer, by a good deal. I was captain and commander of the plane. I am the commanding officer of this party. I'm leaving."[5]

Cherry's firm stance ended the discussion. As the captain prepared to drift away, Rickenbacker, who hated losing the young officer's vitality and calm demeanor, wished him good luck.

AS THEY WATCHED Captain Cherry disappear in the distance, Whittaker and De Angelis wondered if the Texan might be correct and if they should follow his example. After a short discussion—the third person in the raft, Reynolds, was at that time too ill to comprehend the matter—they told Rickenbacker that they, too, would leave. Whittaker and De Angelis could not say if floating away would take them closer to or farther from help, since they had no idea in which direction they should go, but they concluded that any action was better than none. Since remaining as a group had yielded no results in almost three weeks, they figured they had nothing to lose by paddling away.

Rickenbacker predictably exploded at their decision. He argued that the near-comatose Reynolds had no say in the matter, yet they were taking him along. Rickenbacker had already lost one relatively healthy companion with Cherry's departure, and now Whittaker, another comparatively strong man, threatened to leave. If that occurred, he would be left alone with Adamson and Bartek, two of the weakest from their time on the Pacific. What would happen, he asked, if either man tumbled out of the raft and Rickenbacker was unable to grab and lift him back in again?

After a brief debate, Rickenbacker concluded that he could not deter the two from their decision. One hour after Cherry's departure, Whittaker untied the line connecting his raft to Rickenbacker's and said to the aviator, "So long, Rick. I'll be seeing you."

"Good luck to you, Jim,"[6] answered the aviator.

Aided by favorable currents, by nightfall both rafts—Cherry in the smaller one heading in one direction, Whittaker, De Angelis, and Reynolds in another—were out of sight, leaving Rickenbacker in the third with the ailing Colonel Adamson and the weakening Private Bartek. "Now there were three of us—Adamson, Bartek, and myself. Adamson and Bartek were more dead than alive,"[7] said Rickenbacker.

Three tiny rafts, hardly discernible from thousands of feet in the air, now bobbed alone in the currents, hoping to intersect an aircraft's path as it passed above or to come upon an island refuge. They had replaced the teamwork that had, with one exception, kept them alive since their October ditching, with a decision to strike out on individual paths, a risky move that could lead to tragedy.

That evening, a patrol plane flew close to Whittaker's raft, but it raced by without any indication the pilot had spotted it. The moment, however, reaffirmed their decision to part from Rickenbacker and indicated that rescue had to be near. No one in Whittaker's raft slept that night, but all three men inside believed that, one way or another, their ocean journey was nearing its end.

THAT OPTIMISM WAS not matched in the United States, where waning hope for the national hero and his companions prevailed. On November 9, the same day that the three rafts separated, a newspaper reporter painted a dismal scene in Rickenbacker's Eastern Air Lines offices, where workers shied from mentioning their boss. "Today 'Rick's' office is empty and silent," wrote Walter Kiernan in an article that appeared in hundreds of newspapers. Every time a worker entered or left the building, they passed by a "poster in the lobby of the building advertising a motion picture. The name of the picture is *One of Our Aircraft Is Missing*. Rick's employees avert their heads as they pass it."[8]

Marines battled not only the Japanese but also the hidden jungle dangers in the combat on Guadalcanal. At the same time national publications warned that the fighting on that distant Pacific island could take a turn for the worse, they also printed concerns over the possible loss of the country's hero, Eddie Rickenbacker.

THE FRANK CANNISTRACI COLLECTION

The dour mood reflected the nation's attitude toward the war, where news from Guadalcanal also painted a grim situation. American Marines fought gallantly on land, and naval forces slugged it out with Japanese warships in the waters off the island, but no end to the savage combat loomed. The overall military outlook brightened on November 8 with the long-awaited American invasion of North Africa, but no one could predict what would unfold in the coming weeks. The home front needed good news, some tangible event with which people could tell themselves that American ingenuity, courage, and resourcefulness had triumphed. Rickenbacker had always been able to deliver those headlines with his racing and war victories, but now newspapers had begun declaring his all but certain loss to a mighty ocean.

Family and loved ones held on to slim hopes. "How hard I prayed for Alex's safe return and also for the other men in the crew,"⁹ said Coreen Bond, the girl Alex Kaczmarczyk had intended to marry. Each day at work she rushed upstairs to the offices of the WTIC radio station to ask the receptionist if she had any news about Alex, but always walked away empty.

In Freehold, Bartek's New Jersey hometown, a November ceremony in front of the courthouse honored local men in the war. A large banner listed the names of each individual, including Bartek's, and as the organizers thought that hope for the private's safe return had expired, they intended to put a gold star, signifying his death, next to his name. Johnny's sister, Sophie, so vehemently argued that her brother had not perished, however, that they relented and omitted the star.

Adelaide grew more insistent that her husband lived. About the same time that Captain Cherry departed in the smaller raft, Hap Arnold sent a letter informing her of the rescue operation's failure to locate the men and offering his condolences about her missing husband. Adelaide took the missive to mean that the general was about to call off the search. Stifling her rage, she boarded the next train to Washington, DC, to register her disgust that the military would so quickly abandon a Medal of Honor recipient and national hero. After listening politely to Adelaide, Arnold agreed to extend the search into the middle of November and ordered air units at Pacific bases to continue their efforts.

Fortunately, only a few weeks earlier the United States had shifted forces to new island bases that would prove essential to those efforts.

"EDDIE WAS ABOUT GONE, THE COLONEL WAS GONE, AND I WAS ABOUT GONE"

Concerned with the Japanese threat to their supply lines, American units had occupied the Ellice Islands, including Funafuti, in early October, fewer than three weeks before Rickenbacker disappeared. Six warships escorted three transports bringing Marines and supplies to the island group, which would house the aircraft to conduct long-range reconnaissance flights over the Pacific supply lines and the Japanese-held Gilbert Islands to the north. Their main base, under Lieutenant Commander Clayton B. Miller, stood south of the supply lines at Upolu in the Samoan Islands. A second airfield at Wallis Island under Lieutenant

Henry T. Haselton lay almost 300 miles west of Upolu, while a third commanded by Lieutenant William F. Eadie flew out of Funafuti, 700 miles northwest of Samoa.

When word of Rickenbacker's disappearance first came in, Lieutenant Commander Miller diverted only the planes from Upolu and Wallis, the two bases closest to the supply lines, as everyone assumed that the Rickenbacker bomber had most likely ditched near that well-traveled route. Planes from Canton Island and Hawaii joined in those early operations, but they, too, searched locations far from Rickenbacker. Near the end of October, when the aircraft failed to locate any rafts or evidence of a plane crash, most military commanders, including Hap Arnold, figured that Rickenbacker and his companions had either gone down with the plane or had already succumbed at sea.

Lieutenant Eadie and Radioman Boutte, as well as the other four pairs of aviators and radiomen from Squadron VS-1, D14 at Funafuti, had not taken part in that earlier search for Rickenbacker. The squadron of more than twenty aircraft, twenty-six officers, and eighty-six enlisted men had instead conducted routine air patrols in the waters adjoining their atoll. Working in conjunction with four PT boats, and the PT boat tender USS *Hilo* (PG-58), also operating from the atoll, Eadie and his men were now to join the more widespread search that Hap Arnold had ordered after meeting with Adelaide Rickenbacker.

In July *Hilo*, accompanied by the four PT boats of Motor Torpedo Boat Squadron 1B—*PT-21, PT-23, PT-25,* and *PT-26*— had sortied from Pearl Harbor for the 1,100-mile journey southwest to Palmyra Island. Far from the combat zone, the routine duty, though safe, offered scant action for men trained to battle an enemy. A mid-September visit from Admiral Chester Nimitz, who stopped overnight while on his way to Guadalcanal, provided Lieutenant (jg) Alvin P. Cluster, the commander of *PT-21*, a chance to approach the admiral and persuade him that the underutilized PT boats could be better employed if shifted farther south. Nimitz agreed and ordered the unit sent to Funafuti in the Ellice Islands.

Hilo and the PT boats left Palmyra on October 25, one day before home front newspapers printed the names of the men who had accompanied Rickenbacker on his flight, and reached Funafuti eight days later, the same day that Sergeant Kaczmarczyk died. Upon their arrival, they settled into what appeared to be another lackluster routine in a station that, although closer to the Solomons and the bitter fighting then rumbling through Guadalcanal's jungles, still offered little more than tedious patrol and scouting missions.

Arnold's order changed that. The ground crews at Funafuti began working around the clock to keep the Kingfisher pilots in the air looking for the famous aviator. They rotated the planes, with some searching thousands of square miles of ocean in their sector, while others refueled before heading back into one of the three sectors adjoining Funafuti. Flying at altitudes ranging from 1,000 to 2,000 feet, and operating under radio silence that was to be broken only if they spotted either Rickenbacker or the enemy, the pilots crisscrossed the waters lying in every direction but the southeast, which planes from Upolu and Wallis Island covered.

———

FOR ALL RICKENBACKER knew, after almost three weeks of fruitless searches by multiple naval bases, ships, and aircraft, the military had ceased trying to locate his group, and with Cherry's and Whittaker's rafts gone, he was on his own with two other men who could offer little help. "Rick's world had been narrowed down to one raft and two near-dead men," said Colonel Adamson, referring to himself and Johnny Bartek. Rickenbacker had nothing for company, he wrote later, but "Adamson's labored breath and the swish of the sea. Bartek lay across the raft as dead." Eddie admitted that even if they had drifted past land, he and his two comrades had little chance of surviving. "I was terribly worried that night,"[10] Rickenbacker mentioned of that November 9 moment.

Despite the anxiety, he managed to drift off to sleep, where he dreamed about the day of his dad's funeral many years ago. He saw his mother slumped in a chair at the kitchen table, crying over the loss of her husband. When he awoke, Rickenbacker thought of the night that he began transforming from a boy to a man. He remembered hugging his mother and vowing to take care of her, and of his sitting in the chair once occupied by his father as his way of conveying to Lizzie that he was now the man of the family and she need not worry about the future. Mostly, though, he recalled his pledge never to make her cry, and grieved that he was now the cause of indescribable grief for his aging mother in San Francisco.

Bartek was on the verge of despair when Rickenbacker issued

a water ration. Adamson and Bartek could barely lift their heads to drink, but Rickenbacker urged them not to give in. "Anything you want to try, you've got to try a hundred percent," he told them, "and then if you're licked, it's different. But if you don't try for anything, you'll never get anything. You've got to fight in order to get it."[11]

Rickenbacker maintained his composure despite his pain. He tried to scoop up some small fish, but his hands shook so severely that he could only gather a few. He attempted to collect rain that fell that day, but the simple act of wringing water from a shirt sent bolts of pain through his raw hands, as if hundreds of tiny needles had pierced the surface.

The three men stood on the verge of death. Bartek described the day after Cherry, Whittaker, and the others had left as "the loneliest day of my whole life." He said that "Eddie was about gone, the colonel was gone, and I was about gone." They drifted aimlessly, "baking [in the sun], and the ulcers on my feet were getting larger and the ulcers on my back were getting larger. So I figured this was the end."[12]

"RICKENBACKER'S PILOT PICKED UP; HOPE FOR OTHERS"

In the meantime, now isolated from his companions, Cherry hoped that he had made the correct choice in leaving the others, though he never doubted that taking this drastic step increased everyone's chances of rescue. Besides, it freed him from watching Eddie Rickenbacker slowly seize a command that was by rights his. Cherry nudged those thoughts aside, stripped naked, and entered the water for a swim he hoped would rejuvenate him and ease the discomfort caused by the painful sores covering his body. Exhausted upon climbing back into the raft, he quickly fell asleep.

When a noise suddenly roused him late that afternoon, Cherry, wearing nothing but his shorts, glanced up to see a plane coming straight toward him. He hurriedly slipped off his underwear and, "naked as a bird,"[13] waved his garment and hollered as loud as he could. He hardly cared who piloted the aircraft. If it meant he might see Bobbie again, he would happily spend the remainder of the war in a squalid Japanese prison camp. His only fear was that the pilot would fail to see him and fly away, leaving him to face another indeterminate period of pain, hunger, and thirst.

NO SUCH CONCERNS pestered Lieutenant Woodward, who flew his OS2U-3 Kingfisher observation floatplane with observer, Radioman Boutte, as part of a five-plane scout unit launched for the November 11 evening patrol from Funafuti. They expected a tranquil time, as nothing had interrupted their scouting flights in recent days. Superiors had ordered them to keep an eye out for the Rickenbacker party, but they doubted that they would spot anyone this far south when other aircraft had without success combed the ocean for more than two weeks.

Less than an hour into the flight, Boutte spotted a yellow object on the surface and immediately alerted Woodward on the intercom. When the pilot dropped the Kingfisher to investigate, he and the radio operator realized that they had come across a solitary man in a tiny raft. Woodward veered into a left descending turn, dropped close to the surface, and buzzed over the man's head. They could not be certain that the unidentified individual was part of the Rickenbacker group, but whoever it was needed immediate assistance. Since he was now under orders to maintain radio silence in case the enemy was listening, Woodward dropped a smoke flare near the raft and gained altitude for a return to Funafuti to alert them about the sighting.

Cherry alternately laughed and cried, but watched in disbelief when, after the pilot dropped the flare, the aircraft turned and flew over the horizon. He was certain they were Americans and had spotted him, but the captain worried that as he might drift far from his present position, they would be unable to locate him when they returned.

Woodward and Boutte had no intention of leaving the man stranded on the ocean. They hurried back to Funafuti, where they dropped a message informing their commander that they had located one individual in a raft about ten miles north of the island. They also stated that they were heading back to the location to await further rescue forces. After delivering the message, Woodward and Boutte sped back and began circling the raft, much to Cherry's relief.

The unit commander immediately ordered Lieutenant Commander Frank A. Munroe Jr., in charge of the USS *Hilo*, to dispatch a PT boat to the area. Commissioned by the Navy in June, the PT tender prowled the seas with a crew of nine officers and ninety-six men. *Hilo* provided gasoline, food stocks, medical assistance, and other items for which the smaller PT boat lacked space, and offered machine shops and a repair unit to ensure that PT boats could operate when posted to distant locales lacking shore facilities.

Munroe ordered *PT-21*, commanded by Lieutenant Cluster, to the scene. After spotting Woodward's plane, Cluster located the raft, but in case it carried an enemy soldier, he posted a man on the bow with a rifle.

Captain Cherry's chest tightened when he saw the vessel over the horizon. He knew it could be Japanese but thought, "I'll work in the salt mines. It won't bother me at all! Just pick me up and give me water!" As *PT-21* neared the raft, an aircraft flown by Lieutenant Eadie arrived as a replacement for Woodward's plane, which had to return to Funafuti to refuel. When he reached the atoll, the other pilots teased him that if he had indeed located Eddie Rickenbacker, the military would award him the Medal of Honor and send him home on a lengthy speaking tour.

Cluster maneuvered his PT boat within a few yards of the raft, where he heard Cherry's voice from inside weakly muttering, "Don't shoot! Don't shoot!" Crew members reached down and helped lift the underweight man aboard, where the aviator identified himself and exclaimed, "Boy, I'm sure glad to see the Navy!"[14] Cherry's eyes widened when a crew member handed him a bowl of hot tomato soup, the first warm meal he had enjoyed since Hawaii.

Hilo's diary entry at 9:15 p.m. on November 11 became the first official indication that at least part of Rickenbacker's party had been plucked from the Pacific. "*PT-21* returned with Capt. William T. Cherry, Jr. U.S.A. aboard, a survivor of U.S. Army B-17 plane carrying Capt. 'Eddie' Rickenbacker, reported lost on October 21, 1942."[15] Cluster, who the next year would assist in the rescue of future president John F. Kennedy after a Japanese destroyer rammed Kennedy's *PT-109,* also transmitted the latitude and longitude for Cherry's location as 8°22'20"S and 178°39'10"E.

Hilo's medical officer, Lieutenant Richard W. Garrity, treated Cherry and concluded that the survivor was in surprisingly good condition considering what he had been through. The captain informed them that other survivors floated in two rafts somewhere in the vicinity and mentioned that the rafts had split up two or three days earlier—he could not be certain after more than twenty days under the sun.

Cluster gunned the PT boat's engines to reach Funafuti as quickly as possible and deliver the news that Rickenbacker and other men floated in their search area. During the return Cherry, exhausted and confused by his weeks on the ocean, suffered a mental lapse and thought that Lieutenant Garrity wanted to kill him. "Son," the physician whispered kindly, "I'm trying to save you. Don't worry. I'm going to take care of you."[16]

Cherry reached Funafuti early the next morning. Medics cautiously transferred him to a bed in a small hospital, but he had difficulty sleeping. He joked that, even though he knew he was on land, his bed swayed back and forth as if he were still in the raft. Corpsman Elmer Sanders, on duty that night, sat by Cherry's bedside and held his hand until he drifted off, but each

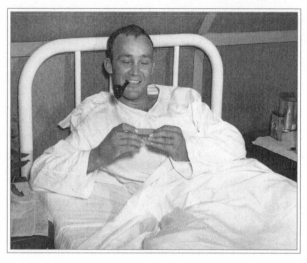

Captain William T. Cherry Jr. enjoys his pipe and rest in a military hospital following his rescue in November 1942.

time Sanders took his hand away, the pilot awakened in alarm. For the remainder of his watch, Sanders sat next to the pilot, holding his hand to ensure that he enjoyed a few hours' rest.

AFTER THREE WEEKS of riding an emotional roller coaster and all but abandoning hope that Eddie Rickenbacker and his companions would return, over the next few days the home front jubilantly greeted the news of Captain Cherry's rescue. A headline in the *New York Times* declared, "Rickenbacker's Pilot Found Alive on Raft, New Pacific Hunt Begins," and Cherry's hometown newspaper, the *Abilene Reporter-News*, revealed in its opening paragraph that "The War Department announced today

(November 13) the rescue of a flier from Capt. Eddie Ricken-backer's missing plane in the Pacific." The article, which also appeared in newspapers across the nation, added that "it is be-lieved possible that other survivors may be on life rafts in the same general vicinity." The reporter described the Abilene citizen as being "in good condition, but weak,"[17] and said that in light of Cherry's rescue, the military had immediately intensified its search in the Pacific, with both surface vessels and long-range aircraft joining the scout planes that checked the waters between Funafuti and the location where Cherry was first spotted.

Cherry was the hero of the moment, the first to be found, and as newspaper articles were delighted to proclaim, Cherry temporarily became the symbol of renewed hope for Ricken-backer's safe return. Accompanying the headline, "Rickenback-er's Pilot Picked Up; Hope for Others," the *Chicago Tribune* informed its readers that Cherry's "rescue spurred the searchers to new efforts."[18]

Upon learning that her husband had been picked up in the Pacific, Bobbie Cherry asserted that Friday the 13th "must be my luckiest day." She said that while her bosses offered her the rest of the day off to celebrate with family, she declined, men-tioning, "I can go back to my work with much more vigor and certainly with a lighter heart now."[19]

Adelaide and the families of the missing men believed that the rescue of Captain Cherry portended well for their loved ones. In Connecticut, the parents of Sergeant Kaczmarczyk, both devout Catholics, had prayed daily for Alex's safe return. Unaware of his fate, they saw in the news of Cherry's return a sign that they would see their son again. "We all pray often and place our trust in God," said Mrs. Kaczmarczyk. "God is good, and we hope Alex will come back alive."[20]

"THERE WERE OTHER HANDS THAN MINE ON THOSE OARS"

On the same day that a PT boat crew lifted Captain Cherry out of the ocean, Lieutenant De Angelis awoke, glanced as usual toward the horizon, and thought he saw land. Assuming that his mind had once again played tricks with him, he awakened Lieutenant Whittaker.

"Jim, I think you'd better take a look. It may be a mirage, but I think I see something." Whittaker sat up, peered in the direction De Angelis pointed, and saw a line of palm trees stretching across the horizon. "We thought he had flipped when he told us he saw palm trees,"[21] said Sergeant Reynolds, but within a few minutes all doubts were dispelled. Land, and with it the prospect of survival, lay not far away.

The three had come across the shoreline of Nukufetau, sixty miles northwest of Funafuti. Whittaker, the strongest of the three, grabbed the two aluminum oars and began rowing toward the island. De Angelis, in slightly better condition than Reynolds, was able to row a few minutes at a time, but if the men were going to reach the island, the lieutenant would have to be the one who muscled them ashore.

Reynolds, lying prone in the bottom of the raft, tried to assist. Even though, according to Whittaker, the sergeant's eyes

Almost at the limit of their endurance, Lieutenant James C. Whittaker, Second Lieutenant John J. De Angelis, and Staff Sergeant James W. Reynolds stare at the island of Nukufetau. They came across it after separating from the men in the other two rafts.

<small>DRAWING COURTESY OF DUTTON</small>

had sunk into their sockets, his weight had plunged below 100 pounds, "and his resemblance to a death's head was startling," Reynolds propped himself up as far as possible, reached over the raft's side to scoop up water with a flare shell, and poured it on Whittaker's neck to cool the copilot as he rowed. By noon Whittaker had progressed to within 300 yards of shore, and even joked with De Angelis and Reynolds about what they might want to order for dinner. "Then something happened," Whittaker said.

The raft, caught in a reverse current, swayed out of control and shot back out to sea. Instead of continuing toward the island and setting foot on land for the first time in three weeks, the men watched helplessly as the raft whisked them away from a welcome refuge. Whittaker had expended every ounce of strength just to advance the raft to within three football fields of the island, only to see his exertions go to naught because, at the last second, a wicked current blocked his path. Weary from his exertions, Whittaker doubted he had enough energy to paddle them landward, but from a mile out he took up the oars and tried to counter the flow that swept them toward open waters. Five minutes later, however, as the current carried the raft farther from the island, Whittaker feared he might never overcome its fierce pull seaward. "If ever I have cried out in anguish it was then. I was done, finished, washed up. I called to Heaven to witness that I was whipped. I could hardly hold on to the light oars. Yet there within reach was the land—and life. And while I watched, that line of majestic palms continued to move away, with terrible deliberation. If we were to reach land at all it would have to be now."

With the island and safety receding, the atheist turned to the one entity he had denied his entire life—God. "Only a miracle could set our feet on that island, I thought; only a miracle." As if his soul had erupted from his body, "I cried out to Him to give me strength. I shouted it above the rising wind in the fear He might not hear. I caught a glimpse of De Angelis's startled face. Still shouting, I lifted the oars. I rowed."

And rowed . . . and rowed. He rowed even though his mus-

In the second of the two miracles convincing James C. Whittaker of God's existence, the exhausted lieutenant suddenly possessed enough strength to paddle the raft toward Nukufetau. He battled high seas, strong winds, sharks, and tricky currents to reach land.

DRAWING COURTESY OF DUTTON

cles felt as if they were about to split into shreds, and he rowed despite an overtaxed heart that seemed ready to burst from his chest. He rowed even when a storm blew in a deluge of rain that nearly blotted out the island, and he rowed when, just as he thought that he had finally overcome the current and was closing the distance to the beach, sharks swarmed the raft and bumped into his oars. Lieutenant De Angelis worried that two of the largest sharks, who seemed to take a particular interest in the occupants and kept snapping at the oars, might capsize the raft and dump the three into the ocean, but Whittaker kept rowing.

"These sharks were not the droll dullards that had plagued us earlier," Whittaker wrote. "These were man eater. If they should attack the raft, we were gone." Pleading, "God! Don't quit me now!" he once again asked God to come to his aid. "The prayer I uttered that afternoon was more than desperate. It was an anguished supplication, shouted above the wind and the rain. It came from the depths of my soul."[22]

Whittaker had earlier experienced what he regarded as the first of two miracles when, with the parched survivors speaking through cracked lips and sorely needing fresh water, a favorable wind had altered the path of a rainstorm and blown it their way. A second miracle now reenergized his weary arms and shoulders. He alternately rowed and slashed at the sharks with his oars. The predators regrouped and bumped into the raft again and again, but Whittaker rowed as if propelled by an unseen force. "Indeed, it was as though the oars were working automatically, and my hands merely following their motions. There were other hands than mine on those oars." Despite the torrential rain, despite the sharks and an ache that tortured every fiber of his body, Whittaker narrowed the distance to shore. "On that day, thoroughly exhausted and with three weeks of thirst and hunger behind me, I accomplished a feat that would have tried a well man. It was the second miracle and I recognized it for what it was."[23]

Reynolds and De Angelis had tried to help, but according to Reynolds, "we didn't have the strength. How Whittaker found the strength, I don't know. He had someone else helping him, believe me."[24] In a final surge toward Nukufetau, Whittaker fended off a jarring surf that threatened to smash the raft against sharp coral reefs protecting the island. Man-eating sharks attacked, and the current refused to yield, but still he paddled. Finally, Whittaker rode the breakers over the reef into the calmer, shallow waters of the beach side.

"All ashore that's going ashore,"[25] he jested in a voice hushed from his exertions. Whittaker helped his two companions climb out of the raft, but when they tried to stand, all three collapsed. In the next few minutes, Whittaker attempted to rise and walk eight times, and in each instance he found himself face down in the surf.

Grateful to be breathing and safely ashore, Lieutenant James C. Whittaker (right), Second Lieutenant John J. De Angelis, and Staff Sergeant James W. Reynolds enjoy their first moments on solid ground since having left Hawaii the previous month.

With forty feet remaining to the beach, Whittaker and De Angelis dragged the raft while Reynolds inched in the sand alongside. The radioman, who had lost fifty pounds in the three weeks, crawled right out of his trousers, and Whittaker propped himself upright with an oar, but in the early afternoon on November 11, after completing an extraordinary seven-and-a-half-hour journey to shore, the trio finally collapsed on a rocky beach, as squalid and ghastly a threesome as ever emerged from the sea, yet grateful for the solid land beneath them.

"I REMEMBER THE WOMEN WEEPING AT OUR EMACIATED CONDITION"

They lay awhile on the first land they had touched in three weeks, trying to catch their breath, before Whittaker and De Angelis dragged Reynolds and the raft off the beach to a cluster of palm trees. Exhausted, Whittaker slumped to the soil. "I thanked God briefly," he said. "I pledged that I would thank Him at length during the remainder of my days, thru thought, word, and deed."[26]

Whittaker spotted several pockets of fresh rainwater and, shoeless, gingerly moved across the sharp rocks, dropped to his knees, and gulped liquid that he later declared was the best beverage he had ever swallowed. Refreshed, the lieutenant helped move his companions to other pockets of water, after which he and De Angelis dragged Reynolds and the raft to a sandy beach a few hundred feet away on the lee side, the side of the island facing away from the wind. After collapsing on the soft beach,

Whittaker muttered another quick thank-you to God before rising to search for food and shelter.

Whittaker and De Angelis propped up Reynolds against a palm tree, then scavenged the nearby area for food. Numerous coconuts lay on the ground, but it took Whittaker an hour to cut through the thick shells with his sheath knife. After quaffing the small amount of nourishing milk each coconut held, and devouring the coconut meat, the pair found a partially finished hut and the remnants of a canoe hull that had been carved from the trunk of a coconut tree. Though dead bugs floated in the rainwater that had collected inside the canoe, Whittaker and De Angelis skimmed them off and drank their fill. Whittaker pulled out his knife and killed several of the ratlike animals scurrying about, while De Angelis used an oar to club others to death. They rejoined Reynolds, and without benefit of a fire, the three tore into the raw rodents.

That evening a Kingfisher plane flew over, but its pilot failed to spot the trio. They assumed that other Kingfishers on patrol would likely return the next morning and evening, and sooner or later, one of those was bound to sight the stranded survivors.

November 11 had been an eventful day for the three. Their gamble in separating from the group had paid off, and instead of bobbing on a Pacific raft with Rickenbacker, they stretched out on solid ground. They might have reached land, but as Cherry experienced in the Funafuti hospital, the men slept fitfully because of the swaying sensation left over from three arduous weeks on the ocean.

———

THE NEXT MORNING, while Captain Cherry recovered in a comfortable bed, a second Kingfisher flew over Nukufetau. Although the pilot noticed nothing unusual, his appearance confirmed that an American base had to exist within reach. The group consumed additional coconuts and rodents to regain strength, but Whittaker worried about Reynolds, as the radioman had not shown any improvement. The three decided to rest for a day instead of exploring the island.

The appearance in mid-afternoon of five aircraft flying in formation interrupted their respite, but the pilots droned on to the northwest, unaware of Whittaker's group on the tiny island below. On one of their subsequent passes the next day, they descended to 300 feet and dropped a message for a New Zealand coastwatcher, Colin Davis, to search the atoll for signs of any shipwrecked Americans. Davis immediately sent out islanders in canoes to inspect the beaches.

In the meantime, Whittaker's group, having rested for a day, returned to their raft and paddled to the southern portion of the island. They had rowed a half mile when they noticed a hut on the beach, and while the thatched structure was simple in comparison to their homes in the United States, to them it looked like a luxurious Manhattan apartment complex.

They hoped to find someone who might assist them, but the dilapidated dwelling was empty. To add to their disappointment, another single aircraft raced directly above at a low altitude without giving any indication the pilot had seen the three men.

Exhausted from paddling, the trio soon drifted into a deep sleep. Noises from the ocean awoke the men, who at first feared that a Japanese naval unit approached, but when De Angelis looked more closely, he thought that the vessels were too small to be destroyers. Whittaker shrugged off the possibility that he might become an easy target for Japanese machine gun bullets, hopped in the raft, and paddled out to meet the mysterious objects. When he was a quarter mile from shore, he discerned the outlines of outriggers manned by native islanders.

In one of those boats, a twenty-one-year-old named Toma had watched Whittaker leave the beach. Standing six and a half feet tall and towering over the other residents, the native of Nukufetau had to be wary about the stranger's identity, but alerted by Davis's message, he believed this must be one of the Americans they sought.

When the islanders paddled close enough to the raft, the stranger asked if anyone spoke English. Toma replied that he did and told the man he had reached the island of Nukufetau and that three other white people, New Zealanders, also lived on the island. When the stranger indicated he had no idea where Nukufetau was, Toma added, "It is part of the Gilbert and Ellice Island Colony." The group tossed Whittaker a line so that he could tie his raft to their outrigger and be taken ashore. Upon reaching the beach, Toma carried Whittaker to land while his companions hurried over to aid Reynolds and De Angelis.

Reynolds, eager to express his gratitude, stood, took a step toward Toma, and collapsed. Toma and a man named Popu rushed forward to assist Reynolds, and while Popu cleaned the sand from Reynolds's eyes and mouth, Toma climbed a palm tree to cut down ripe coconuts. "Do not be afraid," he comforted Reynolds as he handed the radioman a sliced coconut. "You have been rescued now, and we will do our best to look after you." Reynolds quaffed the fresh milk, which enabled him to mutter, "Thank you very much. I feel much alive now."[27]

In late afternoon, the natives transported them to a village across a lagoon. As they neared the settlement, Toma raised a makeshift flag on a mast to indicate that they had found the men. Upon seeing Toma's signal, villagers and the New Zealand coastwatchers flocked to the water to greet the Americans and to help carry them ashore. The whole village gathered around the three as if they were long-lost relatives, and though bare-breasted native women freely approached them, at that stage the three were more interested in food and water.

The islanders led the trio to a thatched hut, gently placed them on cots, and bathed them. All three badly required medical attention. "I remember the women weeping at our emaciated condition," said Whittaker. "Our beards were long and unkempt. Jimmy Reynolds looked like a dying man." Whittaker thought the radioman looked worse now than while on the ocean and that he "needed the best medical attention and quickly." Colin Davis concluded that Reynolds, whom he described as "a skeleton and covered in sores,"[28] had at best a fifty-fifty chance of making it through the night and was certain he would not survive two days.

The islanders and New Zealand personnel next gave Reynolds and De Angelis fruit juices to rebuild their strength. Whit-

Nukufetau's native islanders treated Lieutenant James C. Whittaker, Second Lieutenant John J. De Angelis, and Staff Sergeant James W. Reynolds with great care until they were strong enough to be transported to an island hospital.

DRAWING COURTESY OF DUTTON

taker seemed healthy enough to consume something more substantial, and when they asked what he wanted to eat, he wondered if they could boil a chicken and make a rich broth for him. His mouth watered at the scent of the chicken cooking in the pot, and he had to restrain his impulse to reach into the scalding water and yank out a piece of the fowl.

Bolstered by the broth, the copilot felt much improved. Before long a group of islanders arrived and, bearing mats, fans, shells, and hula skirts, bowed to the three as if the Americans were native chieftains. Whittaker relayed through Toma's father, who also spoke English from his time on a trading steamer that had often stopped in San Francisco, that they would spread word of the islanders' kindness once the three reached the United States.

WHILE THE ISLANDERS nursed the three Americans, the New Zealand coastwatchers transmitted a message to Funafuti that they had picked up a raft with three men aboard and asked that a physician be dispatched. Within an hour Lieutenant Woodward and a doctor, Lieutenant William J. Hall, had loaded blankets, soup, water, glucose, and other medical supplies onto Woodward's Kingfisher and left Funafuti.

When the plane landed in the waters off Nukufetau, Lieutenant Hall hurried ashore and administered plasma and glucose to the men, who suffered from exposure, thirst, lack of nutrition, body sores, and sunburn. Reynolds, he observed, teetered on the brink of death and probably would not have lived much longer without the medicine. Lieutenant De Angelis was a bit better, Hall thought, and Lieutenant Whittaker, for what he had been through, remained in amazingly good condition and should quickly recover.

On November 13 the *Hilo* arrived to transport the three survivors to the base on Funafuti. Lieutenant Commander Munroe sent a whaleboat to shore with the medical officer, Lieutenant Garrity, who had already treated Captain Cherry. Lieutenant Edward M. Gordon, *Hilo*'s executive officer, said that Whittaker, Reynolds, and De Angelis were "very delighted to see us. Whittaker was really in amazing shape for the length of time that he had been exposed." In contrast De Angelis "was in very, very bad shape, and we were afraid that he might not pull through after we took him back to the *Hilo*."[29] Lieutenant Garrity examined each of the survivors and agreed with Lieutenant Hall that while Whittaker appeared to be in decent shape, the other two required more intensive care. He recommended that all three be immediately evacuated from Nukufetau.

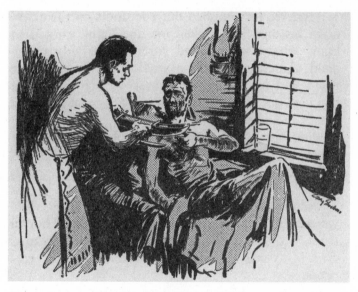

Toma, the native islander who helped bring Lieutenant James C. Whittaker, Second Lieutenant John J. De Angelis, and Staff Sergeant James W. Reynolds to the island's village, presents a model of his outrigger to Lieutenant Whittaker. Once back in the United States, the American sent a parcel of goods to Toma as a way of thanking him.

<small>DRAWING COURTESY OF DUTTON</small>

The Nukufetau islanders, chanting and singing as they carried three stretchers to the boat, staged a touching farewell.

Whittaker said goodbye to Toma, who had given the American his sole pack of cigarettes along with a model of his outrigger canoe. Island custom held that when a native builds a boat, he also constructs a small-scale model of the outrigger. If he keeps the model safe and whole, the islander believes that while at sea on the larger boat, he will be protected from the ocean's hazards. The islanders cherished their models, but Toma made an exception for the American. "Toma told me with great earnestness that I must keep it safe," said a grateful Whittaker. "If anything should happen to it, he assured me, disaster would overtake the big outrigger." On the model's bow, Toma had carved the inscription "Jim America, from Toma."[30] Now about to leave Nukufetau, Whittaker asked if he could send something to Toma once he reached the United States. Toma politely declined, but when Whittaker insisted, he quietly asked for soap and trousers.

As the motor launch left the island to return to the *Hilo*, Lieutenant Whittaker waved goodbye to the islanders and watched the village slowly fade, thankful for the care the kind people had lavished on him and his two companions. Now handed over to the care of the United States Navy, the three men, aided by *Hilo's* crew, boarded the torpedo boat tender, shocking with their skeletal appearance the handful of sailors who gathered to view the subjects of such a widespread search.

Hilo arrived off Funafuti that night, but waited for daylight on November 14, Whittaker's forty-first birthday, to enter the lagoon and dock. Crew members carried De Angelis to the small Marine emergency field hospital, but Lieutenant Garrity hesitated to move Reynolds from the *Hilo*. He would instead remain aboard and receive more plasma and glucose to build his strength. Brimming with renewed vigor, Whittaker insisted on walking.

The copilot noticed that a photographer strangely followed ten feet behind, snapping pictures of De Angelis and him. He wondered why any publication would be interested in two weather-beaten, anonymous bomber crew members, but when Whittaker entered the hospital, he received a surprising answer.

The photographer's presence was an indication that his life, and the lives of the other survivors, were about to drastically change.

CHAPTER 10

"Listen, Captain—Planes!"

Rickenbacker Rescued, November 12–13

OUT ON THE ocean, the third raft bearing Eddie Rickenbacker, Colonel Adamson, and Johnny Bartek had drifted within forty-five miles northwest of Funafuti. They had no way of knowing that Captain Cherry was already safe in the atoll's hospital, that the Whittaker group had landed on Nukufetau, or that if they drifted by the Ellice Island chain without being rescued, they would enter a 600-mile gap devoid of islands, all but assuring their deaths on the Pacific. As far as they were concerned, when November 12 dawned they faced yet another long day under the equatorial sun, famished and thirsty, drifting ever closer to the end.

Although Rickenbacker had weathered the three-week ordeal better than his raft companions, no one was inured to the debilitating impact of the previous twenty-three days. Private Bartek sat in the raft "more dead than alive," while feet away, the nearly comatose Colonel Adamson clutched in his hand the religious medal Rosalind Russell had asked him to keep. Rickenbacker rested at one end of the raft with a ragged handkerchief covering the lower half of his face that, according to Adamson, made his friend "look like a down-at-the-heels bandit"[1] trying to mask his identity.

"We were in a stupor, all of us," said Private Bartek. "Eddie Rickenbacker was in a stupor and I was in a stupor. We weren't communicating. We had our heads down. We could hardly hold our heads up. The colonel [Adamson] was still lying in the bottom of the raft like he was dead."[2]

In late afternoon an unusual noise penetrated Bartek's lethargy. He thought he heard a plane, and at first dismissed it as yet another of nature's cruel tricks, but when the sounds of engines grew louder, he feebly lifted his head and saw through blurry eyes a pair of aircraft. "The silence of sea and space was suddenly ripped apart by the roar of airplane engines,"[3] said Adamson of the two Kingfishers two miles out and a few hundred feet above the ocean surface flying toward them.

Rickenbacker, either asleep or semiconscious, had not yet stirred. Bartek reached over, tugged the aviator's shirt, and muttered, "Listen, Captain—planes! They're back. They're very near." Suddenly alert, Rickenbacker observed the aircraft approaching from the southeast. He waved his hat and yelled as loud as he could, while Bartek thought that the planes were "so near we could touch them and yet so far."[4]

THE SEARCH FROM Funafuti had begun that dawn when five Kingfishers lifted off from the base. The aviators spread out in a scouting line spaced one mile apart and flew at just 300 feet to enhance their chances of spotting a raft in the regions northwest of Funafuti. At the same time, in heavy rain that hampered their surface search, four PT boats accompanied *Hilo* out of the lagoon.

Each man involved in the operation tried to suppress the excitement that the famous Eddie Rickenbacker might be in their search area. He had been given up for lost, but with Cherry's rescue near Nukufetau to the northwest, logic indicated that the other members of that B-17 should be drifting in the same area. Before taking off from Funafuti, the aviators had wagered over who would be the lucky flier to locate the nation's hero, and they joked about the medals that fortunate individual would receive and the national attention he would enjoy. The prospect of hunting the seas for Eddie Rickenbacker broke the monotony of routine air patrols over the Pacific supply lines and handed them a mission worth noting.

In late afternoon, Kingfisher pilot Lieutenant (jg) John G. Boyd thought that he detected an object on the water. He dipped his wing to signal Lieutenant (jg) G. T. Forrest, accompanying Boyd in another Kingfisher, who peered down and saw a raft holding three people.

The aviators descended close to the surface and flew over the raft to display their United States insignias, dropped flares to mark the location, and veered off for Funafuti. The aviators could not conclude whether Rickenbacker occupied the raft, but two people feebly waved as the planes raced by, while a third vigorously gestured with a fedora while remaining on his knees.

Aviators out of Funafuti conducting the November search for Eddie Rickenbacker flew the Vought OS2U Kingfisher floatplane. Lieutenant William F. Eadie landed his Kingfisher near Rickenbacker's raft, where he and Radioman 2/c Lester H. Boutte placed the seriously injured Colonel Hans Christian Adamson into the cabin. Lacking room inside for Eddie Rickenbacker and Private Johnny Bartek, but not wanting to leave them behind in the darkness, Eadie and Boutte lifted Bartek onto the right wing, Rickenbacker onto the left wing, and secured them in sitting positions with their legs dangling over the wings' edges. While Eadie taxied the flying boat through choppy waters, Boutte straddled the rear cockpit area and held on to Rickenbacker and Bartek by their collars.

NATIONAL ARCHIVES PHOTO #80-G-K-1374

"They were U.S. Navy planes, the prettiest sight in the world," said Private Bartek. The Navy insignia brought Rickenbacker to tears, "and gratitude and happiness filled me. I waved and waved, out of a half-crazy notion that the pilot must be made to understand we were not three dead men on a raft."[5]

The jubilant mood on the surface disintegrated when the planes inexplicably veered away and disappeared. "That is where I almost broke down," said Bartek. He lay his head on the raft, burst into tears, and delivered a plea that God reverse the paths of those planes. "If there is a God above, please send back that plane," he prayed, and promised that "if he [*sic*] did I'd always believe"[6] in the power and goodness of God.

"Keep praying, Johnny,"[7] Rickenbacker prodded the young man. He assumed that the aviators were returning to their base to refuel, but with dusk no more than two hours away, one question loomed large—would they fill their tanks, lift off from their airfield, and locate the raft before darkness enshrouded the three and further complicated the task of finding them?

A rain squall in the distance threatened to disrupt any possible rescue attempt. If it engulfed them, the storm would prevent aircraft from landing on the ocean, and if that were so, the three would have to remain in the raft for another night—a prospect that Rickenbacker feared could be deadly for both Colonel Adamson and Private Bartek. Furthermore, the storm's wind velocity could sweep them away from their original location, making it more difficult for search craft to trace them the following morning. He needed the aviators to return before dark, when they still had the chance to land on the ocean and lift them aboard. As he gazed at the setting sun, Rickenbacker's initial joy evaporated to despair.

"Are they coming back? Are they coming back?"[8] Bartek

frantically asked. Captain Eddie assured him that as the Navy now had the location of their raft, the planes would return, but with the sun rapidly setting, he was uncertain whether the pilots would arrive before dark or wait until the following morning.

FROM HIS RAFT, Rickenbacker was unable to see that only one of the two planes had left. While Lieutenant Boyd returned to Funafuti to refuel, Lieutenant Forrest circled at higher altitudes to serve as a beacon guiding subsequent aircraft to the rafts. What looked like muddled mayhem to Rickenbacker, Adamson, and Bartek was, in actuality, an organized tag team system established by the aviators of Squadron VS-1, D14, an aerial ballet orchestrated to ensure that they would not lose the three men on the surface. They knew from Captain Cherry's rescue that other men, including Captain Eddie, were alive and in rafts in the same area. With Forrest and Boyd having sighted a raft that possibly carried the nation's hero, those aviators and their superiors were not about to allow Eddie Rickenbacker to slip away.

Lieutenant Forrest soon reappeared and circled the raft while Lieutenant Boyd raced to Funafuti to deliver their news. "We certainly did not want the raft occupants to think our aircraft had left them, knowing what this would do to their morale!"[9] said Lieutenant Forrest. He leaned out the engine for maximum fuel economy, dropped to a lower altitude, and took station above the raft, knowing that his presence comforted the men below.

The sun had already begun its speedy descent to the horizon, indicating that unless a relief plane soon arrived, Forrest would leave and the occupants of the raft would have to endure another night on the ocean. That concern ended when Lieutenant Eadie arrived as the first relief plane of what turned into a continuous shuttle from Funafuti. Eadie took over for Forrest, who flew back to Funafuti to refuel.

While the aviators performed their aerial dance, a storm swept in. When Rickenbacker told Bartek to begin collecting rainwater, just as they had done every time a storm had passed their way in the last three weeks, Bartek said, "Rickenbacker, we don't need no more water. Didn't you see those planes, they saw us. We're saved already. We're picked up." Rickenbacker replied that rescue was not yet certain and explained that they might need the water in case the storm strengthened, blew them into a different sector, and caused the rescue planes to lose sight of them.

Meanwhile, Lieutenant Eadie faced a crucial decision. His fuel gauge toyed alarmingly close to empty, and, even worse, during the heavy squall he had lost sight of the raft. Since darkness would soon postpone operations until the morning, he worried that some might hold him responsible for losing the nation's hero. Uncertain whether his relief from Funafuti had taken off, he trusted that he could rely on Lieutenant Boyd and that his squadron mate was already on his way back to circle the raft. Eadie reluctantly left the Rickenbacker group, but exhaled a sigh of relief when ten miles from the raft he passed Lieutenant Boyd speeding in the opposite direction. Eadie continued toward Funafuti, where Lieutenant (jg) Warner Clark had already lifted off to relieve Boyd and circle the raft.

Once the storm abated, Rickenbacker and Bartek spotted Lieutenant Clark's Kingfisher droning their way. Clark took station and circled the raft, hoping that a rescue vessel from Funafuti would arrive before dark compounded an already demanding mission.

"WHY, CAPTAIN EDDIE, YOU FELLOWS ARE GOING TOO"

Marine Colonel L. L. Leech, commander at Funafuti, jumped into action. Unwilling to risk losing the hero, at 5:40 p.m. he broke radio silence, something he had not done since arriving on the atoll six weeks earlier, to order the *Hilo*'s senior officer, Lieutenant Commander Munroe, to send PT boats to the raft's location.

Leech faced unfavorable odds. Only one hour of daylight remained, and once darkness set in, Eadie, Clark, and the other aviators would lose visual contact with the raft. Even if they dropped flares to illuminate the area and keep the raft in sight, the aviators would have to land on a choppy ocean in the dark, a tricky tactic even in daylight.

On Funafuti, Lieutenant Eadie and Radioman Boutte looked forward to a break, some hot food, and interaction with buddies, but once they climbed out of their Kingfisher and learned of the dilemma at sea, they volunteered to fly back and pick up the three occupants of the raft. "After having been made fully aware of the situation, and being cognizant of the dangers involved," stated the official military report of the rescue operation, "Lt. Eadie volunteered to fly his plane to the raft, land, take the survivors aboard the plane and taxi back to Funafuti on the surface if unable to contact a PT boat."[10]

He and every other aviator at the base were not about to allow a raft that possibly held Rickenbacker to drift alone in the dark for another night, when Captain Eddie and his two companions were most likely in dire need of medical care. The nation would never forgive them if they rested while the national hero disappeared, possibly forever. The air rescue group would never abandon one of its own, and Eadie figured he could do nothing less than the same for America's most famous World War I aviator. He collected two canteens filled with water and another with hot soup before returning to his Kingfisher for a dangerous race with dusk, a contest in which he and Boutte could wind up dead from an unsuccessful attempt to land on a barely discernible and choppy ocean surface.

Eadie lifted off, and at his cruising speed of 152 miles per hour, reached the raft's site forty-five miles from Funafuti within sixteen minutes. Knowing that he was the raft occupants' sole chance to avoid another night at sea, Eadie dropped two flares to bathe the raft in enough light for the aviator to attempt his landing into the wave crests and troughs, straightened out the Kingfisher, and at 7:30 p.m. touched down on the sea not far from the raft.

Watching the proceedings from his raft, Rickenbacker was impressed with Eadie's piloting skills, courage, and willingness to land in the turbulent waters. He was not surprised that Eadie ignored the obvious hazards to nimbly alight his Kingfisher amidst those heavy swells, for that was his job, but the aviator reminded Rickenbacker of those gallant World War I fliers who risked life and limb to save others. He smiled contentedly as Eadie descended to the surface, while Private Bartek uttered a quick prayer of thanks.

Lieutenant Eadie aligned the Kingfisher so he could steer it into the wind for a more controlled approach to the raft, cut the engine, and allowed the plane to float toward the three men. At the same time, Rickenbacker paddled the raft closer to the Kingfisher and grasped onto the pontoon as Lester Boutte, aided by Eadie once the plane stopped, climbed down to help. The radioman reached toward Rickenbacker, grabbed the raft's line, and tied the raft to the plane. The three had been plucked from the ocean in the early evening of Thursday, November 12.

After giving thanks to God and placing his hands on the Kingfisher for stability, Rickenbacker stood, extended a hand to the two rescuers, and introduced himself. "I'm Captain Eddie Rickenbacker, this is Colonel Adamson, and this is Private Bartek," he said to the naval aviator and radioman. Rickenbacker thought that he had never seen such clean-shaven and handsome men as Lieutenant Eadie and Radioman Boutte, and was proud that his nation had produced such high-caliber men. "They were the finest-looking young men I had ever seen."[11]

Rickenbacker and his companions could hardly contain their glee at being joined by the two Americans. "Naturally we were all bubbling with gratitude, with every kind of expression of gratitude that we knew how to give," said Rickenbacker. The three kept repeating, "Oh, this is heaven," and "Thank God for the U.S. Navy and these boys."[12]

Lieutenant Eadie, who was later awarded an Air Medal for landing the plane, informed Rickenbacker that a PT boat was on its way to the scene. However, he had no idea when it might arrive or, with the flares extinguished, if the boat could locate them in the dark. Eadie hesitated to fire a third flare out of fear that the Japanese, who controlled the Gilbert Islands uncomfortably close to the northwest, might be in the area, so instead of waiting for the PT boat to find them, Eadie chose to taxi the forty-five-mile distance toward Funafuti and, hopefully, meet the boat on the way.

The lieutenant needed only one glance to determine that the three Americans required medical attention. Eadie thought that "Adamson was completely irrational, and Bartek seemed to be in a semi-stupor from exposure and fatigue. Rickenbacker had stood the ordeal better than the others."[13] Hoping good news might be a tonic, Eadie told them that Captain Cherry had already been transported to a hospital, and that a little more than an hour ago, a raft with three men had washed ashore on Nukufetau.

Since the Kingfisher's cockpit had room for only one of the three, Boutte lifted Adamson, the weakest, to wing height, where Eadie grabbed onto his shoulder. With Rickenbacker and Bartek pushing from below, the four hoisted the colonel up eight feet onto the wing and then into the rear cockpit, where Boutte normally sat.

Rickenbacker thought that Eadie and Boutte, battling rough seas, "showed the strength of Hercules" in lifting Adamson into the cabin, but wondered where he and Bartek would sit. Lacking cockpit space for everyone, the two would have to wait in the raft until another airplane or a PT boat came along, a thought that petrified Rickenbacker. Not wanting to drift alone in the blackness, he asked Eadie, "Would you mind waiting until the PT does come up? I don't want them to miss us in the dark."

Taken aback by this unexpected query, Eadie replied, "Why, Captain Eddie, you fellows are going too." When Rickenbacker asked where they would fit in the cramped Kingfisher, the pilot answered, "On the wing."[14]

Working slowly and cautiously in choppy seas that bounced the raft about, Eadie and Boutte boosted Bartek onto one wing, lifted him over the cockpit, and sat him on the right side with his legs dangling over the front edge of the wing. Once Bartek was in place, Eadie and Boutte tightly secured him into a sitting position. They then turned to Rickenbacker, still waiting in the raft, lifted him up to the left wing, and tied him in place. As an added precaution to prevent either man from slipping off the wing while Eadie taxied the plane across the ocean surface, the pilot and radioman tied a rope around Bartek's waist, threaded it through the cockpit, and fastened it around Rickenbacker's waist so that if one toppled off the wing, the man on the other wing would act as an anchor.

After making sure the two were fastened in, Boutte straddled the tiny rear cockpit area between the wings, near and above where he normally sat as radioman. In an upright stance, he then reached out his hands, grabbed their collars, and held on to Rickenbacker on his left and Bartek to his right. Boutte was happy to provide stability for the exhausted pair but wondered if his arms could withstand the strain of traversing forty-five miles across the ocean to Funafuti in that awkward position. Before leaving, he and Eadie gave their passengers a small amount of water and soup. While he supped the welcome broth, Rickenbacker thought that he had rarely come across two such impressive aviators.

After securing the raft to the airplane, and with Boutte clutching each man by the collar, around 9:00 p.m. Lieutenant Eadie, praying that a storm would not cross his path in the darkness, began taxiing toward Funafuti. The propeller wash drenched Rickenbacker and Bartek as the Kingfisher slowly churned across the Pacific, and both winced from pain as the aircraft bounced upward with each wave crest, but it was a jaunt they happily endured. "It was blacker than the inside of a miner's hip pocket," recalled Bartek, but they shrugged off the discomfort of a ride Rickenbacker described as "the most comfortable seat I ever had in my life, lashed to the wing against the fuselage."[15]

Fortunately for the five men, their trip to Funafuti ended quicker than expected. Help in the form of a PT boat was then churning toward them.

"JUST CALL ME EDDIE, BOYS, BUT GET ME ON THIS DAMNED BOAT!"

Coordinated by Lieutenant Commander Munroe in *Hilo*, since dawn four PT boats and four Navy patrol planes had been scouring hundreds of square miles of ocean hunting for the missing raft. Crew aboard the PT boats had so intensely scrutinized the ocean surface that their eyes burned and their heads ached, but no one gave up. Eddie Rickenbacker was out there, and every sailor wanted to be the person who first spotted his raft.

Shortly before sunset, *Hilo* received a message from Lieutenant Eadie informing them that he had located a raft forty-five miles northwest of Funafuti and that he intended to land near it. Lieutenant Commander Munroe immediately relayed the message to his nearest boat, *PT-26,* under the command of Ensign John M. Weeks, who around 7:00 p.m. increased speed and set a course for the raft. Bouncing along the surface at top speed taxed the engines' water jackets, which began spitting out sprays of hot water, but three machinist's mates formed a bucket brigade to keep water flowing into the stressed engines. As they still had thirty-five miles to go before reaching the raft's location, they hoped the engines would hold under the strain.

Fortunately, seventy-five minutes after receiving Munroe's order, *PT-26* sighted Eadie's seaplane, its running lights illuminating the area as it taxied along the surface. After maneuvering his boat closer to the Kingfisher and cutting the engines, Weeks joined Rickenbacker and Eadie to discuss transferring the three. They agreed that Bartek and Rickenbacker were strong enough to be moved to the boat, but fearing that the switch might be too hard on Adamson, they concluded that the colonel should remain in the plane, which would follow in the wake of the PT boat back to Funafuti.

Eadie and Boutte detached the raft from the Kingfisher and lowered Rickenbacker and Bartek back into what had been their home for three torturous weeks. Rickenbacker could barely hold his head up, but he picked up an oar and began paddling toward

PT-26, *which picked up Eddie Rickenbacker and Private Johnny Bartek from Lieutenant William F. Eadie and Radioman 2/c Lester H. Boutte's Vought OS2U Kingfisher floatplane, was similar to the boat pictured here. While* PT-26, *with Rickenbacker and Bartek aboard, slowly churned toward Funafuti, Eadie taxied his Kingfisher in the boat's wake, bringing with him Colonel Hans Christian Adamson.*

THE BARTEK FAMILY COLLECTION

the PT boat, spurred by the thought that each stroke moved him closer to the end of his traumatic ocean nightmare.

The PT boat's crew, who had already contributed money to a pot that would be awarded to the first man who helped the famous Eddie Rickenbacker out of the water to safety, watched as the man steadily advanced toward the vessel. A few shouted greetings to the famed aviator, who replied in a firm voice, "Just call me Eddie, boys, but get me on this damned boat!" Eddie moved the raft close enough to the vessel, from where three of the crew hoisted him aboard. "Planting my feet upon an American deck was the next-best thing to being home," recalled Rickenbacker. "The crew gave us a cheer."[16]

For the first time in three weeks, at 8:15 p.m. on November 12, Funafuti time, Rickenbacker and Bartek felt a solid surface beneath them. "Took aboard from seaplane two missing army aviators, Capt. E. V. Rickenbacker and Pvt. Bartek, J. B., U.S.A.," stated the boat's log, "suffering from exhaustion, exposure, hunger, & thirst. Administered bouillon and shock treatment." As soon as Rickenbacker and Bartek were safely aboard and treatment had begun, Ensign Weeks turned the vessel toward Funafuti to deliver his famous passenger to waiting doctors, warm food, and rest. "Underway on course 120°T, for Funafuti Island, Ellice Group,"[17] added the PT boat's log. Weeks purposely limited the speed of his PT boat to give Rickenbacker and Bartek a smoother ride.

The bearded survivors had lost so much weight that the crew thought they had taken aboard a pair of skeletons. Eddie Rickenbacker looked nothing like the photographs they had seen in newspapers, and while they were unfamiliar with Bartek, his body, too, displayed the unmistakable ravages of their time on the ocean. Knowing that the two would be exhausted and ready to sleep from their weeks on the Pacific, the crew handed out bedrolls and blankets.

Bartek immediately fell asleep, but Rickenbacker was too excited to drift off. After being treated by the naval medical officer, Lieutenant Commander James Fuller, Rickenbacker drank mugs of beef broth, pineapple juice, and water so hurriedly that Weeks and some of the crew cautioned him to slow down. As usual, the aviator ignored their suggestions, but the rich liquid affected his bowels, forcing Eddie to ask directions to the washroom. He slowly rose and, holding on to items to avoid collapsing because of his wobbly leg muscles, enjoyed his first normal bowel movement in more than three weeks.

Refreshed from the liquids, Rickenbacker asked Weeks if he would give him a tour of the PT boat. The ensign obliged, even though he wondered if the fifty-two-year-old should exert himself in such a way. Weeks showed Rickenbacker the three engines, the four twenty-one-inch-long torpedoes, the two twin .50-caliber Browning machine guns, and every other feature of the craft. After the tour, with adrenaline still keeping him awake, for two hours Rickenbacker sat on Weeks's bunk and told him and others about his three weeks adrift on the Pacific.

While Rickenbacker entertained the crew, Bartek had collapsed on the foredeck and asked not to be bothered. "I'm not going to move for another year," he groaned to crew members who rushed to help him. "I'm not going to move even a finger." When the crew brought extra blankets to keep him warm, the young man from Freehold was finally able to let down his guard. "I was in good hands then. I was warm now for the first time and it was the first time I was able to rest. I just laid there and went to sleep."[18]

When thirty minutes later the fatigued private awakened from his first, albeit brief, nap, Lieutenant Commander Fuller examined Bartek before permitting the crew to bring him pineapple juice, water, and two pieces of pineapple. Fuller warned him to drink and eat slowly, even though the radioman wanted to devour everything brought forward.

After assisting Rickenbacker and Bartek onto the PT boat, Lester Boutte's labors were far from complete. He swam through the choppy waters back to the plane, climbed onto the right wing, and perched there while Lieutenant Eadie slowly taxied in *PT-26*'s wake, which created a smoother surface upon which Eadie could maneuver. During the eight hours it took to traverse the distance back to Funafuti, Eadie idled the engines every hour or so to allow Boutte to check on Adamson in the rear cockpit and to give him a few sips of hot soup or water. Sitting in the more sheltered pilot's seat, Eadie had the easier part, but it was an arduous journey for Boutte, already weary from a long day's search and from holding on to Rickenbacker and Bartek before rendezvousing with *PT-26*.

AFTER TALKING TO the PT boat crew, Rickenbacker returned to the deck to check on Bartek. "I'll never forget how Rick walked out on the deck of the boat where Bartek was lying," recalled Lieutenant Commander Fuller. "He stood there a moment, then said quietly to Bartek, who still carried a pocket Bible, 'Johnny, you can thank God for your Testament. Now you can see faith has been rewarded.'"[19]

Rickenbacker's words indicated that both men had been affected by their mutual experiences. Neither would later admit to instant religious conversions, but both had witnessed too many unexplained events in three weeks not to be altered. Something had inexplicably helped them survive, and whether they labeled that "something" as God, fate, or karma mattered little. They were willing to admit that, at least in part, an outside source had offered a supporting hand.

Bartek's mother had been right. Maybe, the private was willing to admit, Mary possessed a wisdom beyond her years.

"THEY ARE LUCKY TO BE ALIVE"

Colonel Leech hoped he exhibited the same astuteness as Bartek's mother. Shortly after 8:00 p.m., he ordered that until morning, every quarter hour the island's searchlights should be turned on for five minutes to help *PT-26* and Lieutenant Eadie's aircraft locate Funafuti in the dark.

The PT boat and the Kingfisher bounced slowly along the surface at eight miles per hour, feeling their way in the shadows and hoping that nothing interfered with the delivery of their important passengers. Ensign Weeks knew that somewhere in the dark loomed the jagged coral rocks of Funafuti's reef, but trusted that Leech had thought of turning on the searchlights to help guide them in. After rescuing Eddie Rickenbacker from the ocean, Weeks dreaded the thought that he might lose his famous passenger to the sea by slamming into the sharp reef. Happily, as they neared the island, they spied searchlights through the darkness.

The lighting provided Funafuti's location, but Ensign Weeks and Lieutenant Eadie still had to find and navigate an opening through the reef, which remained shrouded by the dark. "For a while it was mostly by guess and by gosh," said Eadie of their attempt to locate the lagoon entrance. "So I chugged along beside the reef, watching the white of breakers on my wing tips. Finally, there seemed an unswerving of the white line of foam which I took to indicate a current passing in from the ocean to the lagoon."[20]

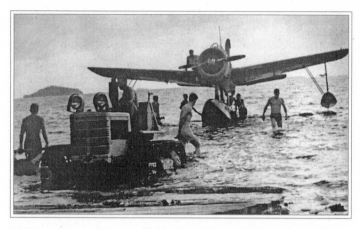

Military personnel at Funafuti bring Lieutenant William F. Eadie and Radioman 2/c Lester H. Boutte's Vought OS2U Kingfisher floatplane ashore after the pair plucked Eddie Rickenbacker, Colonel Hans Christian Adamson, and Private Johnny Bartek from the Pacific.

THE BARTEK FAMILY COLLECTION

The PT boat and airplane passed through the reef at 2:30 a.m. on Friday, November 13. They needed another hour to taxi to the base, where a ground crew stood ready to rush the three men from Rickenbacker's raft to the island hospital. With Captain Cherry's rescue and transport to Funafuti, and with the Whittaker group safe at Nukufetau, the twenty-four-day ocean nightmare on the Pacific had at long last ended for Eddie Rickenbacker and his six companions.

TO PREPARE FOR their famous guest, the Funafuti medical staff had determined that their previous facilities would be inadequate for treating Rickenbacker and the others. They had also been concerned that once the news broke that the renowned aviator had been rescued and was recuperating on the island, swarms of newspaper reporters and photographers would descend on Funafuti. To prevent the press from gathering around a ramshackle medical structure, Colonel Leech had ordered the swift construction of a new one-story frame hospital. As soon as Ensign Weeks docked *PT-26*, the crew placed Rickenbacker and Bartek on stretchers and lowered them into a boat that had come out to bring the pair to shore. Once the boat reached the beach, Navy corpsmen waiting with stretchers carried them to the hospital along a path lined with palm trees.

Rickenbacker called this Friday the 13th "my lucky day," and said that they were taken "through the most beautiful palm trees I have ever seen in my life." Bartek agreed, and declared that "it was the most beautiful island in the whole world," mainly because Funafuti "was the first land we had seen in three weeks. To me it was heaven on earth and then we were brought into the hospital."[21]

Their physical conditions contrasted with the picturesque palm trees. "Capt. Rickenbacker and his party certainly looked as though they had been through the gates of Hades," said Major Peter Altpeter, a Marine stationed on the island. "They are lucky to be alive." Pharmacist's mates carefully undressed the aviator, whom they treated as if he were royalty. Rickenbacker had lost forty pounds in three weeks, and claimed "my clothes literally fell off my back due to the threads in the seams being rotted and eaten away by salt water."[22] The medics gently washed and applied a heavy coating of ointment to their ulcer-covered bodies, and administered sulfa to provide a little comfort.

In a nearby cot, Johnny Bartek overheard Lieutenant Commander Fuller discuss the private's poor condition with the staff. In addition to boils and sunburn, Bartek suffered from badly swollen feet and, like Rickenbacker, had lost significant weight. After Fuller injected plasma to help him regain strength, Bartek felt much better.

The once robust Hans Adamson had seen his weight plummet from 195 to 119 pounds, and his medical situation had so deteriorated that Fuller had to administer a blood transfusion as men carried the colonel to the hospital. "The thing that really saved my life was the miracle that on this little sandspit of an island," Colonel Adamson later explained, the hospital staff "already had blood plasma available." He concluded that "I would have died within several hours if I hadn't had the plasma."[23]

Lieutenant Commander Fuller believed that without the plasma, Bartek, too, would have been dead within a day, and said that Reynolds, who was so weak that he could not lift a hand or speak, would most likely have succumbed within twelve hours. Even though the older Eddie Rickenbacker also suffered from severe dehydration and saltwater ulcers, Fuller thought that the aging aviator could have lasted another three or four days on the ocean.

During that first day and night, Fuller limited the men to sips of tea and beef broth, plus two ounces of water every two hours, to prevent them from overeating. That did not sit well with Rickenbacker, who was so thirsty he felt as if his throat were on fire. His eyes were practically swollen shut from the sun's daily scorching glare, and, aching from head to toe, he slept poorly.

When he did slumber, he dreamed that he was still on the raft and of again visiting that beautiful home. "Even after we were picked up," he said, "for many, many nights in the hospital I would awaken with that same hallucination and dream, with the everlasting rocking and swinging of the raft under me."[24]

WHEN RICKENBACKER LOOKED in a mirror the next morning, a specter stared back at him. Mentally he was still the Eddie Rickenbacker of the month before, but this physical version, with a skeletal frame, sunken cheeks, dulled eyes, and a filthy mustache and brown beard, was almost unrecognizable. Rickenbacker expected that sooner or later photographers and reporters, eager to wire to the States the first photographs and stories about the home front hero, would swamp Funafuti. Borrowing a razor, he sheared his beard and mustache so that he at least looked more like Eddie Rickenbacker than a vagabond, donned fresh clothes handed out by the hospital staff, and waited for the avalanche of press to appear.

Lieutenant Forrest, who had helped search for Rickenbacker, had never seen anything like the feverish activity that overwhelmed the tiny Pacific outpost. Funafuti, he wrote on November 14, "became a Mecca for media and senior military personnel as the word was flashed around the world that Capt. Eddie Rickenbacker had been rescued and was safe. Planes poured in, media were busy and Funafuti was definitely on the map—although designated as 'a forward naval operations base' due to wartime censorship."[25]

When the photographers arrived, the hospital staff brought in Adamson and Cherry—who had by now been brought to the island—to sit for photographs with Rickenbacker. In another section of the hospital, Bartek argued that he should be included as well, but the physicians denied his request, claiming he was too weak for the heightened excitement. When Bartek continued to resist, Rickenbacker told him it was more important for him to recover than it was to sit for a photograph or two. "Do you want me to get on another of my mads?" Rickenbacker threatened. Bartek halted his objections, but as he later wrote, "I was very unhappy with his answer."[26]

Later that day, the four men at Funafuti enjoyed a reunion with the Whittaker group when *Hilo* docked. For the first time since the seven men in three rafts separated, the entire group, save for Sergeant Kaczmarczyk, was together.

Whittaker walked in and thought Bartek appeared "pretty wan." He spotted Rickenbacker, who as he recalled, "looked much weaker and much sicker than when I had seen him last." The lieutenant figured that since their watery saga had ended, Rickenbacker could allow himself to relax and would no longer carry the burdens of commanding the group, but nonetheless, added Whittaker, he was the same leader "whose indomitable spirit brought more than one of our company thru alive."

"What's the matter, Rick? Been sick?" the copilot joked. Rickenbacker smiled and held out his hand to greet his fellow survivor. "I marveled again at this man,"[27] wrote Whittaker of a person who had endured two near-death airplane crashes in less than two years.

On November 13, 1942, a bearded Second Lieutenant James C. Whittaker (right) and Second Lieutenant John J. De Angelis, exhibiting significant weight loss, end their twenty-four agonizing days on the ocean. The PT boat tender USS Hilo (PG-58) transported the two men to Funafuti Island for treatment.

Rickenbacker thought that Whittaker looked surprisingly good, but claimed that Reynolds, who had remained aboard the *Hilo,* "was an emaciated wreck." When Whittaker learned that many in the military and in the press had given them up for lost, he brusquely replied, "Everybody knows that Eddie Ricken-backer always comes back, and I figured my wife thought the same thing about me."[28]

Three unidentified military officers accompany Second Lieutenant John J. De Angelis after his arrival on Funafuti Island in November 1942. He had lost significant weight from his time on the ocean.

AUBURN UNIVERSITY, SPECIAL COLLECTIONS & ARCHIVES

The seven men—six in the hospital and Reynolds aboard the *Hilo*—spent November 14 and 15 recuperating. Cherry and Whittaker made speedy progress, and physicians thought that Rickenbacker was steadily gaining strength. Even Adamson, who had been lifeless and depressed on November 13, and Bartek, displayed signs of renewed strength.

A steady diet of nourishing food and liquids so quickly revitalized Rickenbacker, Adamson, Cherry, Whittaker, and De Angelis that physicians who flew up from Samoa deemed them strong enough for a plane hop to that island and its better-equipped facility. They concluded that Private Bartek and Sergeant Reynolds should remain in the Funafuti hospital and *Hilo* respectively until they had recovered sufficiently for them to fly out.

A COMBINATION OF factors brought the seven survivors safely to Funafuti. Rickenbacker's hard-nosed determination to survive, and in the process bring the other six with him, played a major role, but faith and prayer contributed as well.

Although Eddie Rickenbacker might disagree, Captain Cherry's insistence on leaving the cluster of rafts and dispersing the survivors to a wider plot of ocean led to his discovery by Lieutenant Woodward, which in turn gave Cherry the chance to direct forces to the remaining two rafts. Had the men not disbanded, they might never have been rescued. Shortly after returning to the United States, Lieutenant Whittaker said that everyone owed a debt of gratitude to the pilot, for "Cherry's rescue led to all the others."[29]

WHILE RICKENBACKER FLEW to Samoa, in the United States news broke that the nation's hero had been found. Other than military officials involved in the rescue, Adelaide Rickenbacker was the first to know that her husband had been picked up, but within hours, newspapers had spread the information to the entire nation.

PART V

Home from the Pacific

CHAPTER 11

"Make Me Plenty of Apple Pie"
Home, November–December

EDDIE RICKENBACKER, JOHNNY BARTEK, and the other five survivors were not the only ones celebrating their rescue from a likely Pacific grave. Newspaper headlines and articles in the United States exploded with the news that the nation's hero had been located, and gave his return equal status on front pages with positive news from the war against Hitler, where an American assault into North Africa had begun, and bulletins from the Pacific, where the nation's naval forces were then engaged in a critical slugfest off the shores of Guadalcanal to determine who would seize control of that vital island.

The American public had received heavy tidings with Eddie Rickenbacker's October disappearance. By mid-November, however, heartening news from both theaters and Rickenbacker's reemergence imparted a renewed sense of optimism.

"HE MUST HAVE A RABBIT'S FOOT OR SOMETHING"

Other than her brief visit to Washington, DC, to spur Hap Arnold to action, Adelaide Rickenbacker had spent most of her time at their New York apartment, waiting for word of her husband. During the morning of November 13, Marguerite Shepherd, Eddie's secretary, arrived to keep her company. Around 9:00 a.m. the telephone rang, and when Adelaide answered, she heard Hap Arnold saying, "I have good news for you." She waited until the general provided more details before replying, "God bless you." When Hap offered to transmit any message she might want to send to her husband, Adelaide promptly scribbled a hasty note before hanging up.

Adelaide immediately telephoned her mother-in-law, who resided in Beverly Hills, to relay the glad news. The phone awakened Eddie's brother Dewey, who had been staying with his mother, and when he heard the news, Dewey muttered a quiet "Thank God" before calling to her.

Dewey's holler let Lizzie know that her prayers had been answered. For the past three weeks, she had refused to believe that her son, who had so often survived events that probably should have killed him, had succumbed in a desolate part of the Pacific. When Dewey informed her that Eddie had been found and transported to an island hospital, she broke down in tears. "None of us had given up hope," she said, "and we were sure all the time that he would be located."[1]

"I never knew Eddie to give up on anything," Dewey said later. "Maybe that's why we never gave up on him. Of course,

I'm overjoyed to learn he's safe, but I can't say I'm surprised." As he explained, "There's something about Eddie that makes you believe that he'll rise to any occasion. He's done it before, and he can do it again—and again."[2]

Adelaide next notified their two sons, fourteen-year-old William, a student in Asheville, North Carolina, and eighteen-year-old David, a first-year cadet at the Admiral Farragut Naval Academy in New Jersey. David joined a wild celebration in the hallway as word spread, and later said that he "felt from the beginning that dad's luck would hold out and that he would be found."

Rickenbacker's two sisters, Mrs. Emma Hanson and Mrs. Mary Pflaum, celebrated in the family's hometown of Columbus. In Detroit, Rickenbacker's brother William pointed out that fate had happily always favored his brother. "He must have a rabbit's foot or something. It's just marvelous that they found him safe."[3]

Two hours after receiving Hap Arnold's call, Adelaide walked down to the apartment lobby to talk to the throng of reporters eager to capture her words. In a formal statement, she told them, "I have just been advised by Gen. H. H. Arnold of my husband's rescue." Adelaide said that "I never lost faith and knew that he would be rescued," but she admitted, "I was worried in the last few days because he burns so and I kept thinking about him on a raft. I'd dream about him on a raft and wake up and still think I was seeing him." Now confident that her husband, although underweight and sunburned, was in good shape and on his way to recovery, she added, "Now I'm so happy it's hard to describe my feelings."[4]

On November 13, after learning that her husband has been rescued, Adelaide Rickenbacker meets with members of the press in the lobby of her New York City apartment building.

Adelaide credited the successful outcome to the public's support and the coordinated effort by the nation's military in finding her husband. "As stated before, my belief in the resourcefulness of this wonderful group of men, to say nothing of the constant prayers of Eddie's thousands of admirers and friends, would make it possible for them to withstand the strain until the War Department's thorough and efficient search brought about their ultimate rescue. I can't speak too highly of the wonderful cooperation of the Army and Navy, and wish I could thank every one who participated personally."[5]

The Bartek and Adamson families received government telegrams announcing the good news. A November 14 communication from the adjutant general to Bartek's parents informed them that he was "GRATIFIED TO INFORM YOU THE COMMANDING GENERAL HAWAIIAN DEPARTMENT REPORTS YOUR SON PRIVATE JOHN F. BARTEK AIR CORPS HAS BEEN FOUND IN POOR CONDITION BUT RECOVERY EXPECTED. PROGRESS REPORTS WILL BE FURNISHED AS NEEDED."[6]

Hundreds of publications, in large metropolitan centers as

Charles and Mary Bartek express relief and thanksgiving after learning that their son, Johnny, had been found alive.

THE BARTEK FAMILY COLLECTION

well as in small towns offering only weekly editions, plastered headlines across their front pages to inform the public that their hero had been found. Movietone News, Pathé News, and other newsreels disseminated the information throughout the nation's theaters, and popular radio commentators, such as Walter Winchell, praised the military's effort in bringing home America's most famous aviator.

"Here, surely, is a miracle; a miracle of good fortune, but a miracle also of courage and stamina and great faith," declared the *New York Times*. "It is a story that will take its place among the great sagas of the sea and the great tales of heroism in this war. A gallant soldier of the First World War comes back to us to fight again."[7]

"Once More the Editors Revise Rick's Obituary" dominated the *Chicago Tribune*'s front page, while the *Charlotte Observer* offered the headline "Rickenbacker Again Cheats Grim Reaper."[8] *Time* magazine celebrated that the despair felt by the nation after Rickenbacker disappeared had now been replaced by a newfound sense of national pride over yet another heroic exploit by the aviator.

Each publication placed its own spin on the story, but because reporters lacked sufficient knowledge of what the men had experienced, they could only craft sanitized versions. They knew nothing of the sun, the sharks, the tern that landed on Rickenbacker's head, Alex Kaczmarczyk's dying, the Rickenbacker-Cherry dispute, or Rickenbacker and Bartek being strapped to the wing of a plane.

A Navy spokesman said that no new details would be divulged until the men returned to the States. According to *Time* magazine, as one of the country's most popular personages, Rickenbacker would naturally dominate the narrative, and any details of noble deeds and perilous moments, "the Navy left for Hero Rickenbacker to tell himself."[9]

Until he could, others spoke for him. W. L. White, the son of William Allen White, the prominent Pulitzer Prize–winning editor and publisher of the *Emporia Gazette* in Kansas, who would succeed his father after his death in two years, epitomized the home front reaction. "There is a limit to everything," White wrote. "Even the tough old Pacific, after battling Eddie Rickenbacker for twenty-one days, finally gave him up to the skies. I would imagine with a weary sigh of relief along its white beaches." Damon Runyon, one of the most celebrated writers of the time and a good friend of the hero, wrote that people from coast to coast "were electrified out of their worries, and shouted happily to strangers. It seemed that nothing except the surrender of Hitler could have cheered them more as the news went rippling along their tongues—Eddie Rickenbacker has been found alive!"[10]

THE NEWS OF Eddie Rickenbacker's rescue handed the home front a third positive event within a week. Sharing the front pages were articles about the Naval Battle of Guadalcanal in the Pacific that would by November 15 end in an American triumph and spark a turning point in the Southwest Pacific, as well as stories that highlighted the American Army advancing against German forces in North Africa. Rickenbacker's Friday the 13th rescue enabled the nation to celebrate a trio of encouraging events that made people think that, at long last, the war might be slowly turning in their favor.

On the island of Samoa, on December 12, 1942, after recuperating from his twenty-four days on the Pacific Ocean, Captain Eddie Rickenbacker shakes hands with Lieutenant William F. Eadie, the aviator who landed near Rickenbacker's raft and transported him to PT-26. Rickenbacker was on his way home to the United States when he stopped in Samoa to pick up his friend and fellow survivor Colonel Hans Christian Adamson.

National Archives Photo #80-G-31350

In locating Eddie Rickenbacker, Lieutenant Eadie and Radioman 2/c Boutte had not merely saved a hero. They had helped revitalize a nation that, until recent days, had grown weary of hard blows delivered by Hitler in Europe and his Japanese ally in the Pacific. Everyone understood that frequent, bloody battles lay before them in the coming years, but they could now face those with renewed resolution and optimism. The country's armed forces had begun to respond to the dual threats posed by Germany and Japan, and the nation's hero was once again safe and in friendly hands.

"I AM TRYING TO GET A NEW OUTLOOK ON LIFE"

After initial treatment at Funafuti, Rickenbacker and the others would require enhanced care in a better-equipped military hospital in Samoa before flying home. Physicians deemed Bartek and Reynolds too weak to endure the daylong flight to Samoa and opted to keep Reynolds in the *Hilo*'s sick bay and Bartek in Funafuti's field hospital. The doctors wavered about putting Colonel Adamson aboard an aircraft, but Rickenbacker insisted that his friend would not last much longer than a week if the two were separated. His argument tipped the scales, and the physicians reluctantly approved his request.

In the early morning of November 15, outfitted with uniforms donated by Funafuti Marines, Rickenbacker, Cherry, Whittaker, Adamson, and De Angelis boarded Catalina flying boats for the trip southeast to Tutuila, the main island in American Samoa. After departing Funafuti, the aircraft flew 450 miles southeast to Wallis Island, where they enjoyed a two-hour lay-over. The Rickenbacker group so heartily attacked the bowls of meat soup and pineapple ice cream that two physicians traveling with them put a stop to it before they became ill from the rich food. After a brief rest, the five continued east 400 miles to British Samoa for a second breather before making a short hop to American Samoa.

As he sat in the Catalina and watched the Pacific below, Eddie Rickenbacker marveled that in one day, this aircraft covered more miles than the rafts had drifted in twenty-four days. One month ago, aboard the B-17, he had gazed in awe at the ocean's beauty, but he now knew all too well that on the surface, beauty became the beast.

While the Catalina droned across the ocean, Whittaker recalled his flight to Hawaii before joining Rickenbacker the previous month. He had then stared at the water 5,000 feet below, its apparently tranquil surface sparkling in the October afternoon sun, and thought he had rarely seen such magnificence, but by mid-November, after being adrift on the Pacific, he no longer harbored such delusions. "During that flight, I looked down at the Pacific—smooth and blue; cool and inviting. But Mrs. Whittaker's son James was not fooled," he later wrote. "I wonder how I ever could have seen anything of beauty in that shark-ridden waste of mountainous swells and scalding heat. It took the life of one of my companions and clutched at the rest of us, who were saved only by the intervention of God and two divine miracles."[11]

When the planes touched down in Samoa, hospital personnel

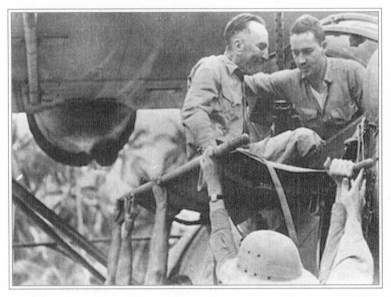

Military personnel assist Captain Eddie Rickenbacker in exiting the plane upon landing at Samoa for further treatment.

NATIONAL ARCHIVES PHOTO #127-GW-785

took the five men to Mobile Hospital No. 3. Once Lieutenant Whittaker entered the modern facility, complete with an air-conditioned operating room, he protested about being put immediately to bed, but the copilot finally relented when he realized the doctors were stricter than the ones he had checkmated on Funafuti.

A feast awaited. The men ate steak at every meal, and the Red Cross handed out cigarettes, uniforms, and moccasins. Ricken-backer, Cherry, Whittaker, and De Angelis improved sufficiently that the doctors told them that none should experience any lasting effects from the twenty-four days on the Pacific.

As for Adamson, his slow recovery perplexed the physicians

until tests showed that he had diabetes, of which even the colonel had been unaware. The hospital lacked insulin, but fortunately another diabetic, an Army physician aboard a ship that had just arrived while on its way to the United States, gave Adamson most of his supply, retaining only enough for his own immediate needs. A few days later, though, a bout with pneumonia halted his recovery. When doctors administered sulfa drugs to combat the illness, Adamson suffered a severe reaction that required three transfusions of blood that had been donated by hospital attendants.

Colonel Adamson was well enough, however, to write to his beloved Helen. He informed her that "it would be difficult, or in fact impossible, for me to recall all our experiences. Just now I am trying to get a new outlook on life. I need this badly, since sitting on a rubber life raft for more than three weeks is pretty 'tough turkey.'" He explained that "on Friday afternoon we were spotted by a marine corps [*sic*] plane and later in the evening we were picked up, and you can't imagine the prayers of thanks we offered."

The colonel made certain to let Helen know how important she had been to his survival. "As we had neither food nor water, all I can say is that thru the hell of it all your presence was an everlasting beacon that gave me the hope and will and determination to live." He empathized with the emotions that had assailed her and claimed that "even when we almost went out, one of the things that made me suffer most was the torture which I knew you were facing. Rick and I knew we were alive, but you did not, and there was no way we could get word to you."

He told Helen not to worry and that he would soon be in her arms. "Meanwhile, I am lying flat on my back in the hospital here trying to readjust all the things that went out of adjustment plus the effort of getting rid of too many saltwater sores."[12]

WHILE THE FIVE had been recovering in Samoa, Private Bartek and Sergeant Reynolds remained at Funafuti for another week, where the Marines and islanders accorded them royal treatment. Each day islanders offered Bartek and the long-bearded Reynolds flowers and well wishes, while Marines brought cakes and pies, soft-boiled eggs, and ice cream to supplement the heaping mounds of roast beef. After a few days Bartek assumed he was strong enough to walk, but he collapsed after taking only three steps. One week later, however, Private Bartek was strong enough to leave Funafuti and rejoin his five comrades. Although he was on his way back to full recovery, he informed the group that Sergeant Reynolds was still too weak to make the flight.

Within two weeks, the Samoan patients had improved to the point where they could walk around on their own. Until the end of November, staff kept a close watch on their temperatures, pulses, and breathing, but no one seemed in danger of succumbing. Lieutenant De Angelis made such rapid gains that the Pennsylvania native returned to one of his favorite hobbies, dancing. Four days after reaching Samoa, the veteran of Nesquehoning dance halls delighted hospital attendants and patients by jitterbugging with Samoan natives.

Each Sunday Rickenbacker sat in the front row at church

services. He had never been a devoted churchgoer, but he believed he owed thanks to God for helping him through the time at sea. To his surprise Lieutenant Whittaker, the lifelong atheist who had early in the three-week odyssey at sea mocked the importance of prayer, walked in and sat next to him. Afterward, Whittaker told Rickenbacker that he had never before attended a church service, but he had witnessed too much on the Pacific to dismiss the notions of a God and faith.

Rickenbacker regained half of the forty pounds he had lost, mainly because he drank gallons of fruit juices and ate everything they placed before him. He recovered so quickly that he informed Secretary Stimson that he intended to complete his mission and visit General MacArthur in early December. When Stimson relayed the note to Hap Arnold, the general wrote Rickenbacker that he would immediately make available a transport to fly him to Australia.

Eddie was not pleased, however, when he scanned the headlines filed during the darkest period of his time adrift, a stretch when many at home, including the military, had lost hope. He scoffed at the obituaries, at a *New York Daily News* editorial cartoon titled "So Long, Eddie," and at the same publication's editorial "Good-By Rickenbacker?" He ripped out one cartoon sketched by his friend Burris Jenkins Jr. of the *New York Journal* depicting Rickenbacker's face, flanked by racing cars and airplanes, all beneath the words "The End of the Roaring Road?" Rickenbacker angrily scribbled "Hell, No!"[13] across it and mailed it to Jenkins.

A writer and photographer from *Life* magazine visited the

Samoan hospital to feature Eddie Rickenbacker's story in its December 7, 1942, issue commemorating the one-year anniversary of the Pearl Harbor attack. Inserted between news of the infamous assault that wrenched America into war, the article stressed Rickenbacker's talent for squeezing out of life-threatening situations.

"Rickenbacker, the World War I flying ace with the charmed life, looked like a pugilist who had just gone ten rounds with Joe Louis," stated the article. "Although both his hands were carefully wrapped in bandages and his eyes were badly puffed and swollen, 'Rick' insisted he was 'feeling great'" after enduring moments on the Pacific when he doubted he would pull through. "I know I came within hearing distance of the Old Fellow this trip, because his approach, always the same, is unmistakable. One hears beautiful soft music and everything is extremely pleasant just as heaven should be."[14]

Other major news outlets also dispatched reporters to interview Rickenbacker, and before long, the normally quiet island turned feverish with activity. Men who had been stationed at this base far from the combat zone enjoyed the interruptions, for as one wrote, "for a brief moment the spotlights of the world were focused on our area"[15] instead of on Guadalcanal or North Africa.

When a *New York Times* reporter asked which factors were crucial to the return of the seven men, Rickenbacker replied that a combination of faith, his own inner qualities, and his willingness to utilize anger to provoke his companions brought them back.

Rickenbacker continued to look after the others in Samoa. He made certain that a car was placed at their disposal so that they, too, could enjoy the island. He convinced superiors into allowing each man to send two cables home to family, and when a general arranged for a bounteous Thanksgiving dinner for the hero, Rickenbacker insisted that the other men attend.

"Captain Rickenbacker always checked every day what needs the boys had," said Lieutenant De Angelis. "If we needed anything he thought perhaps he could come nearer getting it than the boys." De Angelis added, "He was as much concerned about our health after we were picked up as he was while we were out there floating around."[16]

"THIS IS THE HAPPIEST DAY OF MY LIFE"

In the first week of December, Cherry, Whittaker, Bartek, and De Angelis boarded a Consolidated B-24 Liberator for the flight from Samoa to Hawaii, their final stop before continuing to the United States, while Adamson and Reynolds remained in the Pacific until they were strong enough to endure the long flight out of the war zone. After completing the second of three legs to the mainland, Lieutenant Whittaker had two objectives while in Hawaii. The first was to indulge in the malted milkshakes he had dreamed of in the rafts. The other was to purchase a second silk Hawaiian dress for his wife, as the one he had purchased for her there in mid-October was among the many personal items he and the others aboard the B-17 had tossed out the hatch to lighten the bomber's load shortly before ditching.

Before the week was out, the quartet boarded a second airplane for the trip to Treasure Island in San Francisco Bay. Military officials and family members greeted the survivors, who over the next few days sat through interrogations from the military. After the questioning ended, the military provided transport to their homes, and for the first time since the ditching, other than the brief split on the ocean, the men went their separate ways.

Due to Eddie Rickenbacker's lofty status in the United States, he received most of the national press coverage. The other survivors were either briefly mentioned in the many stories about Rickenbacker or in short sidebar pieces.

A joyous family is reunited. Bobbie Cherry (left) and daughter Paula (right) welcome Captain William T. Cherry Jr. as he arrives in Dallas after flying home from the Pacific. Captain Cherry stopped in Texas for the brief reunion before continuing to Washington, DC, to report to his military superiors.

THE CHERRY FAMILY COLLECTION

However, hometown publications compensated by featuring articles about their now famous residents. In Captain Cherry's home area, the *Fort Worth Star-Telegram* ran headlines such as "Friday, the 13th, Brought Back a War Hero Daddy to Paula Cherry and Her Mother," and "Yesterday Made Their Prayers Come True." The headline "A 'Hello' from the Heart"[17] accompanied a photograph of the aviator standing beside his wife and holding two-year-old Paula after they greeted the hometown hero at Dallas's airport.

Reporters had initially swamped the family when news broke of Captain Cherry's rescue. The national media reappeared in mid-December when Cherry stopped in Dallas while on his way to Washington to be interviewed again by military authorities. He returned the Tuesday before Christmas, and he, Bobbie, and Paula celebrated the holiday with Captain Cherry's parents and relatives in Quail, Texas. New Year's Eve found them back in Fort Worth, ringing in 1943 with their good friends Lieutenant and Mrs. E. A. Smith.

LIEUTENANT WHITTAKER RECEIVED a similarly warm reception in Burlingame, California. National publications heralded Whittaker's early account of the weeks adrift and printed his suggestions to address the problems the men experienced with the inadequate size of the life rafts and the malfunctioning flares. He explained that Rickenbacker assumed control over the group at a crucial moment, and that most of the survivors were willing to place their trust in the hands of a man who had pulled through so many tight situations. "There are 10 great men in this world," he said, "and Rickenbacker is right in the middle of that list of 10. When we started out I thought he was just another man on the bandwagon who had influence enough to get a free ride. But there we were—eight men on rafts. We all started even. There was no rank there, no property, no medium of exchange, no authority except the authority of a better and finer intellect. There was only one value—the preservation of one's life. Toward this end, Capt. Rickenbacker took the leadership and pulled us thru."[18]

THE PRESS NEAR Johnny Bartek's hometown had begun casting a spotlight on the local boy as soon as the government announced his rescue. The main headline on the front page of the November 14 edition of the *Asbury Park Press*, a newspaper published in a community only seventeen miles from Bartek's Freehold home, read RICKENBACKER, BARTEK RESCUED. The accompanying article reported that the young private had been rescued from a life raft in the Pacific "along with dauntless Capt. Eddie Rickenbacker and an army colonel," and explained that while Bartek was in serious condition, he "was expected to recover from the ravages of exposure, the navy announcement said."

Neighbors who had heard the news rushed over to share the tidings with his mother. Mary Bartek said that even during the worst of a nerve-wracking time, she knew "Christ was with my boy. When young men go off to war, they can't take their mothers with them. They can't take their fathers with them and they can't take their sweethearts with them. The only one who goes along with them is Jesus Christ."[19]

The family appreciated the letters from Hap Arnold and Adelaide Rickenbacker, as well as from people around the nation. General Arnold wrote, "I was certainly happy to learn of the safety of your son, Private John F. Bartek. I am informed that Private Bartek has exercised unusual diligence and intelligence in disposing of his assignments. The fact that he was chosen to accompany Captain Rickenbacker on his important flight is indicative of the high regard in which he was held by his military superiors. Let me offer my sincere congratulations to you as I join with Private Bartek's comrades in welcoming his return."

Adelaide took time from her hectic schedule to craft a thoughtful note to Mary Bartek, writing, "How happy you must be over the rescue of your son, despite the fact that he apparently suffered dreadfully. However, he must have a wonderful constitution because I understand from the War Department he will be all right after a period of rest and he will have a very interesting story to tell."[20]

After writing his mother that he would soon be home on a thirty-day furlough and asking her to "make me plenty of apple pie and cabbage and meatballs,"[21] on December 15 Private Bartek surprised family and friends by stepping off a bus in Freehold. A warm reception ensued, with tears of joy, kisses, and hugs, and when he asked about his sister's death earlier in the year, his parents explained that while roller-skating at a rink, Ruth had bumped her head. Although she complained of a bad headache, no one suspected anything, but on her way to school the next morning, the girl collapsed and died only four blocks from her home.

In answer to his mother's query if he had kept his copy of the New Testament that the local church had presented, Bartek pulled out the book that had kept him company through the long days and nights. Even though it had been enclosed in a waterproof case, the book's now weather-beaten binding and marred pages showed the effects of the constant dousing from Pacific swells. When Mary asked her son if God had provided help, as she had vowed He would, Johnny told her about the fish that hopped into the raft and the bird that landed on Rickenbacker's head. "Praise the Lord,"[22] quietly uttered the grateful mother.

CITIZENS OF JOHN De Angelis's hometown erupted when the news arrived that the lieutenant had been rescued. People rushed from their homes to celebrate the good fortune of a resident they now lauded as a hero, and the Reverend Michael Angelini, pastor of the Church of Our Lady of Mount Carmel, ordered Angelus bells rung in celebration and announced that he would officiate at a thanksgiving Mass the next day for the former altar boy.

His parents, Mr. and Mrs. Philip De Angelis, received confirmation that their son was well when a radiogram from Lieutenant De Angelis arrived a few days after Father Angelini's Mass, the first time they had heard anything from him since early October. "Surroundings most comfortable," he wrote. "Feeling fine and recuperating nicely. As soon as physical condition permits will be home. Tell Mary. Love to all. Johnny." Upon receiving the news, Lieutenant De Angelis's aunt, Tessie Cerimele, said, "I never gave up hope. I always said Johnny would come back. And I'm going to have a big steak for him when he comes home."[23]

His twenty-three-year-old bride, Mary, had at long last heard the words she had awaited when a War Department telegram informed her that "your husband, Second Lieutenant John Jean De Angelis, Air Corps, has been found. Additional information will be furnished as received." Clutching the note to her heart, she said, "This is the happiest day of my life. This is the message I have been praying for night and day. Now I can live again." She explained that when Captain Cherry had been found alone at sea, she had almost given up hope for her husband's return. "I knew that Johnny and Capt. Cherry were close friends, and I could not understand why he was not with Capt. Cherry, if he were still alive. And I was so afraid I'd never see him again."[24]

Nesquehoning town leaders announced that once the hometown hero returned, they would hold a testimonial at the East End School House for De Angelis, a 1937 graduate of Nesquehoning High School, where he starred in football and basketball. They assured the citizens that the event would dwarf any previous festivities hosted by the town.

When a healthier De Angelis arrived in mid-December, most of the town's 4,000 residents packed the streets to welcome him. The lieutenant joked that he never knew he had so many friends, and he and Mary waved from an open car as they rode through streets packed with fellow citizens and civic groups. They stopped only for the welcoming ceremony at the Catholic Church of Our Lady of Mount Carmel. De Angelis later told his brother that prayer and his belief in God were the reasons he returned alive.

TRAGICALLY, NO CELEBRATIONS comforted the family of Sergeant Kaczmarczyk. His parents in Torrington, Connecticut, thirty miles west of Hartford, received the painful news from the Navy Department on November 14, just as Lieutenant De Angelis's hometown celebrated his rescue. The *Hartford Courant* reported that seven survivors had been located, "But one, Sergeant Alexander Kaczmarczyk, of Torrington, Conn., died on the raft and was buried at sea." When the United Press, a nationwide syndicate of newspapers, contacted her, Kaczmarczyk's mother said through tears, "He was the only one"[25] who failed to return.

On Sunday, November 15, the parents attended a Requiem Mass for their son, after which they listened to a national radio broadcast in which Adelaide Rickenbacker expressed her sympathy for the sergeant's parents. "It's so kind and thoughtful of them," said Mrs. Kaczmarczyk. "I never expected it, and they thought of it."[26]

Hap Arnold sent a letter expressing his regret "that I learned from Captain Rickenbacker of the death of your son, Sergeant Kaczmarczyk." Hoping to provide some comfort in the midst of their sorrow, Arnold said that their son "was engaged in extremely important duties for the Army Air Forces." The general ended with, "It is my sincere hope that time will cancel your grief and that you will derive increasing consolation in the knowledge that your son died heroically in the service of his country."[27]

Coreen Bond—Alex's beloved "Snooks"—learned of his death shortly after news broke that seven men had been found alive. When she first heard that all but one of the eight men had been located, she rushed upstairs to the radio station to see if they could provide the names of the survivors. "Gee, I hate to tell you," the WTIC receptionist told her, "but your boyfriend was the only one who didn't come back." Coreen refused to admit her love was gone and believed that one day, Alex would be found on some desolate island, similar to what she had seen in Hollywood film romances. "That's the way all the movies ended,"[28] she explained.

Adelaide Rickenbacker extended her sympathies to Coreen. "These are sorrows that come to some who have loved ones in the service of their country," she wrote. "I have been trying all day to think of words to express my sorrow for you."[29]

As the months passed, Coreen reluctantly accepted Alexander's death. She vowed that "we loved very deeply, and, being my first love, he will always be remembered."[30]

"GOD, EDDIE, I'M GLAD TO SEE YOU"

While people in the United States celebrated the safe return of the first four survivors, on the other side of the world Eddie

Rickenbacker tended to the business that had sent him to the Pacific in the first place. He did not look forward to meeting General MacArthur, a man with whom he had heatedly disagreed during the 1925 court-martial of aviation advocate Billy Mitchell for publicly labeling the Army incompetent after the deaths of fellow aviators in air mishaps. Rickenbacker had testified in Mitchell's behalf, and blamed MacArthur for his role in the affair after the Army officer served as one of thirteen members of the court that found Mitchell guilty of conduct detrimental to the military.

On the last day of November, Rickenbacker told Adamson that because his friend still needed to recuperate, he had to leave him behind, but promised that if Adamson continued to improve, he would stop in Samoa and pick him up on the way back to the United States. The next day Rickenbacker boarded a Consolidated B-24 bomber, converted for transport duty, to begin the 2,400-mile flight to Brisbane. The group traveled mostly at night, with Rickenbacker napping on a cot, so that he could use daylight hours to visit air personnel at two stopovers, the Fiji Islands and Nouméa, New Caledonia, where he discussed aviation issues with both officers and enlisted men.

On December 4 Rickenbacker left Nouméa for Brisbane. He arrived there to find that MacArthur had prepared an armed B-17 with a full combat crew to fly him to Port Moresby in New Guinea, the scene of savage combat between the Americans and Japanese. The Army general did not want to endanger the national hero by asking him to fly there in an unprotected plane.

Rickenbacker boarded MacArthur's bomber the next day,

and shortly after sundown landed at Port Moresby without incident. Instead of a cool reception, when Rickenbacker stepped out of the bomber, a group of senior officers waited to greet him. "One of them stood out from the rest; with that familiar cap and dramatic stance, it was MacArthur himself," wrote Rickenbacker. The general moved toward him on the tarmac, hugged the ace, and gushed, "God, Eddie, I'm glad to see you."[31] The surprised aviator reacted similarly and proceeded to have a pleasant stay with MacArthur at his lavish home overlooking the Coral Sea.

The first time Rickenbacker was alone with MacArthur, he delivered the message Stimson had asked him to convey on behalf of the government. While none of the three principals ever divulged the contents—"Stimson and MacArthur took it with them to the grave, and so shall I,"[32] Rickenbacker wrote in his autobiography—it likely contained a harsh admonition against placing his own needs above those of the military's requirements in North Africa and for seeking publicity to buttress a potential 1944 run at the presidency against incumbent Franklin Roosevelt. MacArthur again surprised Rickenbacker by congenially accepting the message.

The pair of national figures spent the next two days relaxing and discussing a variety of topics. Rickenbacker found the general warm and easygoing, even to the point where MacArthur apologized for his earlier opposition to air power when he served as chief of staff of the US Army in the 1930s. MacArthur impressed Rickenbacker with his understanding of air issues in his region, and with his admittance that fighters and bombers greatly assisted his infantry in their assaults against well-entrenched Japanese forces. Rickenbacker, in turn, mesmerized MacArthur with a riveting account of his time adrift on the ocean.

Lieutenant General George C. Kenney, MacArthur's air commander, escorted Rickenbacker to air bases near Port Moresby so that he could chat with the aviators. He compared his battle tactics with the ones currently being used, asked about the aircraft's performances, and answered the young fliers' questions. "Eddie was still a hero to the fighter pilots," recalled Kenney, who especially enjoyed the exchange when one of them asked, "Colonel Rickenbacker, how many victories did you have in the last war?" When Rickenbacker answered that he had recorded twenty-six kills, most of the young pilots, who had downed only two or three Japanese aircraft in the first year of the war, lamented that Eddie's record would stand for a long time.

Sensing a motivational moment, General Kenney piped in, "Eddie, I'm going to offer a case of Scotch to the first one to beat your old record." Not to be overshadowed, Rickenbacker replied, "Put me down for another case."[33] Two years later, when Captain Richard I. Bong recorded his twenty-seventh kill while on his way to a total of forty, Eddie made good on his word and sent Kenney a case of Scotch to be delivered to the new record holder.

ON DECEMBER 7, the first anniversary of the Pacific War's opening battle, General Kenney escorted Rickenbacker back to Brisbane. During a two-day layover, the pair drove to Townsville, where they paid a surprise visit to Major Victor Bertrandias, Rick's crew chief in World War I. Bertrandias showed Rickenbacker his depot and then fed the two men what they both called an excellent meal. In the course of the dinner, Rickenbacker again recounted the details of his ordeal on the Pacific, "adding," as Kenney recalled, a few extra details. "I heard Eddie tell his story again that evening at dinner," said the general. With the new additions, "It was better than ever."[34]

Two days later Rickenbacker flew out of Brisbane for Nouméa, 900 miles to the east. The next day Rickenbacker continued northwest to Guadalcanal, which over the past few months had been the scene of bloody combat between American and Japanese military forces. The island would not be labeled secure for more than a month, and Japanese stalkers and snipers still hounded American units, but Eddie wanted to go where American boys were putting themselves in harm's way so that he could observe conditions and assess problems firsthand.

Henderson Field on Guadalcanal lacked the glamor many back home associated with airfields. Far from being a tidy runway skirted with airplane hangars, the field was little more than a tiny airstrip hacked out of the jungle, littered with damaged aircraft and plane parts. Alighting on the often-bombed strip, Rickenbacker later recalled, was "like trying to land on a roller-coaster track." When he exited the plane, Rickenbacker could hear artillery and machine gun fire in the distance, and battle-scarred Marine dugouts dotted the landscape. The aviator needed no more than a few hours to refer to Guadalcanal as "that tropical island slaughterhouse" and to conclude that "it was difficult to see how men could even exist under such conditions."[35]

Rickenbacker spent the day visiting airmen at Henderson Field and the Marine and Army units manning the perimeter shielding the field. The courage of the young aviators and front-line troops, and the appalling conditions under which they fought, so impressed the old warrior that he vowed that once he returned to the United States, he intended to shake home-front civilians out of their lethargy and prod them to do more for their brethren on the fighting line. Frontline Marines and Army infantrymen needed more supplies, but folks at home remained blissfully unaware of the logjams in production and shipping that slowed essential items from reaching combat zones.

Rickenbacker remained on the island for only twenty-four hours. Seven weeks had elapsed since he had hurried out of the B-17 Flying Fortress and begun his long Pacific journey. After nearly perishing at sea and completing his mission to MacArthur, the nation's hero was ready to go back home, once more in triumph. He was already the hero of land and air during the first four decades of the twentieth century, and now, in 1942, he had also conquered the sea.

CHAPTER 12

"It's an Epic; Let It Stand at That"
Aftermath

ON DECEMBER 11, with the detritus of combat evident, Rickenbacker left Guadalcanal. His plane reached Samoa in time for breakfast, when he learned that the first four Americans— Cherry, Whittaker, De Angelis, and Bartek—had already rejoined their families in the United States. He strolled to the hospital, where he saw that even four weeks after the rescue, horrid open sores still covered James Reynolds's feet and legs.

His friend Colonel Adamson had in the meantime developed a lung abscess that required an operation, and physicians told Rickenbacker that he could not be moved for another ten days. The aviator sat down next to the colonel and cautioned Adamson that unless he soon made significant improvement, he would have to remain behind while Rickenbacker flew home in time for the holidays. Doctors agreed that if Rickenbacker could delay his departure by two days, and if Adamson continued to improve, he could accompany the aviator to the United States.

When Rickenbacker consulted with the Navy doctors forty-eight hours later, however, they explained that Adamson remained so critical they feared he might die if he attempted the arduous 4,700-mile journey from Samoa to the United States. Rickenbacker countered that the welcome sight of his wife and home would rejuvenate his friend, and claimed that even if Adamson was destined to die, the colonel would prefer to do so surrounded by his loved ones.

The physicians relented, but they insisted that a Navy doctor, Commander John Durkin, and an Army nurse accompany them. "It was one of the happiest moments of my life," said Rickenbacker, who was delighted that "I could bring him home in time for Christmas."[1]

"I PROMISED YOU I'D NEVER MAKE YOU CRY AGAIN!"

Eleven days before Christmas, the final three survivors started their journey to the United States. An adjustable bed for Adamson and a cot for Reynolds had been set up in the aircraft's cabin, with Commander Durkin and the nurse at their side. After a brief layover, the pilot flew to Hawaii for a one-day stop.

The interlude handed Rickenbacker time to investigate whether his estimation of a more potent tailwind upon takeoff in mid-October had been more accurate than Cherry's conclusion. Discussions with other aviators who had flown that same October day confirmed Rickenbacker's belief that the wind speed that day approached thirty miles per hour, far stronger than Cherry's ten-mile-per-hour deduction, and it was likely a prime reason why they had overflown Canton Island.

When physicians declared Adamson and Reynolds sturdy enough for the final 2,500-mile leg to California, the aircraft lifted off from Hickam Field for the trip eastward. Reynolds's parents tearfully greeted their son at Oakland, and as photographers captured the arrival, Rickenbacker stood to the side and witnessed the emotional welcome.

THE WARM GREETING in Oakland was a prelude to the happy reception Rickenbacker received at their next stop, Los Angeles. When the bomber door opened and airfield workers rolled out a flight of steps, Eddie stepped out to see his mother. Standing beside her were his brother Dewey, and Dewey's family.

"Mother! Mother!" said an elated Rickenbacker as Elizabeth hurried toward him exclaiming, "Oh, my Eddie! My little Eddie!" The two hugged and kissed, and then Rickenbacker took out one of Adelaide's hand-embroidered handkerchiefs, which he had used to wring rainwater into receptacles while adrift at sea, and wiped away her tears. He repeated the vow he had made to her so long ago. "Remember," said the son to his mother, "I promised you I'd never make you cry again!"[2] Rickenbacker briefly spoke to the press and thanked the military for their role in rescuing the group, and explained that his only regret was his inability to bring Sergeant Kaczmarczyk home with him.

Eddie still had some of the possessions he had carried aboard the bomber on October 21—a handful of silver coins discolored

Eddie Rickenbacker warmly embraces his mother, Elizabeth, in December 1942 after returning from his Pacific odyssey. After hugging her, he reminded his mother that as a youth, he had vowed to never make her cry.

from the Pacific; the familiar old felt hat, badly battered from three weeks on the ocean; his scratched and wrinkled shoes; and a wallet Adelaide had given him shortly before their wedding day. Inside the wallet were a few keepsakes, including frayed bills and a badly faded photograph of his wife. He also retained the leather case given him by that little girl in 1917. Inside the now tattered pouch were the religious items that he subsequently claimed gave him strength on the ocean—the crucifix, the

St. Christopher medal, and a prayer that he had retained since his early racing days.

The reunion ended a few hours later because Eddie had to report to Secretary Stimson in Washington, DC. When his plane landed at Bolling Field outside the nation's capital on the morning of December 19, "just two months to the day after I left San Francisco," Rickenbacker rose from his seat, opened the aircraft's door, and hurried to Adelaide and his sons, David and Billy, embracing the three in tearful welcomes. "Hello, honey," Rickenbacker murmured to Adelaide, "looked as if I'd stepped off the reservation for a while, but I'm still around!"[3]

Assembled military brass, including Hap Arnold and other senior officers, as well as Mrs. Adamson and hundreds of soldiers, reporters, and photographers, waited to welcome him home. While newsreel men cranked their cameras to capture the touching reunions for theater audiences, fighter aircraft soared above, and an Army Air Forces band sounded the first notes of a military march.

Rickenbacker scanned the crowd until he came upon Adamson's wife, Helen, standing not far from General Arnold. "Hi, Helen!" he shouted. Rickenbacker then pointed to the plane and added, "There's an old soldier in there who needs some of your medicine badly."[4]

THE PUBLIC KNEW only a fraction of the torments the men faced on the Pacific, but they could not help but be impressed with how far the group had floated on the ocean, as well as shocked with how close they came to vanishing without a trace. In their twenty-four days, the men had drifted between 550 and 600 miles, about the same distance as traveling from New York City to Detroit, and Radioman Lester Boutte emphasized that the chain of islands near where they were picked up "was the last chain of islands for many, many hundreds of miles. If they hadn't been sighted, then I doubt that they ever would have been found."[5]

Eddie Rickenbacker again received the lion's share of attention from the press and radio commentators. Reporters gathered wherever he went, and the more Eddie spoke, the more details—real or exaggerated—he added, which led to flowery accounts featuring Rickenbacker as the hero.

Once Rickenbacker had given his report to Secretary Stimson in Washington, DC, he met a group of newsmen in Stimson's conference room, where, under the watchful eye of the politician, Rickenbacker delivered the first comprehensive account of the twenty-four days on the Pacific. According to *Time* magazine, Rickenbacker spoke in a low voice as he slowly recounted the successful ditching, which he credited to Captain Cherry's skill as a pilot; the days adrift in three tiny rafts; the rescue and the tern. "If it wasn't for the fact I had seven witnesses, I wouldn't dare tell this story because it seems so fantastic," he told the hushed group. "But within an hour after a prayer meeting a seagull came in and landed on my head."

He told them about Sergeant Kaczmarczyk's death, caused mainly by drinking too much salt water, and how "For two nights, I cuddled him like a mother would hold a child, trying to give him warmth from my body. At 3 a.m. I heard his final gasp." He said of his role in managing the men, "I had to get tough and 'mad' and shout them down several times or some would have cracked completely. We all got to bickering pretty badly among ourselves at times."[6]

He related the excitement of seeing the first rescue aircraft approach and how they frantically waved and yelled to grab the aviator's attention, but "He went by and didn't come back, which was heartbreaking. The next day, two planes again missed us. The next day four more passed us up." Before any reporter could ask if he or anyone else blamed the pilots who had flown so tantalizingly close without spotting them, Rickenbacker added, "I want to emphasize that probably one of the most difficult things in the world is to try and see that small an object when breakers are operating."

As he had vowed to do upon visiting Guadalcanal, Rickenbacker used the occasion to speak to the nation. He graphically painted the conditions under which the military fought on the island and told his audience that if the American people understood "what those boys are doing for us and putting up with, I think they would take this war more seriously."[7]

He pleaded with the public to sacrifice more and whine less. "The cry and objection to being rationed on rubber and gasoline seem so insignificant, so ridiculous, when we see what the boys at the front have got." As evidence, he offered his recent Pacific odyssey. "If people only knew that the saving of one old rubber tire makes it possible to produce one of those rafts, which might be responsible, as it has been in our case, for saving seven men, they might not worry whether they have their automobiles on weekends." When Rickenbacker finished, Secretary Stimson, who had been quietly listening to every word, stood and simply said, "It's an epic; let it stand at that." As *Time* magazine's account noted, "The newsmen blinked, rose, applauded, quietly filed out."[8]

His initial accounts of the three-week ocean odyssey helped people throughout the United States understand what he and his seven companions had endured. More descriptions would follow, in article, book, and film format, but Rickenbacker had set the tone in drawing the image of himself as an unrelenting manager whose skills had pulled them through.

That message reached an adoring audience, but when combined with the press's efforts to magnify Rickenbacker's talents in evading the Grim Reaper, it left some survivors seething.

"PERHAPS ONLY LINDBERGH SURPASSES EDDIE RICKENBACKER"

Each of the seven had to make accommodations for the publicity he received after returning to his hometown. Rickenbacker, accustomed to national attention, slipped back into his life with ease, but the others ranged from Lieutenant Whittaker, who embarked on a speaking tour, to Captain Cherry, who rarely spoke of what had occurred on the Pacific.

AN ENTIRE NATION celebrated Eddie Rickenbacker's return, but those who loved Sergeant Kaczmarczyk could only grieve. Mrs. Kaczmarczyk appreciated Rickenbacker's kind words about her son in his comments to the press, but since Alex had been buried at sea, she lacked closure and for years mourned his loss.

Coreen joined the WAVES (Women Accepted for Volunteer Emergency Service), the female branch of the United States Naval Reserve, and after the war married Elmer Schwenk. The couple enjoyed a long life in Corona, California, surrounded by children and grandchildren, but she never forgot her first intended.

SERGEANT JAMES REYNOLDS, although uncomfortable with the attention, granted an interview with the major newspaper in his area, the *Oakland Tribune*. In a soft, low voice, he told the reporter that he would rather be back on duty than answering these questions, that people made too big a fuss over the incident, and that all he wanted was to get back to a normal life as soon as possible.

He talked about their turning to prayer and God when all seemed hopeless, about the incident with the tern landing on Rickenbacker's head, and about their belief that help would eventually come. After recuperating in San Francisco, Reynolds wed his fiancée, Margaret Nassau. He returned to the Pacific, where he served for eighteen months in the China-Burma-India Theater before leaving the Army at the war's end. Seven years later the Korean conflict called him back to duty, after which he returned to civilian life in Oakland with Margaret and their son, Daniel.

EACH YEAR LIEUTENANT John De Angelis's hometown conducted memorial services and a Mass of thanksgiving at Our Lady of Mount Carmel, where De Angelis had served as an altar boy in his youth. He remained in Nesquehoning most of his life, and other than a 1943 interview with Twentieth Century–Fox for a film based on the event, he rarely discussed the matter. Keith De Angelis, a member of the family who still resides in the area, said that the Rickenbacker story "was kept very hush-hush in the family"[9] out of respect for the former Army officer.

AFTER HIS RECOVERY, Colonel Hans Adamson remained in the Army until his 1945 retirement. Afterward, he authored radio drama scripts and books, including a 1946 biography of his friend, titled *Eddie Rickenbacker*, in which he credited Rickenbacker's leadership for bringing the men back. "This fast-moving and excellently written biography brings the Rickenbacker legend to life," summed the *Lexington Herald* in Kentucky. "As a hero of American youth, perhaps only Lindbergh surpasses Eddie Rickenbacker."[10]

Colonel Adamson also joined his friend to produce a thirteen-week radio drama series titled *The World's Most Honored Flights*. The episodes, written by Adamson and featuring Rickenbacker as historian-narrator, told the tales of major air events, such as the Wright Brothers at Kitty Hawk, North Carolina, and the disappearance of Amelia Earhart. The series kicked off with two episodes centering on Rickenbacker's and Adamson's experiences in the Pacific.

THE CITIZENS OF Freehold, New Jersey, staged a rousing reception upon Johnny Bartek's return in December. His church hosted a celebration during which, before packed pews, the pastor presented Bartek with a new Bible to replace the waterlogged one he had used in the Pacific.

Bartek enjoyed Freehold's adulation, but he was never at ease with the press converging on his home. His mother had difficulty washing and drying the family's clothes because each time she stepped outside to hang the wash on their clothesline, a handful of reporters materialized. He agreed to appear at a few functions, where he met New York singers and Hollywood actresses, but he preferred to remain in Freehold as much as possible.

He received hundreds of letters, some praising his courage and others asking for autographs, but soon had to cut back on replying to the vast amount of correspondence, which disrupted both his work and family time. Bartek could not enjoy a cup of coffee or a meal in a diner because so many people wanted to shake his hand or ask him about his story.

Bartek admitted that after spending those harrowing days on the ocean with his hero, his admiration for Rickenbacker increased. "That man is the greatest man I ever met and I'm sure I'll never meet another like him," he told a reporter. "He's got more courage than anybody I ever knew. We were all scared out there, but Eddie helped keep us going with his encouragement and his lack of fear."[11] He claimed that he learned more about courage and leadership in twenty-four days with Rickenbacker than he had ever learned from anyone else.

Publishers asked Bartek to put his story on paper. He obliged with two books, *Life Out There: A Story of Faith and Courage*, published by Charles Scribner's Sons in 1943, and a second in

2003 titled *My Raft Episode,* a privately printed volume completed for family and friends.

After his discharge from the Army in December 1945, Johnny Bartek married Mildred Sentman and lived in a modest home twenty miles east of Freehold. He turned to his first love, the camera, and enjoyed a long career as a photographer for the New Jersey State Police. Following his retirement in 1985, he focused on his family. "I don't want to be a celebrity," he told a reporter in 1958. "The thing we're talking about happened a long time ago. I don't see why people should want to keep writing about it. I don't want to be a hero anymore. I just want to relax and enjoy the wonderful family I have."[12]

AFTER RESTING WITH family during a thirty-day sick leave, Lieutenant James Whittaker embarked on a two-month Army-sponsored tour of war production plants, where he spoke to workers about his time on the Pacific and how crucial to the war were their efforts in producing a stream of weapons and war goods to defeat the enemy.

In the latter half of January 1943 the *Chicago Tribune* ran a thirteen-part series of articles written by reporter Charles Leavelle in which Whittaker told his story to the country. Newspapers around the United States ran the installments, which formed the foundation for Whittaker's 1945 book published by E. P. Dutton & Company, *We Thought We Heard the Angels Sing.*

Whittaker included praise for the man who, he said, pulled him through those twenty-four days. "The world knows him as a daredevil automobile racer who turned aviator and became the nation's greatest ace of the first World War," he wrote. "Out on the trackless Pacific our little band met the Rickenbacker the world doesn't know; the human man, the undoubting leader." He said that whenever someone seemed on the verge of giving up, "Rick handed him such a cussing that he'd usually vow to live if only to spite Rick. And Rick loved it." He then claimed, "I, for one, hope that if ever I have to go through hell like that again, Eddie Rickenbacker or someone like him will be along."[13]

As a way of expressing his gratitude to Toma, the islander from Nukufetau who had asked him for soap and clothing, the copilot sent Toma three suits, a carton of soap, and cigarettes. Also remembering his pledge to keep safe the model of the outrigger canoe Toma had given him, Whittaker placed the canoe in his California home, where it rested beside one of the empty flare shells the group had used to store rainwater.

AT THE BEHEST of his superiors, Captain Bill Cherry flew to Washington, DC, to help redesign rubber rafts that would be placed in newly constructed bombers. Among other suggestions, the pilot promoted the need to have canvaslike material beneath which they could seek refuge from the sun during the day and shelter from the nighttime cold, improved medical kits, a hand pump, better fishlines and hooks, a four-inch flange of rubberized material attached about the rafts to block sea spray, a water distilling unit capable of producing one quart of water every twenty minutes, rations for thirty days, and, most importantly, the urgency to produce more spacious rafts than the tiny ones in which they lived for twenty-four days. The government responded in February 1943 that an improved life raft was in production and would soon be a permanent fixture on bombers. Among the modifications were larger and sturdier rafts, a small sail with a staff that could be used as a mast, and a radio transmitter set on a predetermined frequency that would automatically send SOS signals. Since Captain Cherry and other survivors had provided such valuable input, the government added that the rafts would be known as "Rickenbackers."

Captain Cherry commanded a squadron in the China-Burma-India Theater, where his aircraft towed gliders from India to Burma and China through unpredictable weather over the dangerous eastern portion of the Himalayan Mountains, known to Allied aviators as the "Hump." After the war, Cherry returned to his post with American Airlines, remaining there until his retirement in 1975.

Unlike the other survivors, Captain Cherry was never able to forgive Eddie Rickenbacker for assuming command at sea. His distaste for the national hero had begun as early as Hawaii, when Rickenbacker insisted on leaving Hickam Field in the second bomber as soon as possible even though Cherry argued that it needed to be inspected. The bitterness intensified when, in the midst of the worst travails on the ocean, Rickenbacker took over instead of allowing Cherry to do his job as ranking active-duty officer. As Cherry viewed the matter, military custom dictated that the pilot of a bomber remained in charge in any emergency, but instead a civilian had abrogated command that was rightfully Cherry's.

When the survivors later shared their stories with the press, most spread the credit for their return—Cherry for his piloting skills, Bartek for his role in bringing faith and God into the group, and Rickenbacker for his determined, and sometimes hostile, refusal to admit defeat. Only Rickenbacker, aided by an adoring press, centered the story mostly on himself, emphasizing the point by frequently using in his newspaper interviews and in his subsequent books phrases such as "I did this" or "I refused to allow that." For instance, in his 1967 autobiography, titled simply *Rickenbacker*, he stated that not everyone in the rafts was religious, "but I insisted that they participate."[14]

In a December 1942 interview conducted by the government about his weeks on the Pacific, Captain Cherry so bitterly criticized Rickenbacker for overstepping his bounds that senior officers insisted the original interview be destroyed and a less caustic one be substituted. A cover sheet on the second interview transcript, dated January 5, 1943, bore the note that "in the original report, Cherry was 'a little too outspoken,' that all copies of that original have been burned, and that this [amended] is the report as sent to General Arnold."[15] In effect, the military censored Cherry's interview because the pilot had been too harsh toward the nation's hero.

Private Bartek empathized with Captain Cherry. He put in his own book that both the reporters and the country's populace wanted Eddie to be the hero, but Bartek insisted that others had contributed as well. Bartek contended that while Rickenbacker's presence was a calming factor that helped everyone, "I haven't read hardly a thing about Captain Cherry and he was the skipper and my boss under whom I worked many times. He is a wonderful guy too. I admit Rickenbacker has been through a lot, he's got great courage and he was mighty nice to have around. But there were other strong men with us."[16]

Twenty years after their return, a reporter tried to schedule an interview with Cherry, but the pilot declined. In two recent interviews his daughter, Diane Stacy, told the author that her father rebuffed money from Hollywood producers who had hoped to gain his participation in a film because he saw that they planned to make Rickenbacker the hero. She added that while "Dad never talked much about his time on the ocean," he did state that "Eddie Rickenbacker was the most arrogant son-of-a-bitch alive" and that in her father's opinion, the issue of command was simple—it belonged to him, not Rickenbacker. "Daddy was a no-bull person. Everything was black and white."[17]

Captain Cherry's ire is reasonable, but unrealistic. The nation wanted to read about Captain Eddie, the Ace of Aces who had again defied death, not the unheralded captain from Fort Worth. This all but ensured that the press would once more elevate the Medal of Honor recipient to hero status, and in the process relegate the others to secondary roles.

Cherry correctly asserted that, per military custom, he should have been in charge during the twenty-four days at sea. His decision to drift off alone in the smaller raft, which led to rescue planes spotting him and obtaining locations from Cherry about the other two rafts, validated his expertise in command.

However, on the ocean, daily facing death from any number of sources, there was simply no possibility that Eddie Rickenbacker would shrink to the sidelines and willingly yield control of his fate to another person. His indomitable spirit, courage, and determination had brushed aside every death threat, both on the ground and in the air, and now, faced with a likely demise at sea, he was not about to abandon those traits. Eddie Rickenbacker would live or die because of what Eddie Rickenbacker did or said, not because of another person's words or actions.

As far as the other five survivors were concerned, Rickenbacker knew what it took to survive these kinds of moments, and it was only natural for them to seek guidance from a man who had repeatedly displayed a talent for survival. They meant no insult to Captain Cherry, who had proven his skills in the cockpit, but it was only a matter of time after Cherry ditched the plane before Rickenbacker stepped up and the other survivors turned to him to lead them back home.

"ONCE AGAIN, I HAD FACED THE GRIM REAPER"

After his meeting with Stimson, on December 19 Rickenbacker and his family flew to New York City, where Mayor Fiorello LaGuardia had arranged a warm welcome at the airport. The next evening he addressed the nation in a speech broadcast on all major radio networks. In a statement with which the other six survivors might disagree, he boasted, "Once again, I had faced the Grim Reaper and had not only bested him myself but had also brought six others through with me."[18]

Rickenbacker spoke at war bond rallies and toured defense plants, where he recounted some of the events from the Pacific and asked union members to put aside their demands for better conditions and focus on building the items their fellow citizens

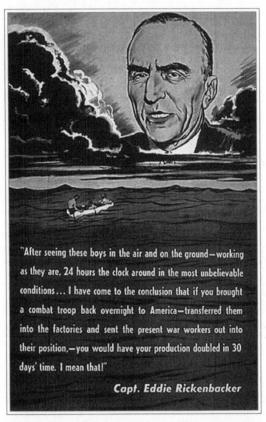

"After seeing these boys in the air and on the ground—working as they are, 24 hours the clock around in the most unbelievable conditions... I have come to the conclusion that if you brought a combat troop back overnight to America—transferred them into the factories and sent the present war workers out into their position,—you would have your production doubled in 30 days' time. I mean that!"

Capt. Eddie Rickenbacker

Following Eddie Rickenbacker's safe return from another of his many death-defying events, the United States government used his time adrift in the Pacific to spur workers to do more for their country. This 1943 war poster shows Rickenbacker above a small raft bearing Captain Eddie and two others, accompanied by his words encouraging war workers to increased effort.

National Archives Photo #513756

in the war zones needed. With each speech, Eddie drew more attention to the three weeks on the ocean. Priests, ministers, and rabbis inserted certain moments, such as the bird landing on Rickenbacker's hat, in their sermons as evidence that if people refused to give up, God would come to their aid.

President Roosevelt and his wife, Eleanor, were driven to the Church of the Epiphany in the heart of Washington, DC, for a special Christmas prayer service, where they listened to a sermon delivered by Reverend Howard Stone Anderson, pastor of the First Congregational Church. Anderson mentioned Rickenbacker's story and told the congregation that the country's future was bright if people would emulate Rickenbacker's actions.

The nation's hero turned to the written word to advance the interests of the military as well as his own. When *Life* magazine asked Rickenbacker in early 1943 to pen a three-part series about his time on the ocean, he donated the $25,000 fee to Hap Arnold's Army Air Forces Aid Society, which supported the families of lost airmen. His subsequent 1943 book, *Seven Came Through*, boosted his reputation with fellow Americans.

Already a nationally renowned figure, Eddie's popularity and influence exploded. The saga of the World War I aviator and his seven companions at sea was so powerful that the editors of the Associated Press, despite a spate of war news in Europe and the Pacific, selected it as one of the year's ten best stories. It was yet another example, the editors explained, that "the man who always comes back had done it again."[19]

The Boy Scouts of America presented Rickenbacker with the organization's Silver Beaver Award at the Waldorf-Astoria in early 1943. "We are very glad and very proud of your safe return," said George Tolson, senior patrol leader of Troop 90 in Queens, New York. "You are a hero—our hero. You represent to us the spirit of America. You are the kind of man we'd like to be."[20]

Even the popular *New York Daily News* cartoonist C. D. Batchelor, who during the darkest days of the loss at sea had drawn the cartoon beneath the headline "So Long Eddie," admitted he had erred in doubting the country's idol. When he met Rickenbacker in New York, he handed Eddie the original drawing of the cartoon, with one minor alteration. Across the image was an inscription in large letters, "Beg Pardon, Eddie."[21]

Hollywood producers and actors, including Gary Cooper and Howard Hawks, bid for his story. The 1945 film *Captain Eddie*, directed by Lloyd Bacon and starring Fred MacMurray as Rickenbacker, leaned on Rickenbacker's *Seven Came Through* as well as Lieutenant Whittaker's *We Thought We Heard the Angels Sing*.

Rickenbacker returned to his post with Eastern Air Lines shortly before the end of 1942, guiding the company to profitable years until 1959, when Eastern's fortunes sagged and Rickenbacker was forced out as chief executive officer. Four years later, the seventy-three-year-old resigned as chairman of the board to spend more time with his wife and to enjoy his favorite pursuits. During the warm seasons he and Adelaide resided in New York, where Eddie loved golfing with associates, but they spent the winter either in a Coconut Grove, Florida, home or traveling overseas.

Rickenbacker never lost the desire to excel that had rocketed him to the top. A painting of the young Rickenbacker hung from a wall in the foyer of his ten-room Manhattan apartment. A cap angled downward over his eyes, reminiscent of the cocky flier he had been in World War I, an expensive camel's hair coat rested on his shoulders, and aircraft filled the blue background behind him. During an interview with *Time* magazine, Rickenbacker gazed at the image of his younger self and mentioned to the reporter, "I was quite a fellow in those days." He then grinned and said, "I'll fight like a wildcat until they nail the lid of my pine box down on me."[22]

"IT'S ALL RIGHT, ROZ. I UNDERSTAND AT LAST"

Although the seven survivors went their own ways after returning from the Pacific, a teacher in Ames, Iowa, sparked an informal reunion. For many years, Mrs. Suzanne Kelly at Meeker Elementary School had read Lieutenant Whittaker's book, *We Thought We Heard the Angels Sing,* to her sixth graders. The students loved the story, which contained many of the same elements as a fictional adventure story while presenting a factual account.

The impetus for hosting a reunion of the survivors came when one student asked Mrs. Kelly what had happened to the men. The query turned into a class research project, and when the students learned that four of the survivors were alive—by 1985 Rickenbacker, Adamson, and Whittaker had died—they sent letters to each man and to their rescuers, including the native of Nukufetau, Toma, asking if they could attend a reunion at their school.

Three survivors enjoy a lighthearted moment during the 1985 reunion in Ames, Iowa. From left to right are Mrs. Suzanne Kelly, who, with her sixth-grade students organized the gathering; Johnny Bartek; William T. Cherry Jr.; and James W. Reynolds.

THE BARTEK FAMILY COLLECTION

IN APRIL 1985 Sergeant Reynolds and Private Bartek joined Captain Cherry, who dropped his reluctance to talk about the event for the students' benefit, in the Rescue Reunion at Meeker Elementary School (Lieutenant John De Angelis was unable to attend). American Airlines arranged free transportation to Iowa, the Gateway Center–Holiday Inn provided complimentary lodging, and reporters from the *Des Moines Register* covered the event, writing articles that were reprinted in newspapers around the nation. The trio renewed old ties and enjoyed talking to students eager to learn about an event that occurred decades before their births.

———

THE SEVEN SURVIVORS might not have agreed on the precise timing of specific actions taken during their three weeks on the Pacific, but they could not deny one reality—each man had been affected by their shared ordeal. Rickenbacker said ten years later that the experience made him realize "more than ever, how little the material things of life really count." Colonel Adamson claimed that after surviving the nightmarish days at sea, he would never again walk by homeless people on the street as if they were invisible, and Lieutenant Whittaker explained that before the rescue, "I couldn't be with any one 15 minutes without an argument or a fight. I saw little good in any one, and believed only in Jim Whittaker. Now I accept every one as being decent and good until he proves otherwise."[23] One of his initial steps was to mend a fifteen-year split with his brother.

For the rest of his life, Sergeant Reynolds considered Friday the 13th, the day he was rescued, as a lucky day, and said that while he suffered no permanent physical damage, each time he read or heard of a plane ditching, "You live it all over again with them." Lieutenant De Angelis's troubles centered around Sergeant Kaczmarczyk. "I can't bear extreme quiet," he said. "I am not scared or anything, but as soon as it gets quiet I think about this kid that died. Like now, I can't go to bed too early. I have to be real tired or else I toss around all night. The death of the boy left the greatest impression on me."[24]

Private Bartek claimed that his tenure in the Pacific "was something that will stay with me for the rest of my life." He added that it put matters into perspective, and that while he loved photography and leisurely pastimes, "The most important thing in my life is my family and my home. My experience in the war made me appreciate the things I have."[25]

Above all, the survivors agreed that their views on faith and God had changed. Other than to the Iowa schoolchildren and to a handful of newspaper reporters, Captain Cherry refused to comment through the years, but in a December 1942 report to his military superiors, the pilot asserted that something of a religious nature had unfolded on the Pacific. "Several things happened on this trip of such a miraculous nature that Captain Cherry feels they should be recorded for the general interest of all," stated the report. Each man who was rescued claimed that "A man may start as an atheist passenger in a rubber boat, but if he returns, he will return a Christian."[26]

"We all got religion," acknowledged Johnny Bartek. He said that for the first twenty-three years of his life, he had attended religious services from a sense of duty, mainly out of respect for his mother, rather than from a deep need to be there, and never thought how his preacher's words might relate to his life. After returning with Eddie Rickenbacker, however, his faith and his belief in God had deepened from witnessing the bird landing atop Rickenbacker, the initial storm that quenched their thirst, and the last-ditch rescue by aircraft and PT boats. He wrote that "for twenty-three years, I've never realized what religion was," but "in twenty-one days, I found out."[27]

Almost eighty years later Bernadette Rogoff, a museum archivist in Johnny Bartek's hometown, talked about the city's most renowned World War II hero, a man residents still remember. "He had such a faith in God. He lit up inside, a peaceful glow, when he talked about the New Testament. I think it was a result of his time on the ocean. If people remembered two things about him, he'd want it to be his faith, and that he survived."[28]

Men who had not spoken to God in years, on the ocean readily turned to the prayers they had learned as children in efforts to attain His help. James Reynolds explained that while he was a baptized Baptist, "It was on the raft, though, where I learned what religion meant."[29]

Eddie Rickenbacker claimed that his faith and belief in God became more integral to his daily life, but the aviator stretched the truth a bit. He had survived every other mishap without admitting that a higher power had come to his aid, and while he accorded a role to a divine entity, Rickenbacker would always believe that his own inner qualities had been the major factor in bringing him through the mishaps.

On the other hand, Lieutenant Whittaker freely conceded that God had saved him from perishing at sea. After help inexplicably arrived in a handful of perilous moments—the tern, the rainwater, and the favorable currents off Nukufetau—the lifelong atheist embraced faith and gave God credit in his *Chicago Tribune* series. Shortly after he returned to the United States, Whittaker wrote in his series of articles for the paper that Private Bartek's New Testament had coalesced the eight individuals into a faith community, and claimed that prayer and the series of miracles at sea had redeemed him.

Large crowds flocked to auditoriums and churches to hear

Lieutenant Whittaker deliver his message of newly found faith and salvation. Because of what he saw and experienced on the ocean, a forty-year-old atheist who had scoffed at the notion of God now not only believed but also spread his message from coast to coast in frequent speeches to religious groups and other audiences. Clergy praised Whittaker for his conversion to religion and urged their congregations to follow his example in this time of worldwide carnage. Numerous ministers cited Whittaker's account in their sermons, and largely due to Whittaker's writings and speeches, ministers asserted that sales of the Bible increased dramatically over the previous year's numbers. As Johnny Bartek wrote, Whittaker might have begun the ocean ordeal as an atheist, but "he ended up with great faith in God and prayer."[30]

THE AGNOSTIC, COLONEL Adamson, was also transformed. Unlike Whittaker, he had never denied the existence of God, but the fifty-two-year-old intellectual returned with a newfound belief in the Supreme Being because of the evidence he witnessed while on the ocean. In a letter to his wife, Colonel Adamson explained that "I have found a nearness to our Creator which I have never known before, and I am certain that this new feeling is going to deeply affect both of our lives in the future."[31]

A few days before Christmas 1942, Rosalind Russell toiled on a film in a Hollywood studio when she learned that Adamson would soon be in for a visit. She and her husband, Freddie, warmly welcomed their friend, whose weathered face and bandaged hands still showed the ravages exacted by his recent Pacific ordeal. "I was so upset seeing him and remembering the old Hans," the actress said, "that I tried to keep the conversation on trivial things: welcome home, how good it was to see him alive."

When Freddie inquired about the colonel's bound hand, Adamson slowly unwrapped the bandage to reveal the gift Rosalind Russell had insisted he keep before departing on the trip. "There, cupped in his hand," wrote Russell, "was the medal" of the seventeenth-century Franciscan priest St. Joseph of Cupertino, the patron saint of aviators. Adamson smiled and said softly, "It's all right, Roz. I understand at last."[32]

"IT IS THE GREATEST STORY A MAN CAN TELL"

A history of heart ailments ended with Colonel Adamson's death on September 11, 1968, in San Francisco's Children's Hospital at the age of seventy-eight. He was subsequently interred in Arlington National Cemetery. The obituary, as was true with every member of the Rickenbacker party, mentioned Adamson's 1942 experiences on the raft among his other accomplishments.

Seven years later copilot Whittaker died in El Cajon, California, at the age of seventy-three, twenty-five years before his fellow aviator and pilot of the bomber, eighty-four-year-old Captain Cherry, passed away in Torrance, California, in 2000. Cherry's daughter Diane Stacy explained that the impact of her father's life has reached into ensuing generations of the family. She has often retold the story of her father and his seven companions adrift on the Pacific to her twelve grandchildren. To ensure they do not soon forget the event, she placed a World War II photograph of Captain Cherry in specially made dog tags for each grandchild and said to them, "You are here for a reason. I tell them that we would not be alive if Grandfather hadn't made it, but he did, so there must be a reason why we are here. One of us will do something special. There's a reason he was spared."[33]

Sergeant Reynolds succumbed the next year at the age of eighty-three in Alameda, California, while Lieutenant De Angelis followed in 2003, dying at his home in Harrisburg, Pennsylvania, also at eighty-three. Surrounded by his family, Johnny Bartek, the final survivor to die, passed away at age ninety-four in 2013 in his New Jersey home, having fulfilled the promise of a long life pledged by his sister Ruth in Bartek's 1942 dream on the ocean.

EDDIE RICKENBACKER'S DEATH on July 23, 1973, garnered an avalanche of obituaries, articles, and accolades for the eighty-two-year-old. His health had failed steadily since he had suffered a stroke the previous October. Nevertheless, he regained sufficient strength for a trip to Zurich, Switzerland, to seek medical assistance for Adelaide. While there, Eddie suffered another stroke which ultimately led to his death in that European city. His ashes were flown to Miami for a memorial service during which another famous aviator, General James H. "Jimmy" Doolittle, who had led the daring 1942 bombing raid of Tokyo, delivered the eulogy. A short time afterward, Rickenbacker's ashes were flown to Columbus, Ohio, for burial next to his mother in his hometown. A military honor guard stood at attention and fighter aircraft from the 94th Fighter Squadron flew above in the "missing man" formation as signs of the military's respect for the national hero.

"Edward Vernon Rickenbacker was a man whose delight in turning the tables on seemingly hopeless odds took him to the top in three distinct fields," stated the obituary that ran in the *New York Times*. "But in the long run, it will not be his material successes that will be remembered. Rather, he will be recalled as a larger-than-life figure cast in the same mold as legendary folk heroes of the past."[34]

Eddie's son William added his praise for a father who, because of his world travels, speeches, and government missions, missed a large portion of his two sons' lives. "No scorn could match the scorn he had for men who settled for half-measures, uttered half-truths, straddled the issues, or admitted the idea of failure or defeat."[35] A proud son was honored to dwell in his father's shadow and carry his last name.

In recognition of the hometown aviator, in 1974 Lockbourne Air Force Base in Columbus was first renamed Rickenbacker Air Force Base and, subsequently, Rickenbacker International Airport. Twenty-one years later the US Postal Service paid tribute to Rickenbacker with a stamp bearing his image, part of a series of stamps in its "Great Americans" series.

A FEW DAYS after Lieutenant William Eadie and his radioman, Lester Boutte, rescued Johnny Bartek, the *Monmouth Democrat* in Bartek's hometown of Freehold heralded the news that their local boy was safe. The article asserted that his saga on the ocean was "a miracle of good fortune as well as courage, stamina and great faith that will go down in the annals of heroic history of the sea."[36]

Few doubted those words, but it would be an injustice to categorize those twenty-four days on the ocean simply as an adventure story. Far more than men battling the elements to survive, it became a life-altering moment for the seven. Men from

Johnny Bartek stands beside the New Testament and the life jacket that helped him and his six companions survive the Pacific. The items are still on display at the Monmouth County Historical Association Museum in Freehold, New Jersey.

THE BARTEK FAMILY COLLECTION

diverse backgrounds, religions, and financial status found themselves trapped in tiny rubber worlds from which they could escape only with good fortune, grit, and the willingness to work together. They may have come from different social strata, but in the rafts they were all the same, whether it was the famous hero, Eddie Rickenbacker, or the son of immigrant parents, Johnny Bartek.

"Eddie had several hundred dollars with him and I only had two dollars; he was a captain and I was a private, but there we were, both of us in the same predicament,"[37] Bartek said. Social status, wealth, good looks, and fame counted for nothing on the Pacific, but courage, hope, and faith did. They became key characters in a life-threatening event, and once embroiled in dangers, they had to shed their differences and become a team to survive.

In a desolate stretch of the Pacific, a Presbyterian from Ohio, an American Airlines pilot from Texas, a Catholic altar boy from Pennsylvania, a Baptist from New Jersey, an atheist from California, an agnostic from Denmark, and a radioman from Oakland joined forces to return home, grateful and altered. They leaned on the strength and leadership of Eddie Rickenbacker, the results of Johnny Bartek's religious upbringing, and on one another to pull through. In the process they learned that faith in themselves, in one another, and in a higher power could yield results seemingly unattainable to an individual.

Why else would Johnny Bartek have titled his 1943 book *Life Out There: A Story of Faith and Courage*? And why else would Lieutenant Whittaker have selected the words with which to end his 1945 book, *We Thought We Heard the Angels Sing*? On that final page, he described his appearances before audiences, where he depicted the events of those twenty-four days drifting at the whim of nature and the ocean. "And I told them the story of the rafts; how during those blazing days out there I found my God." Those words led into the book's final sentence, "It was the greatest adventure a man can have. It is the greatest story a man can tell."[38]

ACKNOWLEDGMENTS

Without my realizing it, for years the concept for this volume stared at me from my bookshelves. When considering topics for this project, I turned to my collection of books about World War II that were written during that war. Volumes by Bill Mauldin and Ernie Pyle stood beside Richard Tregaskis's memorable *Guadalcanal Diary*, John Hersey's moving *Into the Valley*, and Robert Sherrod's graphic portrait of battle, *Tarawa*.

In the midst of these stalwarts was the slender book *Seven Came Through*. Published in 1943 and written by the famous automobile racer and World War I ace Eddie Rickenbacker, the volume depicts his twenty-four-day odyssey adrift on the Pacific with seven other men after they had to ditch their out-of-fuel and lost B-17 Flying Fortress bomber in a remote sector of the ocean. Although it had nothing to do with a major sea or land clash with the Japanese, I was drawn to Rickenbacker's descriptions of men from various walks of life and notoriety cast together in a seagoing drama and forced to collaborate to survive. Other than newspaper and magazine articles written at the time and three books penned in the 1940s by fellow survivors, little had been published in the intervening years. Only Rickenbacker's 1967 autobiography, occasional articles marking the anniversaries of the event, or a chapter or two in a pair of Rickenbacker biographies cast any light on this extraordinary, and overlooked, oceanic saga.

Subsequent research handed me additional reasons for writing this book. Rickenbacker's undeniable charisma, take-charge attitude, and astounding skill and luck in repeatedly surviving multiple automobile and airplane accidents that should have marked his demise captivated me. I thrilled at discovering the civilian and military exploits that marked Eddie as one of the nation's foremost heroes, a man who occupied a rare lofty status alongside Charles Lindbergh and Babe Ruth. Most of all, the role played by faith and God in bringing home most of the group surprised, and moved, me. Although not a prime feature when I commenced my research, the religious aspect to this story gained importance as I read the words of the survivors, all of whom admitted that they had been altered by their shared ordeal. More than offering a riveting sea odyssey, which it certainly is, the saga of eight men in three tiny rafts became a metaphor for people struggling to meet difficult times wherever and whenever they occur.

Many people deserve my thanks. The families of the eight men, especially those related to Captain William Cherry, Second Lieutenant John J. De Angelis, Sergeant Alexander Kaczmarczyk, and Private Johnny Bartek, were most accommodating in answering questions and providing letters and photographs that enabled me to present a more complete account of that period in 1942. A special mention goes to John Bartek's daughter, Cathy Weed, and her son David; to Captain Cherry's daughter Diane Cherry Stacy; to Glenda Cherry, his daughter-in-law; to William T. Cherry IV, the pilot's grandson; and to Henry Kaczmarczyk, the nephew of Alex Kaczmarczyk.

Auburn University's Special Collections & Archives houses the Eddie Rickenbacker Papers as well as material from other men involved in the Pacific story, including John Bartek, Lester Boutte, and members of the Rickenbacker family. The able staff, especially Greg Schmidt, Jennifer Wiggins, Amanda Decker, and Dr. Tommy Brown, made research easier in this time of Covid-19. William McLaughlin at the National Museum of the United States Air Force in Dayton, Ohio, helped guide me through the photographs and other information they possess about the event, as did Jonathan Eaker and Lewis Wyman at the Library of Congress in Washington, DC, which holds a vast collection on the famous aviator. The National Archives and Records Administration offers military action reports and additional photographs relating to this Pacific saga, and the Billy Rose Theatre Division at the New York Public Library has information illuminating the friendship between Colonel Hans Christian Adamson and actress Rosalind Russell.

Neil Hodge, Public Services Coordinator, and Simon Elliott, Public Services/Licensing, UCLA Library Special Collections, made available copies of the Rosalind Russell/Frederick Brisson

Collection, while Bernadette Rogoff, Kim Bedetti, and Dana Howell of the Monmouth County Historical Association in Freehold, New Jersey, relayed images of John Bartek's New Testament and life vest that rest in their collection. The inspiring Iowa teacher Suzanne Kelly and her students put hours into arranging the special 1985 reunion of survivors. Articles written about that event, plus a beautifully crafted book by Mrs. Kelly, provided helpful information.

One individual who played a prominent role in my writing career is no longer with us, the victim of an aggressive brain cancer that took him way too early. My agent, historian, and most of all, friend Jim Hornfischer encouraged me at every step of the way, for this book and for every previous volume. In the process, he helped me attain a dream I had long harbored of writing books about the Pacific War. He will always be with me in spirit, motivating me to do my best. I miss you, Jim.

Two other historians influenced my writing career. My mentor, Tom Buell, whose powerful biographies of Pacific commanders fueled my desire to write about that conflict, emptied many a red pen with his enlightening comments on my manuscripts. He also put me in touch with people and organizations that furthered my career. My history adviser at the University of Notre Dame, Dr. Bernard Norling, mailed cogent comments on various topics in his lengthy, single-spaced typewritten letters. I owe much to these two amazing individuals.

The welcome comments of my editor at Dutton, Brent Howard, improved the manuscript, and editorial assistant Grace Layer brought her talents to promoting this book. Also at Dutton, thanks go to LeeAnn Pemberton, Hannah Dragone, Katy Riegel, Tiffany Estreicher, Susan Schwartz, and Ryan Richardson. Cartographer extraordinaire Jeffrey Ward designed the map that accompanies the text.

Last, but certainly not least, my family has been at my side throughout my decades-long literary quest. I love the pride my three daughters, Amy, Julie, and Karen, exhibit whenever I publish another book or deliver a presentation. Their support has been crucial to any success I have attained. That my grandchildren, Matthew, Megan, Emma, and Katie, display similar elation has also buttressed my desire to produce worthwhile volumes.

The memory of my parents, Tom and Grace, and of my two brothers, Tom and Fred, who gave unquestioned support to my endeavors, are a constant in my life. I'm comforted in knowing they are smiling from above. Terri Faitel, my companion of three decades, has read this and every other manuscript with the same dedication and precision that have marked her incredible career in mathematics.

I am fortunate to have their encouragement, and I love them all.

John F. Wukovits
Trenton, Michigan
April 15, 2022

NOTES

CHAPTER 1: "HE HAS CHEATED THE 'GRIM REAPER' ABOUT
AS OFTEN AS ANY LIVING MAN"

1. Captain Edward V. Rickenbacker, "Pacific Mission, Part I: In Which Eight Men Are Cast Adrift in Mid-Pacific on Rubber Rafts," *Life*, January 25, 1943, p. 90; "Pacific Mission, Part II: In Which the Navy Rescues Seven Castaways After 21 Days' Drifting," *Life*, February 1, 1943, p. 79.

2. Captain Edward V. Rickenbacker, *Seven Came Through: Rickenbacker's Full Story* (Garden City, New York: Doubleday, Doran and Company, Inc., 1943), p. ix; "Durable Man," *Time*, April 17, 1950. Found at http://content.time.com/time/subscriber/article/0,33009,805367,00.html. Accessed February 8, 2021.

3. Captain Eddie Rickenbacker, *Rickenbacker* (Englewood Cliffs, New Jersey: Prentice-Hall, Inc., 1967), p. 30; Walter Kiernan, "Rickenbacker Did Work of Man While Only 12," *Miami News*, November 9, 1942, p. 1.

4. Rickenbacker, *Rickenbacker*, pp. 38–39.

5. Capt. Eddie Rickenbacker, "Eddie Rickenbacker Tells His Own Philosophy," *Los Angeles Times*, November 11, 1962, p. 2.

6. Rickenbacker, "Pacific Mission, Part I: In Which Eight Men Are Cast Adrift in Mid-Pacific on Rubber Rafts," p. 25; W. David Lewis, *Eddie Rickenbacker: An American Hero in the Twentieth Century* (Baltimore: Johns Hopkins University Press, 2005), pp. 63, 77.

7. Rickenbacker, *Rickenbacker*, pp. 79–80; "Three Periods in Colorful Life of Great Air Ace of World War I," *Los Angeles Times*, October 24, 1942, p. 6.

8. John F. Ross, *Enduring Courage: Ace Pilot Eddie Rickenbacker and the Dawn of the Age of Speed* (New York: St. Martin's Press, 2014), p. 60.

9. Rickenbacker, "Eddie Rickenbacker Tells His Own Philosophy," p. 2.

10. Rickenbacker, *Rickenbacker*, pp. 127, 143.

11. Ross, *Enduring Courage*, p. 144.

12. Newton C. Parke, "Rickenbacker Gets Fifth Hun Plane," *St. Louis Star and Times*, May 31, 1918, p. 2; "Daredevil Racer Is New Ace," *Oregon Daily Journal*, May 31, 1918, p. 6; "With the American Armies in France," *Chicago Tribune*, June 16, 1918, p. 1.

13. Rickenbacker, *Rickenbacker*, pp. 132–133.

14. "Eddie Rickenbacker Has Narrow Escape," *Akron Beacon Journal*, September 27, 1918, p. 1.

15. J. L. Maloney, "Comrade of '18 Finds Rick the Leader of Yore," *Chicago Tribune*, January 24, 1943, p. 3.

16. "Durable Man," *Time*, April 17, 1950.

17. Lewis, *Eddie Rickenbacker*, p. 227; "How They Welcomed 'Rick,'" *Los Angeles Times*, February 9, 1919, p. 1.

18. "For Rickenbacker Day," *Los Angeles Times*, June 19, 1919, p. 1; William M. Henry, "Rickenbacker Home in the Southland Again," *Los Angeles Times*, June 21, 1919, p. 1; "Diamond Ring Is Given Ace," *Los Angeles Times*, June 24, 1919, p. 3; Rickenbacker, *Rickenbacker*, p. 166.

19. George Kirksey, "Veteran Ace Cheated Death Often," *Pasadena Post*, February 2, 1934, p. 7.

20. Henry McLemore, "The Lighter Side," *Los Angeles Times*, October 29, 1942, p. 11.

21. Walter Kiernan, "'Rick' Often Faced Death," *Palladium-Item* (Richmond, IN), November 11, 1942, p. 2.

22. Rickenbacker, *Rickenbacker*, p. 174.

23. "Durable Man," *Time*, April 17, 1950.

24. "People," *Time*, October 17, 1938. Found at http://content.time.com/time /subscriber/article/0,33009,848345,00.html. Accessed February 8, 2021; Ed Sullivan, "Little Old New York," *New York Daily News*, November 1, 1942, p. 452.

25. Sergeant Johnny Bartek, assisted by Austin Pardue, *Life Out There: A Story of Faith and Courage* (New York: Charles Scribner's Sons, 1943), p. 94.

CHAPTER 2: "WOULD HAVE BEEN AT HOME WITH LANCE AND ARMOR"

1. Rickenbacker, "Eddie Rickenbacker Tells His Own Philosophy," p. 2.
2. Rickenbacker, "Eddie Rickenbacker Tells His Own Philosophy," p. 2; J. S. Rosenfeld, "Victim Tells of Being Hurled from Plane, Just Missing Stump," *Atlanta Constitution*, February 28, 1941, p. 8.
3. Rosenfeld, "Victim Tells of Being Hurled from Plane, Just Missing Stump," p. 8.
4. Ross, *Enduring Courage*, p. 290.
5. Rosenfeld, "Victim Tells of Being Hurled from Plane, Just Missing Stump," p. 8; Rickenbacker, *Rickenbacker*, pp. 272–273.
6. "Survivors Pay High Tribute to Rickenbacker," *Atlanta Constitution*, February 28, 1941, p. 44.
7. Key, "Rescuers Find Grim Reality at Crash Site," p. 8.
8. Ralph McGill, "Unflinching Courage, Devotion to Duty Found at Crash Site," *Atlanta Constitution*, February 28, 1941, p. 5; "Two Atlantans, Five Others Die as Ship Falls," *Atlanta Constitution*, February 28, 1941, p. 7.
9. William Key, "Rescuers Find Grim Reality at Crash Site," *Atlanta Constitution*, February 28, 1941, p. 8.
10. McGill, "Unflinching Courage, Devotion to Duty Found at Crash Site," p. 1.
11. "Rickenbacker Will Recover, Doctors Report," *Atlanta Constitution*, February 28, 1941, p. 1; Rickenbacker, *Rickenbacker*, pp. 274–275.
12. Rickenbacker, *Rickenbacker*, p. 275; Ross, *Enduring Courage*, p. 290.
13. Louie D. Newton, "Rickenbacker's Life Has Been Full of Action," *Atlanta Constitution*, February 28, 1941, p. 6.
14. "Flyer's Wife Arrives After Dramatic Dash," *Atlanta Constitution*, February 28, 1941, p. 44; Ross, *Enduring Courage*, p. 291; "Two Atlantans, Five Others Die as Ship Falls," p. 7.
15. Rickenbacker, "Eddie Rickenbacker Tells His Own Philosophy," p. 3.
16. Rickenbacker, *Rickenbacker*, pp. 278–279.
17. "Durable Man," *Time*, April 17, 1950.
18. "Flyer's Wife Arrives After Dramatic Dash," *Atlanta Constitution*, February 28, 1941, p. 44.
19. "Rescuer Lauds Fortitude of Rickenbacker," *Atlanta Constitution*, February 28, 1941, p. 7; "Rickenbacker's Life Has Been Full of Action," *Atlanta Constitution*, February 28, 1941, p. 6.
20. McGill, "Unflinching Courage, Devotion to Duty Found at Crash Site," p. 5; Ralph McGill, "One More Word," *Atlanta Constitution*, February 28,

1941, p. 14; Henry Vance, "The Coal Bin," *Birmingham News*, March 4, 1941, p. 8.

21. Rickenbacker, "Eddie Rickenbacker Tells His Own Philosophy," p. 2; Rickenbacker, *Rickenbacker*, pp. 284–285.

22. Rickenbacker, *Rickenbacker*, p. 284.

23. H. Paul Jeffers, *Ace of Aces: The Life of Capt. Eddie Rickenbacker* (New York: Ballantine Books, 2003), p. 275.

24. "Rickenbacker Reviews Today's Pilots of His 94th Squadron," *Los Angeles Times*, March 27, 1942, p. 3.

25. Lewis, *Eddie Rickenbacker*, pp. 389–390.

26. Bill Henry, "By the Way," *Los Angeles Times*, March 23, 1942, p. 1; "War Apathy Flayed by Rickenbacker; Public Letting Army Down, He Says," *Los Angeles Times*, March 26, 1942, p. 6.

27. "It's Civilians Who Need Prodding" *Spokane Chronicle*, March 30, 1942, p. 4; Ross, *Enduring Courage*, p. 293; Lewis, *Eddie Rickenbacker*, p. 390.

28. Rosalind Russell, "A Medal for Freddie," *Lansing (MI) State Journal*, February 20, 1956, p. 1.

29. "Rickenbacker's Mother Had Premonition of Bad Luck," *Los Angeles Times*, October 24, 1942, p. 6.

30. Russell, "A Medal for Freddie," p. 1.

31. John Francis Bartek, *My Raft Episode* (Washington, D.C.: Library of Congress, 2003), p. 23.

32. Lieutenant James C. Whittaker, *We Thought We Heard the Angels Sing* (New York: E. P. Dutton & Company, Inc., 1945), p. 20.

33. Hans Christian Adamson, *Eddie Rickenbacker* (New York: The Macmillan Company, 1946), p. 265.

34. Bartek, *My Raft Episode*, p. 6.

35. Bartek, *My Raft Episode*, p. 6.

36. Whittaker, *We Thought We Heard the Angels Sing*, pp. 19, 21.

CHAPTER 3: "IT WAS OBVIOUS TO ALL OF US THAT WE WERE IN GRAVE DANGER"

1. Bartek, *My Raft Episode,* p. 9.

2. Mark Smidt, "Students Hear Their Story," *Ames (IA) Tribune*, April 20, 1985, no page given.

3. Whittaker, *We Thought We Heard the Angels Sing*, pp. 23–24.

4. "Mother Sobs at News of Flier's Death," *Pittsburgh Press*, November 14, 1942, p. 3; "Finding of Pilot Raises Hopes of Torrington Family," *Hartford Courant*, November 14, 1942, p. 1.

5. Edward Rickenbacker, "Pacific Mission," dictated by Captain Edward V. Rickenbacker to Eureka Pictures, Inc., 1943, p. 8 (hereafter cited as Rickenbacker interview with Eureka Pictures).

6. Edward V. Rickenbacker, interviewed by W. David Lewis, no date given. W. David Lewis Papers, Special Collections & Archives, Auburn University Libraries, Reel #19, p. 2.

7. Whittaker, *We Thought We Heard the Angels Sing*, p. 25.

8. Adamson, *Eddie Rickenbacker*, p. 260.

9. Rickenbacker, "Pacific Mission, Part I: In Which Eight Men Are Cast Adrift in Mid-Pacific on Rubber Rafts," p. 21.

10. Whittaker, *We Thought We Heard the Angels Sing*, p. 27; Rickenbacker, "Pacific Mission, Part I: In Which Eight Men Are Cast Adrift in Mid-Pacific on Rubber Rafts," p. 21.

11. Adamson, *Eddie Rickenbacker*, p. 261.

12. Whittaker, *We Thought We Heard the Angels Sing*, p. 29.

13. Lt. James C. Whittaker, as Told to Charles Leavelle, "How 8 Men Fought the Elements—and 7 Won," *Chicago Tribune*, January 12, 1943, p. 2; Bartek, *My Raft Episode,* p. 11.

14. Whittaker, *We Thought We Heard the Angels Sing*, p. 31.

15. "Statement of Lieutenant John J. De Angelis" to the Twentieth Century–Fox Film Company, Beverly Hills, California, July 8, 1943, p. 22.

16. Rickenbacker, *Rickenbacker*, p. 341.

17. Rickenbacker, *Seven Came Through*, p. 10.

18. Whittaker, *We Thought We Heard the Angels Sing*, p. 32.

19. Whittaker, "How 8 Men Fought the Elements—and 7 Won," p. 2.

20. Rickenbacker, *Rickenbacker*, p. 342.

21. Lt. James C. Whittaker, as Told to Charles Leavelle, "Crashes Rickenbacker Plane in Sea Without Losing Man," *Chicago Tribune*, January 13, 1943, p. 1.

22. John Bartek speech and interview conducted by Dr. David Lewis, November 19, 1998. Special Collections Department, RBD Library, Auburn University, Alabama. Found at https://www.lib.auburn.edu /archive/find-aid/528/speech.htm. Accessed February 18, 2021 (hereafter referred to as Bartek speech, November 19, 1998).

23. Rickenbacker, *Rickenbacker*, p. 343.

24. Rickenbacker, "Pacific Mission, Part I: In Which Eight Men Are Cast Adrift in Mid-Pacific on Rubber Rafts," pp. 23–24.

25. Bartek, *My Raft Episode,* p. 13.
26. Rickenbacker, "Pacific Mission, Part I: In Which Eight Men Are Cast Adrift in Mid-Pacific on Rubber Rafts," p. 24.
27. Bartek speech, November 19, 1998.
28. Whittaker, *We Thought We Heard the Angels Sing,* p. 37.
29. Bartek, *My Raft Episode,* p. 13.

CHAPTER 4: "WE WERE TRULY ALONE IN THE PACIFIC"

1. Adamson, *Eddie Rickenbacker,* p. 276.
2. Rickenbacker, *Rickenbacker,* pp. 343, 345.
3. Bartek, *My Raft Episode,* p. 12.
4. "Statement of Lieutenant John J. De Angelis" to the Twentieth Century–Fox Film Company, p. 27; Ross, *Enduring Courage,* p. 301; Rickenbacker, "Pacific Mission, Part I: In Which Eight Men Are Cast Adrift in Mid-Pacific on Rubber Rafts," p. 24.
5. Whittaker, "Crashes Rickenbacker Plane in Sea Without Losing Man," p. 6; Whittaker, *We Thought We Heard the Angels Sing,* p. 38.
6. Whittaker, *We Thought We Heard the Angels Sing,* p. 39; Bartek and Pardue, *Life Out There: A Story of Faith and Courage,* p. 7.
7. Whittaker, "Crashes Rickenbacker Plane in Sea Without Losing Man," p. 6.
8. Rickenbacker, *Rickenbacker,* p. 345; Bartek and Pardue, *Life Out There: A Story of Faith and Courage,* p. 7.
9. Whittaker, "Crashes Rickenbacker Plane in Sea Without Losing Man," p. 6.
10. Rickenbacker, "Pacific Mission, Part I: In Which Eight Men Are Cast Adrift in Mid-Pacific on Rubber Rafts," p. 24.
11. Bartek and Pardue, *Life Out There: A Story of Faith and Courage,* pp. 9–10.
12. John Bartek, interview conducted by Dr. David Lewis and Dwayne Cox, November 20, 1998, Auburn University, Alabama. Found at https://www.lib.auburn.edu/archive/find-aid/528intv.htm. Accessed February 22, 2021 (hereafter cited as Bartek interview with Dr. David Lewis, November 20, 1998).
13. Rickenbacker, "Pacific Mission, Part I: In Which Eight Men Are Cast Adrift in Mid-Pacific on Rubber Rafts," p. 26.
14. Whittaker, *We Thought We Heard the Angels Sing,* p. 50.
15. Rickenbacker, *Rickenbacker,* p. 347.
16. Whittaker, *We Thought We Heard the Angels Sing,* pp. 42, 50.

17. Rickenbacker, "Pacific Mission, Part I: In Which Eight Men Are Cast Adrift in Mid-Pacific on Rubber Rafts," p. 26; Rickenbacker interview with Eureka Pictures, p. 24.
18. Whittaker, "Crashes Rickenbacker Plane in Sea Without Losing Man," p. 6.
19. Rickenbacker, *Rickenbacker*, p. 349.
20. Bartek, *My Raft Episode,* pp. 15–16.
21. Whittaker, *We Thought We Heard the Angels Sing*, p. 51.
22. Rickenbacker, "Pacific Mission, Part I: In Which Eight Men Are Cast Adrift in Mid-Pacific on Rubber Rafts," p. 90.
23. Rickenbacker interview with Eureka Pictures, p. 29; Rickenbacker, *Rickenbacker*, p. 351.
24. Rickenbacker, *Rickenbacker*, p. 350.
25. Rickenbacker, "Pacific Mission, Part I: In Which Eight Men Are Cast Adrift in Mid-Pacific on Rubber Rafts," p. 90.
26. Rickenbacker, *Rickenbacker*, p. 351.
27. Rickenbacker, "Pacific Mission, Part I: In Which Eight Men Are Cast Adrift in Mid-Pacific on Rubber Rafts," p. 90.
28. Rickenbacker, "Pacific Mission, Part I: In Which Eight Men Are Cast Adrift in Mid-Pacific on Rubber Rafts," p. 90; Bartek, *My Raft Episode,* p. 17.
29. Whittaker, *We Thought We Heard the Angels Sing*, p. 52.
30. "Statement of Lieutenant John J. De Angelis" to the Twentieth Century–Fox Film Company, p. 33.
31. Rickenbacker interview with Eureka Pictures, p. 66.

Chapter 5: "Rickenbacker Flight Down at Sea"

1. Suzanne Zobrist Kelly, *Reaching Beyond the Waves* (Ashland, Oregon: Hellgate Press, 2015), pp. 254–255.
2. Kelly, *Reaching Beyond the Waves*, p. 258.
3. Rickenbacker, *Rickenbacker*, pp. 354–355.
4. Lieutenant General H. H. Arnold letter to Mrs. Edward V. Rickenbacker, October 23, 1942, Edward V. Rickenbacker Collection, Box 29, Library of Congress; "Wife Waits by Phone to Hear of Ace," *New York Daily News*, October 24, 1942, p. 3.
5. "RICKENBACKER LOST AT SEA!" *Chicago Tribune*, October 24, 1942, p. 1; "Rickenbacker Missing in Pacific on Flight Southwest of Hawaii," *New York Times*, October 24, 1942, p. 1; "Rickenbacker Plane Missing in Pacific," *Los Angeles Times*, October 24, 1942, p. 1; "RICKENBACKER

MISSING ON OCEAN FLIGHT," *New York Daily News*, October 24, 1942, p. 1.

6. "Rickenbacker Missing in Pacific on Flight Southwest of Hawaii," *New York Times*, October 24, 1942, pp. 1, 4.

7. "Army and Navy Aircraft Hunt Missing Flyer," *Chicago Tribune*, October 24, 1942, p. 1; "Outlook Gloomy, Washington Says," *New York Daily News*, October 24, 1942, p. 3.

8. "Army and Navy Aircraft Hunt Missing Flyer," p. 1.

9. "Wife Sure 'Eddie Will Turn Up,'" *Chicago Tribune*, October 24, 1942, p. 2.

10. "Rickenbacker's Mother Had Premonition of Bad Luck," *Los Angeles Times*, October 24, 1942, p. 6.

11. "Fear Famous Airman Dies Airman's Death," *New York Daily News*, October 24, 1942, p. 16.

12. Finis Farr, *Rickenbacker's Luck: An American Life* (Boston: Houghton Mifflin Company, 1979), p. 226.

13. Rickenbacker, "Pacific Mission, Part I: In Which Eight Men Are Cast Adrift in Mid-Pacific on Rubber Rafts," p. 90.

14. Rickenbacker, "Pacific Mission, Part I: In Which Eight Men Are Cast Adrift in Mid-Pacific on Rubber Rafts," p. 90.

15. Bartek and Pardue, *Life Out There: A Story of Faith and Courage*, pp. 20–21.

16. Bartek and Pardue, *Life Out There: A Story of Faith and Courage*, pp. 104–106, 110–111.

17. Rickenbacker, "Pacific Mission, Part II: In Which the Navy Rescues Seven Castaways After 21 Days' Drifting," p. 79.

18. Lt. James C. Whittaker, as Told to Charles Leavelle, "How Rickenbacker and Drifting Crew Snare First Meal," *Chicago Tribune*, January 15, 1943, p. 2.

19. Whittaker, "How Rickenbacker and Drifting Crew Snare First Meal," pp. 1–2; Whittaker, *We Thought We Heard the Angels Sing*, p. 59.

CHAPTER 6: "WE WERE ALONE. WE WERE COLD. WE WERE AFRAID."

1. Lt. James C. Whittaker, as Told to Charles Leavelle, "Rickenbacker Crew Saved by Rain on Eighth Day Adrift," *Chicago Tribune*, January 16, 1943, p. 1.

2. Ross, *Enduring Courage*, p. 306.

3. Whittaker, "Rickenbacker Crew Saved by Rain on Eighth Day Adrift," p. 2; Whittaker, *We Thought We Heard the Angels Sing*, pp. 66–67.

4. Rickenbacker, "Pacific Mission, Part I: In Which Eight Men Are Cast Adrift in Mid-Pacific on Rubber Rafts," p. 94.

5. Rickenbacker interview with Eureka Pictures, p. 39.

6. Kelly, *Reaching Beyond the Waves*, pp. 259, 261.

7. "7 of Army in Plane of Rickenbacker," *New York Times*, October 26, 1942, p. 1.

8. "3-Day Hunt Fails to Turn Up Trace of Rickenbacker," *St. Louis Post-Dispatch*, October 25, 1942, p. 17.

9. "Hope Waning for Safety of Ace, Crew," *Fort Worth Star-Telegram*, October 27, 1942, p. 1.

10. "Burlingame Flier with Rickenbacker," *San Mateo (CA) Times*, October 26, 1942, pp. 1, 3.

11. Bartek, *My Raft Episode*, p. 85.

12. "Sends Sympathy to Fiancée," *Indianapolis News*, November 16, 1942, p. 17.

13. Adamson, *Eddie Rickenbacker*, pp. 298–299.

14. Russell, "A Medal for Freddie," p. 1.

15. "Mayor Wants Aid of Landlords, Too," *New York Daily News*, October 26, 1942, p. 16; Ed Sullivan, "Little Old New York," *New York Daily News*, October 26, 1942, p. 26.

16. Farr, *Rickenbacker's Luck: An American Life*, pp. 226–227.

17. C. B. Driscoll, "New York Day by Day," *News-Palladium* (Benton Harbor, MI), November 10, 1942, p. 2.

18. Bill Corum, "Corum Pays Tribute to Eddie Rickenbacker," *Pittsburgh Sun-Telegraph*, October 27, 1942, p. 20.

19. Rickenbacker, *Rickenbacker*, p. 355.

20. Rickenbacker interview with Eureka Pictures, p. 34.

21. Rickenbacker, *Rickenbacker*, p. 356.

22. Whittaker, *We Thought We Heard the Angels Sing*, p. 78.

23. Rickenbacker, *Rickenbacker*, p. 356.

24. Bartek speech, November 19, 1998.

25. Rickenbacker, *Rickenbacker*, pp. 360–361.

26. Whittaker, "How Rickenbacker and Drifting Crew Snare First Meal," p. 2.

27. Rickenbacker, *Rickenbacker*, p. 361; Bartek and Pardue, *Life Out There: A Story of Faith and Courage*, p. 27.

28. "Stimson Still Hopes Rickenbacker Safe," *Los Angeles Times*, October 30, 1942, p. 7.

29. "Captain Eddie," *Time*, November 2, 1942, p. 24.

30. Farr, *Rickenbacker's Luck: An American Life*, p. 234.

31. Farr, *Rickenbacker's Luck: An American Life*, p. 234.

32. "Good-By Rickenbacker?" *New York Daily News*, October 28, 1942, p. 33.

33. Henry McLemore, "The Lighter Side," *Los Angeles Times*, October 29, 1942, p. 11.

34. Lt. James C. Whittaker, as Told to Charles Leavelle, "Rick's Pilot Hooks Shark and Battles It to Death," *Chicago Tribune*, January 17, 1943, p. 1.

35. Whittaker, "Rickenbacker Crew Saved by Rain on Eighth Day Adrift," p. 2; Whittaker, *We Thought We Heard the Angels Sing*, pp. 72, 77–78.

36. Whittaker, "Rickenbacker Crew Saved by Rain on Eighth Day Adrift," p. 2.

37. Rickenbacker, "Pacific Mission, Part I: In Which Eight Men Are Cast Adrift in Mid-Pacific on Rubber Rafts," p. 96; Rickenbacker, *Rickenbacker*, pp. 361–362.

38. Rickenbacker, "Pacific Mission, Part I: In Which Eight Men Are Cast Adrift in Mid-Pacific on Rubber Rafts," p. 96.

39. Rickenbacker, "Pacific Mission, Part I: In Which Eight Men Are Cast Adrift in Mid-Pacific on Rubber Rafts," p. 99.

40. Rickenbacker interview with Eureka Pictures, p. 61.

CHAPTER 7: "IT WAS THEN THAT RICK TOOK OVER"

1. Rickenbacker interview with Eureka Pictures, pp. 46–47.

2. Rickenbacker, *Rickenbacker*, p. 366.

3. Bartek speech, November 19, 1998.

4. Bartek, *My Raft Episode,* p. 21; Bartek interview with Dr. David Lewis, November 20, 1998.

5. Rickenbacker, "Pacific Mission, Part II: In Which the Navy Rescues Seven Castaways After 21 Days' Drifting," p. 81.

6. Whittaker, *We Thought We Heard the Angels Sing*, p. 69.

7. Rickenbacker, "Eddie Rickenbacker Tells His Own Philosophy," p. 2.

8. Bartek and Pardue, *Life Out There: A Story of Faith and Courage*, p. 26.

9. Adamson, *Eddie Rickenbacker*, p. 299.

10. Adamson, *Eddie Rickenbacker*, p. 299

11. Bartek and Pardue, *Life Out There: A Story of Faith and Courage*, pp. 103, 106–107, 113.

12. Whittaker, "Rick's Pilot Hooks Shark and Battles It to Death," p. 2; Rickenbacker, "Pacific Mission, Part II: In Which the Navy Rescues Seven Castaways After 21 Days' Drifting," p. 79.

13. Whittaker, "Rick's Pilot Hooks Shark and Battles It to Death," p. 2.

14. Rickenbacker, *Rickenbacker*, p. 355.

15. Rickenbacker, *Rickenbacker*, pp. 367–368.

16. Adamson, *Eddie Rickenbacker*, pp. 282–283.
17. Henry L. Stimson letter to Mrs. Edward V. Rickenbacker, November 1, 1942, Edward V. Rickenbacker Collection, Box 29, Library of Congress.
18. Whittaker, *We Thought We Heard the Angels Sing*, pp. 78–79.
19. Rickenbacker, *Rickenbacker*, p. 364.
20. Bartek, *My Raft Episode*, p. 27.
21. Rickenbacker, "Pacific Mission, Part I: In Which Eight Men Are Cast Adrift in Mid-Pacific on Rubber Rafts," p. 100; Rickenbacker, *Rickenbacker*, p. 364.
22. Whittaker, *We Thought We Heard the Angels Sing*, p. 85; "Statement of Lieutenant John J. De Angelis" to the Twentieth Century–Fox Film Company, p. 12.

CHAPTER 8: "WE WILL HELP OURSELVES, IF YOU GIVE US THE CHANCE"

1. Lt. James C. Whittaker, as told to Charles Leavelle, "Rickenbacker's Cussing Boosts Morale on Raft," *Chicago Tribune*, January 19, 1943, p. 2; Whittaker, *We Thought We Heard the Angels Sing*, pp. 92–93.
2. Adamson, *Eddie Rickenbacker*, p. 297.
3. Rickenbacker, "Pacific Mission, Part II: In Which the Navy Rescues Seven Castaways After 21 Days' Drifting," p. 79.
4. Lewis, *Eddie Rickenbacker*, p. 437.
5. Whittaker, *We Thought We Heard the Angels Sing*, p. 93; Whittaker, "Rickenbacker's Cussing Boosts Morale on Raft," p. 2.
6. Rickenbacker interview with Eureka Pictures, p. 48.
7. Whittaker, "Whittaker Tells Tragic Burial from Raft at Sea," *Chicago Tribune*, January 18, 1943, p. 4; Whittaker, *We Thought We Heard the Angels Sing*, p. 87.
8. Bartek, *My Raft Episode*, p. 30.
9. Whittaker, *We Thought We Heard the Angels Sing*, pp. 82–83.
10. Bartek and Pardue, *Life Out There: A Story of Faith and Courage*, p. 117.
11. Bartek and Pardue, *Life Out There: A Story of Faith and Courage*, p. 45; Edward V. Rickenbacker, interviewed by W. David Lewis, no date given. W. David Lewis Papers, Special Collections & Archives, Auburn University Libraries, Reel #19, pp. 17–18.
12. Bartek speech, November 19, 1998; Whittaker, *We Thought We Heard the Angels Sing*, p. 80.
13. Bartek, *My Raft Episode*, p. 31.

14. Lt. James C. Whittaker, as told to Charles Leavelle, "18th Day! Plane Fails to Notice Rick's 3 Rafts," *Chicago Tribune*, January 20, 1943, p. 2; Whittaker, "Rickenbacker's Cussing Boosts Morale on Raft," p. 2.

15. Rickenbacker, *Seven Came Through*, p. 37.

16. Rickenbacker interview with Eureka Pictures, p. 76.

17. Whittaker, "Rickenbacker's Cussing Boosts Morale on Raft," p. 2.

18. Whittaker, "18th Day! Plane Fails to Notice Rick's 3 Rafts," p. 2.

19. Bartek and Pardue, *Life Out There: A Story of Faith and Courage*, p. 22.

20. Bartek and Pardue, *Life Out There: A Story of Faith and Courage*, p. 23.

21. Whittaker, *We Thought We Heard the Angels Sing*, p. 98; "Statement of Lieutenant John J. De Angelis" to the Twentieth Century–Fox Film Company, p. 4.

22. Whittaker, "Rickenbacker's Cussing Boosts Morale on Raft," p. 2; "Statement of Lieutenant John J. De Angelis" to the Twentieth Century–Fox Film Company, p. 37.

CHAPTER 9: "I HEAR AN ENGINE! I HEAR AN ENGINE!"

1. Whittaker, "18th Day! Plane Fails to Notice Rick's 3 Rafts," p. 2.

2. Whittaker, "18th Day! Plane Fails to Notice Rick's 3 Rafts," p. 2.

3. Rickenbacker, "Pacific Mission, Part II: In Which the Navy Rescues Seven Castaways After 21 Days' Drifting," pp. 83, 85.

4. Whittaker, *We Thought We Heard the Angels Sing*, p. 105.

5. Whittaker, *We Thought We Heard the Angels Sing*, p. 106.

6. Whittaker, *We Thought We Heard the Angels Sing*, p. 107.

7. Rickenbacker, "Pacific Mission, Part II: In Which the Navy Rescues Seven Castaways After 21 Days' Drifting," p. 85.

8. Walter Kiernan, "Rickenbacker Did Work of Man While Only 12," *Miami News*, November 9, 1942, p. 2.

9. Bartek, *My Raft Episode*, p. 85.

10. Adamson, *Eddie Rickenbacker*, p. 303; Rickenbacker, "Pacific Mission, Part II: In Which the Navy Rescues Seven Castaways After 21 Days' Drifting," p. 85.

11. Bartek and Pardue, *Life Out There: A Story of Faith and Courage*, p. 50.

12. Bartek speech, November 19, 1998.

13. Kelly, *Reaching Beyond the Waves*, p. 274.

14. Kelly, *Reaching Beyond the Waves*, pp. 41, 275.

15. *U. S. S. Hilo (PG-58) War Diary*, November 11, 1942.

16. Kelly, *Reaching Beyond the Waves*, pp. 41, 275.

17. "Rickenbacker's Pilot Found Alive on Raft, New Pacific Hunt Begins," *New York Times*, November 14, 1942, p. 1; "Rescue Abilene Flier in Pacific," *Abilene Reporter-News*, November 13, 1942, p. 1.

18. Walter Trohan, "Rickenbacker's Pilot Picked Up; Hope for Others," *Chicago Tribune*, November 14, 1942, p. 3.

19. "Wife to Keep on Building Planes," *Abilene Reporter-News*, November 13, 1942, p. 1; "Rickenbacker's Pilot Found Alive on Raft, New Pacific Hunt Begins," p. 7.

20. "Finding of Pilot Raises Hopes of Torrington Family," *Hartford Courant*, November 14, 1942, p. 1.

21. Lt. James C. Whittaker, as told to Charles Leavelle, "21st Day's Dawn Brings Land to 3 of Rick's Crew," *Chicago Tribune*, January 21, 1943, p. 3; John Ferris, "Rickenbacker Raft Ordeal Recalled by Survivor Here," *Oakland Tribune*, November 26, 1962, p. 8.

22. Whittaker, "21st Day's Dawn Brings Land to 3 of Rick's Crew," p. 3; Whittaker, *We Thought We Heard the Angels Sing*, pp. 110–112.

23. Whittaker, *We Thought We Heard the Angels Sing*, pp. 112–113; Whittaker, "21st Day's Dawn Brings Land to 3 of Rick's Crew," p. 3.

24. Ferris, "Rickenbacker Raft Ordeal Recalled by Survivor Here," p. 8.

25. Whittaker, *We Thought We Heard the Angels Sing*, p. 114.

26. Whittaker, "21st Day's Dawn Brings Land to 3 of Rick's Crew," p. 3.

27. "Toma Fakapae," an account by the native islander who assisted the Whittaker group, in the Bartek Family Collection; Bartek, *My Raft Episode*, pp. 90–91.

28. Lt. James C. Whittaker, as told to Charles Leavelle, "Natives Rescue 3 of Rick's Lost Crew on Island," *Chicago Tribune*, January 22, 1943, p. 2; Whittaker, *We Thought We Heard the Angels Sing*, p. 124; Kelly, *Reaching Beyond the Waves*, p. 208.

29. "Narrative of Lt. Edward M. Gordon, Executive Officer, USS *Hilo*, PT Boat Tender," Office of Naval Records and Library, January 20, 1944, p. 2.

30. Lt. James C. Whittaker, as told to Charles Leavelle, "Natives' Chicken Broth Revives Three on Island," *Chicago Tribune*, January 23, 1943, p. 4; Whittaker, *We Thought We Heard the Angels Sing*, pp. 129–130.

CHAPTER 10: "LISTEN, CAPTAIN—PLANES!"

1. Bartek, *My Raft Episode*, p. 36; Adamson, *Eddie Rickenbacker*, pp. 303–304.

2. Bartek interview with Dr. David Lewis, November 20, 1998.

3. Adamson, *Eddie Rickenbacker*, p. 304.

4. Rickenbacker, "Pacific Mission, Part II: In Which the Navy Rescues Seven Castaways After 21 Days' Drifting," p. 86; Bartek, *My Raft Episode*, p. 36.

5. Bartek, *My Raft Episode*, p. 36; Rickenbacker, "Pacific Mission, Part II: In Which the Navy Rescues Seven Castaways After 21 Days' Drifting," p. 86.

6. Bartek and Pardue, *Life Out There: A Story of Faith and Courage*, pp. 61–62.

7. Bartek, *My Raft Episode*, p. 36.

8. Rickenbacker, "Pacific Mission, Part II: In Which the Navy Rescues Seven Castaways After 21 Days' Drifting," p. 86.

9. Bartek, *My Raft Episode*, p. 58.

10. The Commanding Officer to the Commanding General, Straw Area, "Report of Rescue of Captain Rickenbacker and Party, 11, 12 November, 1942," 15 November, 1942.

11. Kelly, *Reaching Beyond the Waves*, p. 278; Rickenbacker, "Pacific Mission, Part II: In Which the Navy Rescues Seven Castaways After 21 Days' Drifting," p. 89; Rickenbacker, *Rickenbacker*, p. 372.

12. Rickenbacker interview with Eureka Pictures, pp. 95–96.

13. Bartek, *My Raft Episode*, p. 50.

14. "Rickenbacker's Story of His Ordeal in Pacific," *Los Angeles Times*, December 20, 1942, p. 11; Rickenbacker, "Pacific Mission, Part II: In Which the Navy Rescues Seven Castaways After 21 Days' Drifting," pp. 89–90.

15. Rickenbacker interview with Eureka Pictures, p. 97; Bartek, *My Raft Episode*, p. 51.

16. Lewis, *Eddie Rickenbacker*, p. 441; Rickenbacker, "Pacific Mission, Part II: In Which the Navy Rescues Seven Castaways After 21 Days' Drifting," p. 90.

17. Kelly, *Reaching Beyond the Waves*, p. 231.

18. Bartek and Pardue, *Life Out There: A Story of Faith and Courage*, p. 65; Bartek speech, November 19, 1998.

19. Charles P. Arnot, "Hospital Built in One Day Saves Rickenbacker Men," *Pittsburgh Press*, May 6, 1943, p. 4.

20. Bartek, *My Raft Episode*, p. 51.

21. Rickenbacker interview with Eureka Pictures, pp. 98–99; Bartek interview with Dr. David Lewis, November 20, 1998.

22. "In the Fight," *Ventura County (CA) Star-Free Press*, December 15, 1942, p. 1; Rickenbacker interview with Eureka Pictures, p. 46.

23. "Aide of Rickenbacker Names Rescue Island," *New York Times*, May 7, 1943.

24. Rickenbacker, *Seven Came Through*, pp. 55–56.

25. Bartek, *My Raft Episode*, p. 60.

26. Lt. James C. Whittaker, as told to Charles Leavelle, "Ordeal at End, 'Iron Man' Has 3 Malted Milks," *Chicago Tribune*, January 24, 1943, p. 2; Bartek, *My Raft Episode*, p. 38.

27. Whittaker, *We Thought We Heard the Angels Sing*, p. 134; Whittaker, "Ordeal at End, 'Iron Man' Has 3 Malted Milks," p. 2.

28. Rickenbacker, *Rickenbacker*, p. 374; Lieut. John W. Thomason, "Half Orange for 22 Days Keeps Fliers Alive at Sea," *Pittsburgh Press*, November 23, 1942, pp. 1, 4.

29. Rickenbacker, *Rickenbacker*, p. 374; Lieut. John W. Thomason, "Half Orange for 22 Days Keep Fliers Alive at Sea," *Pittsburgh Press*, November 23, 1942, pp. 1, 4.

CHAPTER 11: "MAKE ME PLENTY OF APPLE PIE"

1. "Good News Comes to Rickenbackers," *New York Times*, November 15, 1942.

2. "Good News Comes to Rickenbackers," *New York Times*, November 15, 1942; "Ace's Mother Beams Joy," *Los Angeles Times*, November 15, 1942, p. 3.

3. "Good News Comes to Rickenbackers," *New York Times*, November 15, 1942.

4. "Rickenbacker Safe; 6 Others in Party Found," *St. Louis Post-Dispatch*, November 14, 1942, p. 3; "Never Lost Hope for 'Eddie,' Says Thankful Wife," *Chicago Tribune*, November 15, 1942, p. 4; Edna Ferguson, "Diet of Raw Fish Worried His Wife," *New York Daily News*, November 15, 1942, p. 58.

5. "Rickenbacker Safe; 6 Others in Party Found," *St. Louis Post-Dispatch*, November 14, 1942, p. 3.

6. Telegram from the Adjutant General to Mrs. Mary Bartek, November 14, 1942, in the Bartek Family Collection.

7. "Pacific Rescue," *New York Times*, November 15, 1942.

8. "Once More the Editors Revise Rick's Obituary," *Chicago Tribune*, November 15, 1942, p. 4; "Rickenbacker Again Cheats Grim Reaper" and "Man Who Always Comes Back Does It Again," *Charlotte Observer*, November 15, 1942, pp. 1–2.

9. "Rickenbacker Safe," *Time*, November 23, 1942, p. 26.

10. Rickenbacker, *Seven Came Through*, p. x; Damon Runyon and Walter Kiernan, *Capt. Eddie Rickenbacker* (New York: Dell Publishing Co., Inc., 1942), p. 3.

11. Whittaker, *We Thought We Heard the Angels Sing*, pp. 20, 136–137

12. "Faith, Courage of Rickenbacker and His Men Told," *Chicago Tribune*, November 24, 1942, p. 2.

13. Rickenbacker, *Rickenbacker,* p. 375.

14. "Rickenbacker Rescued," *Life*, December 7, 1942, p. 43.

15. Commanding Officer, Marine Observation Squadron One Fifty-Five to The Historical Unit, Office of the Chief of Naval Operations, Washington, D. C., "History of Marine Observation Squadron One Fifty-Five," January 8, 1945, p. 6.

16. "Statement of Lieutenant John J. De Angelis" to the Twentieth Century–Fox Film Company, p. 56.

17. Headlines in the *Fort Worth Star-Telegram*, November 13–14, and December 11, 1942.

18. "Pilot Tells How 'Rick's' Courage Saved 7 at Sea," *Chicago Tribune*, December 21, 1942, p. 5.

19. "Long-Lost Men Found on Raft," *Asbury Park (NJ) Press*, November 14, 1942, p. 1.

20. "Bartek Is Praised by Air Chief in Letter to Family at Freehold," *Long Branch (NJ) Daily Record*, December 4, 1942, p. 1.

21. Bartek and Pardue, *Life Out There: A Story of Faith and Courage*, p. 94.

22. "Rickenbacker Survivor Home," *Wilkes-Barre (PA) Record*, December 15, 1942, p. 18.

23. "De Angelis Family Receives First Word from Son," *Allentown (PA) Morning Call*, November 19, 1942, p. 20; "Rescue Ends Ordeal of Navigator's Bride," *Los Angeles Times*, November 15, 1942, p. 3.

24. "Rescue Ends Ordeal of Navigator's Bride," *Los Angeles Times*, November 15, 1942, p. 3.

25. "Rickenbacker and Men Rescued; Torrington Boy Only One to Die," *Hartford Courant*, November 15, 1942, p. 1; "Mother Sobs at News of Flier's Death," *Pittsburgh Press*, November 14, 1942, p. 3.

26. "Army Sends Kaczmarczyk's Brother Home to Comfort Bereaved Parents," *Hartford Courant*, November 17, 1942, p. 12.

27. "Army Tells Torrington Woman Son Died as Hero," *Hartford Courant*, November 21, 1942, p. 7.

28. Bartek, *My Raft Episode,* p. 85.

29. "Sends Sympathy to Fiancée," *Indianapolis News*, November 16, 1942, p. 17.

30. Bartek, *My Raft Episode,* p. 86.

31. Rickenbacker, *Rickenbacker,* p. 376.

32. Rickenbacker, *Rickenbacker,* p. 376.

33. George C. Kenney, *General Kenney Reports* (New York: Duell, Sloan and Pearce, 1949), pp. 153–154.

34. Kenney, *General Kenney Reports*, p. 154.
35. Captain Edward V. Rickenbacker, "Pacific Mission, Part III: In Which 'Rick' Resumes His Trip and Visits the Fighting Fronts," *Life*, February 8, 1943, p. 100; Rickenbacker, *Rickenbacker*, p. 377.

CHAPTER 12: "IT'S AN EPIC; LET IT STAND AT THAT"

1. Rickenbacker, "Pacific Mission, Part III: In Which 'Rick' Resumes His Trip and Visits the Fighting Fronts," p. 106.
2. Adamson, *Eddie Rickenbacker*, pp. 306–307.
3. Rickenbacker, "Pacific Mission, Part III: In Which 'Rick' Resumes His Trip and Visits the Fighting Fronts," p. 106; Ross, *Enduring Courage*, p. 313; "Rickenbacker Tells Story of His 23 Days on Raft," *New York Times*, December 20, 1942, p. 37.
4. Adamson, *Eddie Rickenbacker*, p. 308; Ross, *Enduring Courage*, p. 313.
5. George Fawcett, "Rickenbacker Rescuer Talks to Students," *Daily Advertiser* (Lafayette, LA), November 16, 1975, pp. 1, 43.
6. "Of Hell and Prayers," *Time*, December 28, 1942, p. 11; Sgt. Richard C. Seither, "Rickenbacker Eats Seagull Raw," *Pittsburgh Press*, November 23, 1942, p. 4.
7. "Rickenbacker Tells of 21 Days Adrift at Sea; Only Oranges to Eat 6 Days, Then Gull, Two Fish," *St. Louis Post-Dispatch*, December 19, 1942, pp. 1–2.
8. "Rickenbacker Tells of 21 Days Adrift at Sea; Only Oranges to Eat 6 Days, Then Gull, Two Fish," pp. 1–2; "Of Hell and Prayers," *Time*, December 28, 1942, p. 11.
9. Author's telephone interview with Keith De Angelis, June 7, 2021.
10. "Rickenbacker Legend Comes to Life in Biography of Air Ace of World War I," *Lexington (KY) Herald*, February 24, 1946, p. 30.
11. W. A. Barnhill, "After 16 Years, Johnny Bartek, Survivor of 21-Day Ordeal During World War II, Wants Quiet Life," *Long Branch (NJ) Daily Record*, December 4, 1958, p. 6; Bartek and Pardue, *Life Out There: A Story of Faith and Courage*, p. 46.
12. Barnhill, "After 16 Years, Johnny Bartek, Survivor of 21-Day Ordeal During World War II, Wants Quiet Life," p. 1.
13. Whittaker, *We Thought We Heard the Angels Sing*, p. 134; Whittaker, "Ordeal at End, 'Iron Man' Has 3 Malted Milks," p. 2.
14. Rickenbacker, *Rickenbacker*, p. 359.

15. Commanding General, Air Transport Command, "Interrogation of Captain William T. Cherry, Jr.," conducted by Col. L. G. Fritz, Lt. Col. Milton W. Arnold, and Maj. E. R. Mandel, December 11, 1942.
16. Bartek and Pardue, *Life Out There: A Story of Faith and Courage*, p. 53.
17. Author's telephone interviews with Diane Stacy, March 23, 2020, and March 4, 2022.
18. Rickenbacker, *Rickenbacker*, p. 382.
19. "Ten Best Stories of Year Listed by Associated Press," *Oakland Tribune*, December 31, 1942, p. 8.
20. "Captain Rickenbacker," *Boys' Life*, March 1943, p. 4.
21. Rickenbacker, *Rickenbacker*, p. 388.
22. "Durable Man," *Time*, April 17, 1950.
23. "It's Easy to Die, Rickenbacker Says," *Los Angeles Times*, October 12, 1952, p. 34; Whittaker, "Rick's Pilot Hooks Shark and Battles It to Death," p. 2.
24. Ferris, "Rickenbacker Raft Ordeal Recalled by Survivor Here," p. 8; "Statement of Lieutenant John J. De Angelis" to the Twentieth Century–Fox Film Company, p. 40.
25. "Cooked Seafood Dinner to Mark Bartek's Survival Anniversary," *Asbury Park (NJ) Press*, November 13, 1960, p. 4.
26. Headquarters, South Pacific Wing, Army Air Forces, Air Transport Command, "Crash Landing at Sea," December 9, 1942.
27. "Rickenbacker Aide Says Party Prayed for Food," *Bridgewater (NJ) Courier News*, December 15, 1942, p. 12; Bartek and Pardue, *Life Out There: A Story of Faith and Courage*, p. 56.
28. Author's telephone interview with Bernadette Rogoff, January 18, 2022.
29. "Rickenbacker Party 'Found God' in Mid-Ocean Aboard Rafts, Says Radio Man in Bay Hospital," *Oakland Tribune*, December 21, 1942, p. 15.
30. Bartek and Pardue, *Life Out There: A Story of Faith and Courage*, p. 53.
31. "Faith, Courage of Rickenbacker and His Men Told," p. 2.
32. Russell, "A Medal for Freddie," p. 1.
33. Author's telephone interview with Diane Stacy, March 23, 2020.
34. "Capt. Eddie Is Dead at 82," *New York Times*, July 24, 1973, p. 38.
35. C. V. Glines, "Captain Eddie Rickenbacker: America's World War I Ace of Aces," *Aviation History*, January 1999.
36. "Pacific Rescue," p. 3.
37. Barnhill, "After 16 Years, Johnny Bartek, Survivor of 21-Day Ordeal During World War II, Wants Quiet Life," p. 6.
38. Whittaker, *We Thought We Heard the Angels Sing*, p. 139.

BIBLIOGRAPHY

COLLECTIONS, ACTION REPORTS AND INTERVIEWS

Collections
Archival

Auburn University Special Collections & Archives holds a vast collection of papers relating to the 1942 episode on the Pacific. They include:

> The Eddie Rickenbacker Papers, 1890–1973
> The Brian Rickenbacker Papers
> The Marcia Rickenbacker Papers
> The Lester Boutte Papers, 1942–1995
> The John Bartek Papers
> The W. David Lewis Papers
> The Floyd McRae Jr. Papers

Library of Congress, Washington, DC, has:

> The Eddie Rickenbacker Collection
> The Henry Harley Arnold Papers

National Archives and Records Administration at College Park, MD, holds a thorough collection of World War II military reports.

The Billy Rose Theatre Division of the New York Public Library houses the
Frederick Brisson Papers.

The National Museum of the United States Air Force Museum in Dayton, Ohio,
has a wide-ranging collection of photographs and documents about Eddie
Rickenbacker.

Individuals

The Bartek Family Collection contains a wide-ranging collection of letters,
photographs, official reports, and other items pertaining to the rescue of the
Rickenbacker group.

The Frank Cannistraci Collection

The Cherry Family Collection possesses photographs and other information
relating to the 1942 saga on the Pacific.

Rosalind Russell/Frederick Brisson Collection, #183, Box 30, "Hans Christian
Adamson," U.C.L.A. Special Collections #183, Los Angeles, California, has
various letters and other pertinent documents.

Action Reports

Commander in Chief, U. S. Pacific Fleet to Commandant, Twelfth Naval
District. "Ship's History of the U.S.S. *Hilo*," November 21, 1945.

Commanding General, Air Transport Command. "Interrogation of Captain
William T. Cherry Jr.," conducted by Col. L. G. Fritz, Lt. Col. Milton W.
Arnold, and Maj. E. R. Mandel, December 11, 1942.

Commanding Officer to Commander in Chief, U. S. Fleet. "U. S. S. *Hilo* War
Diary, October 19, 1942, to January 31, 1943," February 1, 1943.

Commanding Officer to the Commanding General, Straw Area. "Report of
Rescue of Captain Rickenbacker and Party, 11, 12 November, 1942,"
November 15, 1942.

Commanding Officer, Marine Observation Squadron One Fifty-Five to the
Historical Unit, Office of the Chief of Naval Operations, Washington, DC
"History of Marine Observation Squadron One Fifty-Five," January 8, 1945.

Headquarters, Eleventh Ferrying Group, Army Air Forces, Air Transport
Command to Commanding Officer, West Coast Wing, Air Transport
Command. "Narrative Report on Rickenbacker Trip," December 29, 1942.

Headquarters, South Pacific Wing, Army Air Forces, Air Transport Command. "Crash Landing at Sea," December 9, 1942.

"Narrative of Lt. Edward M. Gordon, Executive Officer, USS *Hilo*, PT Boat Tender," Office of Naval Records and Library, January 20, 1944.

INTERVIEWS
Auburn University Special Collections & Archives
John Bartek

John Bartek speech and interview conducted by Dr. W. David Lewis, November 19, 1998. Special Collections Department, RBD Library, Auburn University, Alabama. Found at https://www.lib.auburn.edu/archive/find-aid/528/speech .htm. Accessed February 18, 2021.

John Bartek, interview conducted by Dr. W. David Lewis and Dwayne Cox, November 20, 1998, Auburn University, Alabama. Found at https://www.lib .auburn.edu/archive/find-aid/528intv.htm. Accessed February 22, 2021.

Rickenbacker Family

Brian Rickenbacker, interview conducted by Dr. W. David Lewis, July 17, 1999. Found at https://www.lib.auburn.edu/archive/find-aid/348.htm. Accessed February 18, 2021.

Edward V. Rickenbacker, interviewed by Dr. W. David Lewis, no date given. W. David Lewis Papers, Special Collections & Archives, Auburn University Libraries.

Edward Rickenbacker, "Pacific Mission," dictated by Captain Edward V. Rickenbacker to Eureka Pictures, Inc., 1943.

Marcie Rickenbacker, interview conducted by Dr. W. David Lewis, October 8, 1998. Found at https://www.lib.auburn.edu/archive/find-aid/344.htm. Accessed February 18, 2021.

Other Interviews

Author's telephone interview with Bernadette Rogoff, January 18, 2022.

Author's telephone interviews with Diane Stacy, March 23, 2020, and March 4, 2022.

Author's telephone interview with Glenda Cherry, March 14, 2022.

Author's telephone interview with Keith De Angelis, June 7, 2021.

Author's telephone interview with William Cherry IV, March 14, 2022.

Interview of Frederick La Tour, Bureau of Yards and Docks, June 2, 1943.

"Statement of Lieutenant John J. De Angelis" to the Twentieth Century–Fox Film Company, Beverly Hills, California, July 8, 1943.

BOOKS

Adamson, Hans Christian. *Eddie Rickenbacker*. New York: The Macmillan Company, 1946.

Arnold, H. H. *Global Mission*. New York: Harper & Brothers, Publishers, 1949.

Bartek, John Francis. *My Raft Episode*. Washington, DC: Library of Congress, 2003.

Bartek, Sergeant Johnny, assisted by Austin Pardue. *Life Out There: A Story of Faith and Courage*. New York: Charles Scribner's Sons, 1943.

Breuer, William B. *Devil Boats: The PT War Against Japan*. Novato, California: Presidio Press, 1987.

Bulkley, Captain Robert J., Jr., USNR (Retired). *At Close Quarters: PT Boats in the United States Navy*. Washington, DC: Naval History Division, 1962.

Farmer, Mark. *Flight to Anywhere: A Navigator's Life*. Yountville, California: Coralreef Group, 1998.

Farr, Finis. *Rickenbacker's Luck: An American Life*. Boston: Houghton Mifflin Company, 1979.

Gold, Ned. *Eight Who Wrestled Death*. Milwaukee: Raintree Publishers, 1980.

Groom, Winston. *The Aviators: Eddie Rickenbacker, Jimmy Doolittle, Charles Lindbergh, and the Epic Age of Flight*. Washington, DC: National Geographic Society, 2013.

James, D. Clayton. *The Years of MacArthur*, vol. 2, *1941–1945*. Boston: Houghton Mifflin Company, 1975.

Jeffers, H. Paul. *Ace of Aces: The Life of Capt. Eddie Rickenbacker*. New York: Ballantine Books, 2003.

Kelly, Suzanne Zobrist. *Reaching Beyond the Waves: A Teacher's Sixth Graders' Inspirational Search for the WWII Survivors of a Downed B-17 and the Men Who Rescued Them*. Ashland, Oregon: Hellgate Press, 2015.

Kenney, George C. *General Kenney Reports*. New York: Duell, Sloan and Pearce, 1949.

Lewis, W. David. *Eddie Rickenbacker: An American Hero in the Twentieth Century*. Baltimore: The Johns Hopkins University Press, 2005.

MacArthur, General of the Army Douglas. *Reminiscences*. New York: McGraw-Hill Book Company, 1964.

Manchester, William. *American Caesar: Douglas MacArthur, 1880–1964*. Boston: Little, Brown and Company, 1978.

Morriss, Mack, edited by Ronnie Day. *South Pacific Diary, 1942–1943*. Lexington: The University Press of Kentucky, 1996.

Oates, Carl. *Canton Island: Aerial Crossroads of the South Pacific*. McLean, Virginia: Paladwr Press, 2003.

Perret, Geoffrey. *Old Soldiers Never Die*. Holbrook, Massachusetts: Adams Media Corporation, 1996.

Rickenbacker, Captain Eddie. *Ace Drummond*. Racine, Wisconsin: Whitman Publishing Company, 1935.

_____. *We Prayed*. New York: American Viewpoint, Inc., 1943.

_____. *Seven Came Through Rickenbacker's Full Story*. Garden City, New York: Doubleday, Doran and Company, Inc., 1943.

_____. *Rickenbacker*. Englewood Cliffs, New Jersey: Prentice-Hall, Inc., 1967.

Rickenbacker, William F., editor. *From Father to Son: The Letters of Captain Eddie Rickenbacker to His Son William from Boyhood to Manhood*. New York: Walker and Company, 1970.

Ross, John F. *Enduring Courage: Ace Pilot Eddie Rickenbacker and the Dawn of the Age of Speed*. New York: St. Martin's Press, 2014.

Runyon, Damon, and Walter Kiernan. *Capt. Eddie Rickenbacker*. New York: Dell Publishing Co., Inc., 1942.

Sherrod, Robert. *History of Marine Corps Aviation in World War II*. Washington, DC: Combat Forces Press, 1952.

St. Joseph Edition of the New American Bible (New York: Catholic Book Publishing Co., 1991).

Swarthout, Lind. *Captain Eddie Rickenbacker: God Still Answers Prayers*. Grand Rapids: Zondervan Publishing House, 1944.

Whittaker, Lieutenant James C. *We Thought We Heard the Angels Sing*. New York: E. P. Dutton & Company, Inc., 1945.

Bibliography

ARTICLES

"A Born Leader," *Chicago Tribune*, December 25, 1942, p. 17.

"Adamson on Rickenbacker," *Rochester (NY) Democrat and Chronicle*, February 10, 1946, p. 60.

"Aeronautics 1,000,000," *Time*, June 18, 1923. Found at http://content.time .com/time/subscriber/printout/0,8816,715809,00.html. Accessed February 8, 2021.

"A 'Hello' from the Heart," *Fort Worth Star-Telegram*, December 11, 1942, p. 1.

"A Poem Written for 'Rick' in '18 Holds Good in '42," *Chicago Tribune*, December 19, 1934, p. 9.

"A Worthy Tribute," *Los Angeles Times*, June 27, 1919, p. 1.

"'Ace' Rickenbacher Cables Old Pals at Detroit Speed Meet," *Chicago Tribune*, June 3, 1918, p. 12.

"Ace's Mother Beams Joy," *Los Angeles Times*, November 15, 1942, p. 3.

"Aide of Rickenbacker Names Rescue Island," *New York Times*, May 7, 1943.

"Air Battle Staged for Motion Pictures," *New York Times*, November 25, 1918.

"Air Liner Spans U.S.; 12 Hrs.," *Chicago Tribune*, November 9, 1934, p. 1.

"American Ace Will Be Guest of Local Club," *Dayton Herald*, May 2, 1919, p. 30.

"Army and Navy Aircraft Hunt Missing Flyer," *Chicago Tribune*, October 24, 1942, pp. 1–2.

"Army Colonel Among Seven Missing with Rickenbacker," *St. Louis Post-Dispatch*, October 26, 1942, p. 2.

"Army Gives Credit to Navy," *New York Times*, November 15, 1942, p. 20.

"Army Planes Aiding Rickenbacker Search," *New York Times*, November 2, 1942, p. 1.

"Army Planes Aiding Search for Rickenbacker and Crew," *St. Louis Post-Dispatch*, November 2, 1942, p. 6.

"Army Reveals 7 Airmen with Rickenbacker," *Atlanta Constitution*, October 26, 1942, p. 13.

"Army Sends Kaczmarczyk's Brother Home to Comfort Bereaved Parents," *Hartford Courant*, November 17, p. 12.

"Army Tells Torrington Woman Son Died as Hero," *Hartford Courant*, November 21, 1942, p. 7.

Arnot, Charles P. "Hospital Built in One Day Saves Rickenbacker Men," *Pittsburgh Press*, May 6, 1943, p. 4.

"Author-Hero Tells of Life on Small Raft," *White Plains (NY) Journal News*, March 15, 1951, p. 7.

"Auto Entries Closed," *Munster (IN) Times*, May 2, 1912, p. 3.

"Automobile Race Is Big Money Event," *Chicago Day Book*, May 30, 1912, p. 29.

"Baby Star Buys W. S. S. for U. S. Ace," *Santa Maria Times*, November 23, 1918, p. 8.

"Barney Oldfield Tells of Prayer," *Los Angeles Times*, November 15, 1942, p. 2.

Barnhill, W. A. "After 16 Years, Johnny Bartek, Survivor of 21-Day Ordeal During World War II, Wants Quiet Life," *Long Branch (NJ) Daily Record*, December 4, 1958, pp. 1, 6–7.

"Bartek Is Praised by Air Chief in Letter to Family at Freehold," *Long Branch (NJ) Daily Record*, December 4, 1942, p. 1.

"Bartek Plans to Preach," *New York Daily News*, January 20, 1943, p. 28.

"Bartek Tells Freehold Rotary of Bomb Patches on Airplane," *Long Branch (NJ) Daily Record*, December 16, 1942, p. 1.

"Better Than Luck," *New York Times*, November 16, 1942, p. 1.

"Bill Cherry's Rubber Raft in Fort Worth," *Abilene Reporter-News*, May 27, 1943, p. 6.

"Bill Henry Returns After Journey Through War Zones in South Pacific," *Los Angeles Times*, November 5, 1942, p. 7.

Boyne, Walter J. "Rickenbacker," *Air Force Magazine*, July 7, 2008. Found at https://www.airforcemag.com/article/0900rickenbacker/. Accessed April 9, 2020.

"Boy Scout Notes," *Morning Call* (Paterson, NJ), June 15, 1944, p. 4.

"Brother Thinks He's Safe," *Chicago Tribune*, October 24, 1942, p. 2.

"Burlingame Flier with Rickenbacker," *San Mateo (CA) Times*, October 26, 1942, pp. 1, 3.

Butler, Sheppard. "Most Notable Year in Auto Speed Annals," *Chicago Tribune*, December 30, 1917, p. 11.

—————. "America's Ace Loops Our Loop to Wild Acclaim," *Chicago Tribune*, April 24, 1919, p. 18.

"Capacity Audience Hears Epic Tale of Lieutenant James C. Whittaker," *Hanford (CA) Sentinel*, February 3, 1947, p. 8.

"Capt. Eddie Is Dead at 82," *New York Times*, July 24, 1973, pp. 1, 38.

"Capt. Rickenbacker at San Francisco," *Los Angeles Times*, December 18, 1942, p. 1.

"Capt. Rickenbacker in U.S. as Companion Tells Story," *Pamona (CA) Progress Bulletin*, December 18, 1942, pp. 1–2.

"Capt. Rickenbacker Safe," *Asbury Park (NJ) Press*, November 14, 1942, p. 8.

"Captain Cherry Heard on Radio," *Abilene Reporter-News*, February 10, 1943, p. 2.

"Captain Cherry Speaks Here at Flag Dedication," *Abilene Reporter-News*, January 4, 1943, p. 1.

"Captain Eddie," *Time*, November 2, 1942, p. 24.

"Captain Eddie," *Time*, February 8, 1943, p. 19.

"Captain Rickenbacker," *Boys' Life*, March 1943, pp. 4, 21–22.

Casselman, William. "How 8 Fliers Battled Sea to Be Told by Rickenbacker This Week," *New York Daily News*, December 13, 1942, p. 82–83.

"Ceiling 300," *Time*, March 10, 1941. Found at http://content.time.com/time /subscriber/article/0,33009,790013,00.html. Accessed February 8, 2021.

"Church Groups Clamor to Hear Lt. Whittaker," *Chicago Tribune*, January 25, 1943, p. 2.

Clausen, Walter B. "Rickenbacker Missing 2 Days on Pacific Hop," *New York Daily News*, October 24, 1942, p. 3.

"Col. Adamson Handled Museum's Publicity," *Kingston (NY) Daily Freeman*, October 26, 1942, p. 1.

"Col. Adamson, Veteran Pilot," *San Francisco Examiner*, September 12, 1968, p. 53.

"Col. H. C. Adamson Shares Experience with Student Body," *What's What*, October 29, 1943, p. 3.

"Colonel Rickenbacker Back on Job with Eastern Air," *Chicago Tribune*, December 30, 1942, p. 8.

"Companion Tells of Kaczmarczyk's Death on Raft," *Hartford Courant*, December 15, 1942, p. 1.

"Cooked Seafood Dinner to Mark Bartek's Survival Anniversary," *Asbury Park (NJ) Press*, November 13, 1960, p. 4.

Cope, Willard. "2 Pilots Apparently Unaware of Plane Hitting Small Pines," *Atlanta Constitution*, March 2, 1941, pp. 1, 8.

Corum, Bill. "Corum Pays Tribute to Eddie Rickenbacker," *Pittsburgh Sun-Telegraph*, October 27, 1942, p. 20.

"Crash Victims Are Identified," *Atlanta Constitution*, February 28, 1941, pp. 1, 9.

Crowther, Bosley. "'Captain Eddie,' Sentimental Romance About Rickenbacker, with Fred MacMurray, Makes Its Appearance at the Roxy," *New York Times*, August 9, 1945.

"Daredevil Racer Is New Ace," *Oregon Daily Journal*, May 31, 1918, p. 6.

"Dawson Wins Breaking All Records in Great Indianapolis Auto Meet," *Sacramento Star*, May 30, 1912, p. 1.

"De Angelis, at Capital, Credits All to Prayer," *Allentown (PA) Morning Call*, December 24, 1942, p. 26.

"De Angelis Family Receives First Word from Son," *Allentown (PA) Morning Call*, November 19, 1942, p. 20.

"Death Easier, Says Rickenbacker, Who Has Cheated It," *Richmond Times-Dispatch*, October 12, 1952, p. 24.

"Death on Life Raft Attributed to Thirst," *New York Times*, December 15, 1942, p. 1.

"Death Stared Rick in the Face—and Rick Stared Right Back!" *New York Daily News*, November 23, 1942, p. 24.

"'Deathless Rick' . . . Modern Adventure," *New York Daily News*, November 15, 1942, p. 400.

"Decatur's Diary," *Decatur (AL) Daily*, December 15, 1942, p. 1.

"Diamond Ring Is Given Ace," *Los Angeles Times*, June 24, 1919, p. 3.

"Diary Tells How Bible Comforted Corporal Lost with Rickenbacker," *Los Angeles Times*, December 19, 1942, p. 5.

"Doctor Admits Rickenbacker 'Put One Over'," *Chicago Tribune*, December 25, 1942, p. 7.

Drake, Frank. "Investigation Launched Soon After Incident," *Atlanta Constitution*, February 28, 1941, pp. 1, 9.

Driscoll, C. B. "New York Day by Day," *News-Palladium* (Benton Harbor, MI), November 10, 1942, p. 2.

"Dual Memorial Rites Held in Nesquehoning," *Allentown (PA) Morning Call*, November 15, 1971, p. 18.

Duff, Katharyn. "Page One," *Abilene Reporter-News*, November 26, 1962, p. 1.

"Durable Man," *Time*, April 17, 1950. Found at http://content.time.com/time/subscriber/article/0,33009,805367,00.html. Accessed February 8, 2021.

"Eastern Sold," *Time*, May 2, 1938. Found at http://content.time.com/time/subscriber/printout/0,8816,848949,00.html. Accessed February 8, 2021.

"Eddie Rickenbacker," *Anniston (AL) Star*, October 30, 1942, p. 4.

"Eddie Rickenbacker," *Honolulu Advertiser*, October 28, 1942, p. 18.

"Eddie Rickenbacker," International Motorsports Hall of Fame, Class of 1992. Found at https://www.motorsportshalloffame.com/Hall-of-Fame. Accessed April 9, 2020.

"Eddie Rickenbacker," *New York Times*, November 14, 1942, p. 7.

"Eddie Rickenbacker," *Rutland (VT) Daily Herald*, November 4,
    1942, p. 8.

"Eddie Rickenbacker, 1890–1973," *Time*, August 6, 1973. Found at
http://content.time.com/time/subscriber/article/0,33009,904018,00.html.
    Accessed February 8, 2021.

"Eddie Rickenbacker Broke Eardrums," *Chicago Tribune*, October 6, 1918, p. 13.

"Eddie Rickenbacker Expected to Issue Statement Soon," *St. Louis Post Dispatch*,
    November 16, 1942, p. 1.

"Eddie Rickenbacker Has Narrow Escape," *Akron Beacon Journal*, September 27,
    1918, p. 1.

"Eddie Rickenbacker Has Narrow Escape," *San Pedro News-Pilot*, August 3,
    1920, p. 6.

"Eddie Rickenbacker Outraces Death Again," *St. Louis Post-Dispatch*, November
    22, 1942, p. 2.

"Eddie Rickenbacker Scores 24 Victories," *Akron Beacon Journal*, November 7,
    1918, p. 10.

"Eddie Rickenbacker's Story," *Hartford Courant*, December 21, 1942, p. 8.

"Eddie's Wife Consoles Lost Sergeant's Fiancee," *Boston Globe*, November 16,
    1942, p. 28.

Eddlem, Thomas R. "Miracle at Sea," *The New American*, April 5, 2004. Found
    at https://www.thefreelibrary.com/_/print/PrintArticle.aspx?id=115078280.
    Accessed April 9, 2020.

"Editorial," *Battle Creek (MI) Enquirer*, November 8, 1942, p. 4.

"Editorial," *Enterprise (AL) Ledger*, November 6, 1942, p. 1.

"Eight on Board Missing Plane," *Pittsburgh Press*, October 26, 1942, p. 4.

Evans, Rev. John. "Pastors Praise Pilot's Story of Finding God," *Chicago Tribune*,
    January 13, 1943, p. 6.

——————. "Ministers Cite Faith of Rick's Party on Rafts," *Chicago
Tribune*, January 18, 1943, p. 1.

——————. "Men in Service Abroad Tell in Letters of Their Reunions,"
Chicago Tribune, January 22, 1943, p. 15.

——————. "'It Was Us'—That's All Rick's Rescuer Admits About Feat,"
Chicago Tribune, January 23, 1943, p. 4.

"Faith, Courage of Rickenbacker and His Men Told," *Chicago Tribune*,
    November 24, 1942, p. 2.

Fawcett, George. "Rickenbacker Rescuer Talks to Students," *Daily Advertiser*
    (Lafayette, LA), November 16, 1975, pp. 1, 43.

"Fear Famous Airman Dies Airman's Death," *New York Daily News*, October 24, 1942, p. 16.

"Feels Quite at Home on Death's Doorsteps," *Charlotte Observer*, November 15, 1942, p. 6.

Ferguson, Edna. "Diet of Raw Fish Worried His Wife," *New York Daily News*, November 15, 1942, p. 58.

Ferris, John. "Rickenbacker Raft Ordeal Recalled by Survivor Here," *Oakland Tribune*, November 26, 1962, p. 8.

"15 Others Are Aboard; Liner Hours Overdue." *Chicago Tribune*, February 27, 1941, p. 1.

"Fifty Cars to Start in Big Race Around Indianapolis Track," *Pittsburgh Daily Post*, March 12, 1911, p. 7.

"Find Rickenbacker and 5 Mates Safe; Sixth Died on Raft," *New York Times*, November 15, 1942, pp. 1, 20.

"Find Rickenbacker Dictated Greeting Just Before Flight," *Chicago Tribune*, December 20, 1942, p. 4.

"Finding of Pilot Raises Hopes of Torrington Family," *Hartford Courant*, November 14, 1942, pp. 1–2.

"First Rickenbacker Rescue Story Told," *Los Angeles Times*, November 22, 1942, p. 1.

"1st Story from Rick: Rescued Ace Doesn't Like Raw Sea Gulls!" *New York Daily News*, November 22, 1942, p. 2.

Fisher, John. "Rickenbacker Found; Now on Way to Hawaii," *Chicago Tribune*, November 15, 1942, p. 1.

Fleming, W. S. "Rickenbacker As a Text," *Chicago Tribune*, January 24, 1943, p. 14.

"Flier Declares Luck Guided 'Rick' Rescue," *Salt Lake Tribune*, April 21, 1943, p. 4.

"Flyer's Wife Arrives After Dramatic Dash," *Atlanta Constitution*, February 28, 1941, p. 44.

"400,000 Fotos Free," *Los Angeles Times*, June 17, 1919, p. 4.

"For Rickenbacker Day," *Los Angeles Times*, June 19, 1919, p. 1.

"Form High School War Training Corps," *Nance County Journal* (Fullerton, NE), October 1, 1942, p. 6.

"Former HSU Man with Missing Rickenbacker," *Abilene Reporter-News*, October 26, 1942, p. 1.

"Freehold Youth Was Missing with Rickenbacker on Plane," *Long Branch (NJ) Daily Record*, August 25, 1943, p. 4.

"Freeholder's War Adventure to Be Relived on Air Tonight," *Long Branch (NJ) Daily Record*, April 24, 1951, p. 12.

Glines, C. V. "Captain Eddie Rickenbacker: America's World War I Ace of Aces," *Aviation History*, January 1999.

"Good-By Rickenbacker?" *New York Daily News*, October 28, 1942, p. 33.

"Good News Comes to Rickenbackers," *New York Times*, November 15, 1942.

"Gossip of the Auto Trade," *Chicago Tribune*, March 18, 1917, p. 9.

"Greatest Race in This Country," *Decatur Herald and Review*, March 26, 1911, p. 20.

"Group Kept Alert by Rickenbacker," *New York Times*, November 23, 1942, p. 1.

Hannagan, Steve. "Men Who Knew Rickenbacker Refuse to Believe He's Gone," *Birmingham (AL) News*, October 28, 1942, p. 18.

—————. "'Rick's' Friends Never Gave Up," *Los Angeles Times*, November 15, 1942, p. 3.

"Hans Christian Adamson, 78, Survivor on Rickenbacker Raft," *Miami Herald*, September 13, 1968, p. 71.

"Hans Christian Adamson Dies; With Rickenbacker on Life Raft," *New York Times*, September 12, 1968, p. 47.

Henry, Bill. "By the Way," *Los Angeles Times*, March 23, 1942, p. 1.

—————. "By the Way," *Los Angeles Times*, March 28, 1942, p. 1.

—————. "Capt. Rickenbacker Hugs Mother at Stop Here," *Los Angeles Times*, December 19, 1942, pp. 1, 3.

Henry, William M. "Rickenbacker Home in the Southland Again," *Los Angeles Times*, June 21, 1919, pp. 1, 3.

Hicks, Ida Belle. "Mrs. William T. Cherry Jr. Back from Hollywood Story Conference—Unexcited," *Fort Worth Star Telegram*, August 6, 1943, p. 22.

"High School Pupils Train for Total War," *Daily Tribune* (Wisconsin Rapids, WI), November 7, 1942, p. 7.

Hildebeitel, Valerie. "Former B-17 Crewman 'Found' by Students," *Allentown (PA) Morning Call*, April 19, 1985, p. 19.

Hogan, Charles. "Friday, the 13th, Brought Back a War Hero Daddy to Paula Cherry and Her Mother," *Fort Worth Star-Telegram*, November 14, 1942, pp. 1–2.

"Hope for Capt. Eddie Fades," *The Times Herald* (Port Huron, MI), November 3, 1942, p. 4.

"Hope Waning for Safety of Ace, Crew," *Fort Worth Star-Telegram*, October 27, 1942, p. 1.

Hopper, Hedda. "Hedda Hopper's Hollywood," *Los Angeles Times*, January 1, 1943, p. 11.

_____. "Looking at Hollywood," *Chicago Tribune*, January 29, 1943, p. 16.

"How Bible, Two Fish Aided 'Rick' and Crewmates," *Chicago Tribune*, December 15, 1942, p. 4.

"How They Welcomed 'Rick,'" *Los Angeles Times*, February 9, 1919, p. 1.

"In the Fight," *Ventura County (CA) Star–Free Press*, December 15, 1942, p. 1.

"It's Civilians Who Need Prodding" *Spokane Chronicle*, March 30, 1942, p. 4.

"It's Easy to Die, Rickenbacker Says," *Los Angeles Times*, October 12, 1952, p. 34.

Jacobs, Capt. I. W. "PhM's Aided in Rescue of Survivors," *Hospital Corps Quarterly*, February 1946, p. 27.

"Joke Turns to Reality," *Arizona Republic*, November 18, 1942, p. 7.

Key, William. "Rescuers Find Grim Reality at Crash Site," *Atlanta Constitution*, February 28, 1941, p. 8.

Kieran, John. "All Around the Mulberry Bush," *New York Times*, October 28, 1942.

Kiernan, Walter. "Rickenbacker Did Work of Man While Only 12," *Miami News*, November 9, 1942, pp. 1–2.

_____. "'Rick' Often Faced Death," *Palladium-Item* (Richmond, IN), November 11, 1942, p. 2.

Kirksey, George. "Veteran Ace Cheated Death Often," *Pasadena Post*, February 2, 1934, p. 7.

Klein, Sandor S. "'Our Prayers Heard': Rick Tells His Story," *New York Daily News*, December 20, 1942, pp. 3, 46.

Larsen, Erik. "A Christmas Homecoming for a Freehold Soldier Lost at Sea," *Asbury Park (NJ) Press*, December 24, 2017, pp. 1, 38. Found at https://www.app.com/story/news/history/erik-larsen/2017/12/24/jersey-roots-christmas-homecoming-freehold-soldier-lost-sea/979089001/. Accessed February 8, 2021.

"Lieutenant Boyd Helps Find Rickenbacker," *The Monocle* (Richmond, VA), February 12, 1943, p. 4.

"Local Doctor Revealed as Rescuer," *Pittsburgh Post-Gazette*, February 17, 1943, p. 17.

"Long-Lost Men Found on Raft," *Asbury Park (NJ) Press*, November 14, 1942, p. 1.

"Lost at Sea!" *All Hands*, February 1972, pp. 54–59.

"Lost Flier's Fiancée Gets Wire of Sympathy from Mrs. Rickenbacker," *Meriden (CT) Journal*, November 16, 1942, p. 1.

"Lt. J. C. Whittaker Is Known as U. S. Army's Iron Man," *Chicago Tribune*, January 12, 1943, p. 2.

Maloney, J. L. "Comrade of '18 Finds Rick the Leader of Yore," *Chicago Tribune*, January 24, 1943, p. 3.

"Mayor Wants Aid of Landlords, Too," *New York Daily News*, October 26, 1942, p. 16.

McGill, Ralph. "Unflinching Courage, Devotion to Duty Found at Crash Site," *Atlanta Constitution*, February 28, 1941, pp. 1, 5.

——————. "One More Word," *Atlanta Constitution*, February 28, 1941, p. 14.

McLemore, Henry. "Passenger Liner Spans Continent in 12 Hr. 4 Min.," *Indianapolis Star*, November 9, 1934, pp. 1, 3.

——————. "The Lighter Side," *Los Angeles Times*, October 29, 1942, p. 11.

Miller, John J. "Ace of Aces," *National Review*, June 21, 2018. Found at https://www.nationalreview.com/magazine/2018/07/09/eddie-rickenbacker-ww1-hero-incredible-life/. Accessed April 9, 2020.

"Missing Ace," *Harrisburg Telegraph*, October 31, 1942, pp. 15–16.

Moore, Reuel S. "Rescue Plane Lashed Rickenbacker to Wing," *New York Daily News*, November 18, 1942, p. 3.

"More Sweat, Toil, in U.S., Rick's Plea," *New York Daily News*, December 20, 1942, p. 46.

"Mother of Rescued Flier Never Abandoned Her Hope," *Sacramento Bee*, November 17, 1942, p. 10.

"Mother Sobs at News of Flier's Death," *Pittsburgh Press*, November 14, 1942, p. 3.

"Mother Weeps for Sergeant Lost on Rickenbacker Flight," *Los Angeles Times*, November 15, 1942, p. 2.

"Motorists Break Records," *Sioux City (IA) Journal*, September 3, 1913, p. 8.

"Mrs. Cherry Blesses Friday, the 13th," *New York Daily News*, November 14, 1942, p. 9.

"Mrs. Rickenbacker Tells War Women to Keep Hope," *New York Times*, November 16, p. 1.

Myler, Joseph L. "Rickenbacker Does It Again; Rescue with 5," *New York Daily News*, November 15, 1942, pp. 2, 4.

"Navy Keeps Silence on Rickenbacker," *Morning Call* (Paterson, NJ), November 16, 1942, p. 22.

"Nesquehoning Fete to Lieut. D'Angelis," *Hazelton (PA) Standard-Speaker*, December 15, 1942, p. 9.

"'Never Lost Faith,' Wife of Flyer Declares," *St. Louis Post-Dispatch*, November 15, 1942, p. 3.

"Never Lost Hope for 'Eddie,' Says Thankful Wife," *Chicago Tribune*, November 15, 1942, p. 4.

"New Raft for Flyers Down at Sea," *Chicago Tribune*, February 14, 1943, p. 5.

"New York Airliner Overdue at Atlanta; Rickenbacker and 15 Others Are Aboard," *New York Times*, February 27, 1941.

"New York Airplane Damaged in Tucson," *San Francisco Chronicle*, August 14, 1920, p. 15.

"New York Plans Big Ovation for Rickenbacker," *Chicago Tribune*, December 14, 1942, p. 1.

"News Clips from Studio Town," *Los Angeles Times*, November 20, 1942, p. 10.

Newton, Louie D. "Rickenbacker's Life Has Been Full of Action," *Atlanta Constitution*, February 28, 1941, p. 6.

"No Absenteeism," *Chicago Tribune*, February 2, 1943, p. 1.

"Noted L. A. Ace Falls with Plane," *Los Angeles Evening Post-Record*, August 3, 1920, p. 1.

O'Donnell, John. "Capitol Stuff," *New York Daily News*, November 16, 1942, p. 4.

"Of Hell and Prayers," *Time*, December 28, 1942. Found at http://content.time.com/time/subscriber/article/0,33009,886069,00.html. Accessed February 8, 2021.

"Officials Leave the Story for Captain Rickenbacker to Tell," *Indianapolis News*, November 16, 1942, p. 17.

"Once More the Editors Revise Rick's Obituary," *Chicago Tribune*, November 15, 1942, p. 4.

"One Companion of Rickenbacker Picked Up at Sea; Hope for Others," *St. Louis Post-Dispatch*, November 13, 1942, pp. 1–2.

"Outlook Gloomy, Washington Says," *New York Daily News*, October 24, 1942, pp. 3, 10.

"Pacific Rescue," *Monmouth Democrat* (Freehold, NJ), November 19, 1942, p. 3.

"Pacific Rescue," *New York Times*, November 15, 1942.

"Pair Lashed to Wings, Craft Taxies 40 Miles," *Arizona Republic*, November 18, 1942, p. 7.

Parke, Newton C. "Rickenbacker Gets Fifth Hun Plane," *St. Louis Star and Times*, May 31, 1918, p. 2.

"Patch of Destiny," *Time*, November 2, 1942, pp. 28–32.

"People," *Time*, October 17, 1938. Found at http://content.time.com/time /subscriber/article/0,33009,848345,00.html. Accessed February 8, 2021.

Phillips, H. I. "Johnny Bartek's Bible," *Asbury Park (NJ) Press*, April 5, 1943, p. 6.

"Pilot Tells How 'Rick's' Courage Saved 7 at Sea," *Chicago Tribune*, December 21, 1942, p. 5.

"Pilot's Wife Stays on Job at Plane Plant," *St. Louis Post-Dispatch*, November 14, 1942, p. 3.

"Plane Crashes into House Without Serious Result," *Hanover Evening Sun* (Hanover, PA), August 3, 1920, p. 1.

Powers, Jimmy. "The Power House," *New York Daily News*, May 25, 1942, p. 33.

"President Joins Nation in Prayers for Peace," *Los Angeles Times*, December 26, 1942, p. 2.

"Pvt. Bartek Missing with Rickenbacker," *Monmouth Democrat* (Freehold, NJ), October 29, 1942, p. 1.

Rea, Billy A. "Eddie Rickenbacker and Six Other People Survive a B-17 Crash and Three Weeks Lost in the Pacific Ocean." Found at https://www .historynet.com/eddie-rickenbacker-and-six-other-people-survive-a-b-17 -crash-and-three-weeks-lost-in-the-pacific-ocean.htm Accessed March 5, 2020.

"Recovery Is Quick for Rickenbacker," *New York Times*, November 22, 1942, p. 1.

"Rescue Abilene Flier in Pacific," *Abilene Reporter-News*, November 13, 1942, p. 1.

"Rescue Ends Ordeal of Navigator's Bride," *Los Angeles Times*, November 15, 1942, p. 3.

"Rescue of Airman Delights Millions," *New York Times*, November 15, 1942, p. 20.

"Rescue of Rickenbacker and Five Flyers Related," *Los Angeles Times*, November 15, 1942, pp. 1–2.

"Rescue Pilots," *Chicago Tribune*, January 15, 1943, p. 2.

"Rescued Airman Wins Plaudits," *Allentown (PA) Morning Call*, December 19, 1942, p. 8.

"Rescued Flyer's Birthday Observed," *Los Angeles Times*, November 15, 1942, p. 2.

"Rescuer Lauds Fortitude of Rickenbacker," *Atlanta Constitution*, February 28, 1941, p. 7.

"Rescuer, Lt. Eadie, Is Awarded Air Medal," *Chicago Tribune*, March 15, 1943, p. 7.

"Reunited Cherrys to Visit Here Over the New Year," *Fort Worth Star-Telegram*, December 30, 1942, p. 1.

"Rick an Iron Man," *New York Daily News*, November 29, 1942, p. 93.

"Rick Never Doubted He'd Be Saved," *New York Daily News*, November 23, 1942, p. 2.

"Rick's Raft Survivor Reveals Sea Water Killed Only Victim," *New York Daily News*, December 15, 1942, p. 2.

"Rickenbacker," *Los Angeles Times*, November 15, 1942, p. 4.

"Rickenbacker Again Cheats Grim Reaper," *Charlotte Observer*, November 15, 1942, pp. 1–2.

"Rickenbacker Aide Is Welcomed Home," *New York Times*, December 17, 1942, p. 22.

"Rickenbacker Aide Says Party Prayed for Food," *Bridgewater (NJ) Courier News*, December 15, 1942, p. 12.

"Rickenbacker and Men Rescued; Torrington Boy Only One to Die," *Hartford Courant*, November 15, 1942, pp. 1–2.

"Rickenbacker Ate Only Half Orange in 22 Day Drift," *Fresno Bee*, November 29, 1942, p. 4.

"Rickenbacker, Bartek Recovering from Ordeal, Their Story Awaited," *Asbury Park (NJ) Press*, November 15, 1942, p. 1.

"Rickenbacker Busy Till Last," *Kansas City Star*, November 18, 1918, p. 5.

Rickenbacker, Capt. Eddie. "Bailing Wire and Fabric Crates," *The Airman*, August 1957, pp. 8, 11.

_____. "Eddie Rickenbacker Tells His Own Philosophy," *Los Angeles Times*, November 11, 1962, pp. 2–3.

Rickenbacker, Captain Edward V. "Pacific Mission, Part I: In Which Eight Men Are Cast Adrift in Mid-Pacific on Rubber Rafts," *Life*, January 25, 1943, pp. 19–26, 90–100.

_____. "Pacific Mission, Part II: In Which the Navy Rescues Seven Castaways After 21 Days' Drifting," *Life*, February 1, 1943, pp. 78–86, 89–92.

_____. "Pacific Mission, Part III: In Which 'Rick' Resumes His Trip and Visits the Fighting Fronts," *Life*, February 8, 1943, pp. 94–100, 103–106.

"Rickenbacker Cautioned Against Over-Optimism," *Bridgewater (NJ) Courier News*, December 19, 1942, p. 2.

"Rickenbacker Day June 28," *Los Angeles Times*, May 18, 1919, p. 1.

"Rickenbacker, Edward Vernon," National Aviation Hall of Fame. Found at https://www.nationalaviation.org/our-enshrinees/rickenbacker-edward-vernon. Accessed April 9, 2020.

"Rickenbacker Escapes," *Gettysburg (PA) Times*, May 18, 1918, p. 1.

"Rickenbacker Found in Pacific," *Abilene Reporter-News*, November 14, 1942, pp. 1, 8.

"Rickenbacker, 4 Months in Hospital, Back; He Will Resume His Airline Post on Monday," *New York Times*, June 26, 1941.

"Rickenbacker Goes on Air," *Los Angeles Times*, December 21, 1942, p. 9.

"Rickenbacker Hunt Pushed," *Los Angeles Times*, November 2, 1942, p. 3.

"Rickenbacker Legend Comes to Life in Biography of Air Ace of World War I," *Lexington (KY) Herald*, February 24, 1946, p. 30.

"Rickenbacker Life Will Go on Screen," *New York Times*, January 29, 1943.

"Rickenbacker Missing in Pacific on Flight Southwest of Hawaii," *New York Times*, October 24, 1942, pp. 1, 4.

"Rickenbacker Not Lost, Says His Mother," *San Francisco Chronicle*, August 21, 1920, p. 6.

"Rickenbacker Overdue on Pacific Island Hop," *New York Daily News*, October 24, 1942, p. 3.

"Rickenbacker Party Found," *Abilene Reporter-News*, November 15, 1942, p. 7.

"Rickenbacker Party 'Found God' in Mid-Ocean Aboard Rafts, Says Radio Man in Bay Hospital," *Oakland Tribune*, December 21, 1942, p. 15.

"Rickenbacker Plane Missing in Pacific," *Los Angeles Times*, October 24, 1942, pp. 1, 6.

"Rickenbacker Plane Search Hope Fades," *Fresno (CA) Bee*, October 26, 1942, p. 1.

"Rickenbacker Rescued," *Life*, December 7, 1942, pp. 42–43.

"Rickenbacker Rescued," *New York Times*, November 15, 1942.

"Rickenbacker Rescuer Gets Navy Air Medal," *Allentown (PA) Morning Call*, March 15, 1943, p. 1.

"Rickenbacker Returns to the U.S., Won't Talk About His Experiences," *St. Louis Post-Dispatch*, December 18, 1942, p. 1.

"Rickenbacker Reviews Today's Pilots of His 94th Squadron," *Los Angeles Times*, March 27, 1942, p. 3.

"Rickenbacker Rode Rescue Plane Wing," *Minneapolis Star Tribune*, November 18, 1942, p. 1.

"Rickenbacker Safe," *Time*, November 23, 1942, pp. 25–26.

"Rickenbacker Safe; 6 Others in Party Found," *St. Louis Post-Dispatch*, November 14, 1942, pp. 1, 3.

"Rickenbacker Says He Never Doubted Rescue," *St. Louis Post-Dispatch*, November 22, 1942, pp. 1, 15.

"Rickenbacker Search Fails," *Los Angeles Times*, October 25, 1942, pp. 1, 5.

"Rickenbacker Sees Mother; 'Grateful' for Being Rescued," *Chicago Tribune*, December 19, 1942, p. 9.

"Rickenbacker, 6 of His Plane Crew Rescued," *St. Louis Post-Dispatch*, November 15, 1942, pp. 1, 3.

"Rickenbacker Story Left for Him to Tell," *New York Times*, November 16, 1942, p. 1.

"Rickenbacker Story Stirs School Children," *Los Angeles Times*, January 2, 1943, p. 9.

"Rickenbacker Survivor Home," *Wilkes-Barre Record*, December 15, 1942, p. 18.

"Rickenbacker Tells Horrors of Days at Sea," *Los Angeles Times*, December 20, 1942, pp. 1, 5.

"Rickenbacker Tells of 21 Days Adrift at Sea; Only Oranges to Eat 6 Days, Then Gull, Two Fish," *St. Louis Post-Dispatch*, December 19, 1942, pp. 1–2.

"Rickenbacker Tells of Vigil in Life Boat," *Hartford Courant*, December 20, 1942, pp. 1, 5.

"Rickenbacker Tells Story of His 23 Days on Raft," *New York Times*, December 20, 1942, pp. 1, 37.

"Rickenbacker Will Recover, Doctors Report," *Atlanta Constitution*, February 28, 1941, p. 1.

"Rickenbacker's Companion Tells of His Experiences," *Bridgewater (NJ) Courier News*, January 13, 1943, p. 2.

"Rickenbacker's Health Is 'Very Good,' Says Wife," *Chicago Tribune*, November 17, 1942, p. 5.

"Rickenbacker's Life Has Been Full of Action," *Atlanta Constitution*, February 28, 1941, p. 6.

"Rickenbacker's Mother Had Premonition of Bad Luck," *Los Angeles Times*, October 24, 1942, p. 6.

"Rickenbacker's Pilot Found Alive on Raft, New Pacific Hunt Begins," *New York Times*, November 14, 1942, pp. 1, 7.

"Rickenbacker's Plane Revealed as Scarred Vet," *Chicago Tribune*, December 16, 1942, p. 10.

"Rickenbacker's Record Flight, Los Angeles-Newark, in 13:02," *Brooklyn Times-Union*, February 25, 1934, p. 18.

"Rickenbacker's Story of His Ordeal in Pacific," *Los Angeles Times*, December 20, 1942, pp. 5, 11.

"'Ricky' Writes of 6,000 Foot Fall," *Chicago Tribune*, July 29, 1918, p. 1.

Rigney, Frank. "World War II Heroes," *Sandusky Register*, February 20, 1945, p. 6.

Rosenfeld, J. S. "Victim Tells of Being Hurled from Plane, Just Missing Stump," *Atlanta Constitution*, February 28, 1941, p. 8.

Russell, Rosalind. "A Medal for Freddie," *Lansing (MI) State Journal*, February 20, 1956, p. 1.

"Say Rickenbacker May Lose One Eye," *New York Times*, March 1, 1941.

"Search Continues for Rickenbacker," *Miami News*, October 26, 1942, p. 6.

"Search Continues for Rickenbacker Plane," *Monmouth Democrat* (Freehold, NJ), November 5, 1942, p. 2.

"Second Front Must Await Greater Air Superiority," *Helena (MT) Independent-Record*, October 16, 1942, p. 3.

Seither, Sgt. Richard C. "Rickenbacker Eats Seagull Raw," *Pittsburgh Press*, November 23, 1942, p. 4.

"Send More Planes, Guns, Ships!" *Los Angeles Times*, June 6, 1918, pp. 1, 7.

"Sends Sympathy to Fiancée," *Indianapolis News*, November 16, 1942, p. 17.

"Sends Wire to Sergeant's Fiancée," *Chicago Tribune*, November 17, 1942, p. 5.

"7 Army Fliers Missing with Rickenbacker; No Sign of Men Found," *Philadelphia Inquirer*, October 26, 1942, p. 3.

"7 of Army in Plane of Rickenbacker," *New York Times*, October 26, 1942, p. 1.

Shalit, Sid. "Listening In," *New York Daily News*, January 9, 1946, p. 262.

"Silence Guards Rickenbacker," *Los Angeles Times*, November 16, 1942, p. 9.

"Sixth Grade Brings World War II Drama to Classroom," *Los Angeles Times*, April 19, 1985, p. 2.

Sobol, Louis. "New York Cavalcade," *The Evening News* (Harrisburg, PA), November 20, 1942, p. 20.

"Soldier Got Religion on Rickenbacker Raft," *Marshfield (WI) News Herald*, December 15, 1942, p. 2.

"Spiritual War Film Showing on Tuesday," *Allentown (PA) Morning Call*, November 18, 1944, p. 7.

Stephenson, Bess. "Captain Cherry Tells of 'Cruise,'" *Fort Worth Star-Telegram*, January 12, 1943, p. 2.

"Still No Word from Eddie Rickenbacker," *Bismarck Tribune*, October 30, 1942, p. 4.

"Stimson Hopes Rickenbacker Can Continue Survey Trip," *St. Louis Post-Dispatch*, November 19, 1942, p. 1.

"Stimson Hopes Rickenbacker Will Be Able to Resume Tour," *Los Angeles Times*, November 20, 1942, p. 24.

"Stimson Still Hopes Rickenbacker Safe," *Los Angeles Times*, October 30, 1942, p. 7.

"Story of 'John Bartek 16 Years Later' Told in Issue of Methodist Magazine," *Freehold (NJ) Transcript and Monmouth Inquirer*, September 25, 1958, p. 7.

"Strike Is Treason," *Chicago Tribune*, February 2, 1943, p. 1.

Sullivan, Ed. "Little Old New York," *New York Daily News*, October 26, 1942, p. 26.

——————. "Little Old New York," *New York Daily News*, November 1, 1942, p. 452.

——————. "Little Old New York," *New York Daily News*, November 16, 1942, p. 34.

——————. "Little Old New York," *New York Daily News*, December 31, 1942, p. 23.

"Survivors Get Medical Care," *Los Angeles Times*, November 15, 1942, p. 3.

"Survivors Pay High Tribute to Rickenbacker," *Atlanta Constitution*, February 28, 1941, p. 44.

Taylor, Frank J. "German Aviators Invent New Tricks but They Don't Get Very Far," *Arkansas City (KS) Daily News*, May 18, 1918, p. 1.

Taylor, Michael. "Alvin Cluster—Close Friend of JFK," *San Francisco Chronicle*, March 14, 2004. Found at https://www.sfgate.com/bayarea/article/Alvin-Cluster-close-friend-of-JFK-2809146.php. Accessed January 15, 2022.

"Tells of 24 Day Ordeal in Life Raft on Pacific," *Chicago Tribune*, November 22, 1942, pp. 1, 16.

"Ten Best Stories of Year Listed by Associated Press," *Oakland Tribune*, December 31, 1942, p. 8.

"The 'Music' of Danger," *New York Times*, November 24, 1942.

"The Rescue of Eddie Rickenbacker," *St. Louis Post-Dispatch*, November 14, 1942, p. 4.

Thomason, Lieut. John W. "Half Orange for 22 Days Keeps Fliers Alive at Sea," *Pittsburgh Press*, November 23, 1942, pp. 1, 4.

"3-Day Hunt Fails to Turn Up Trace of Rickenbacker," *St. Louis Post-Dispatch*, October 25, 1942, p. 17.

"3-Day Hunt Finds No Trace of Rickenbacker," *New York Daily News*, October 25, 1942, p. 8.

"Three Periods in Colorful Life of Great Air Ace of World War I," *Los Angeles Times*, October 24, 1942, p. 6.

"3 Rickenbacker Aides Foodless at Sea 22 Days," *St. Louis Post-Dispatch*, November 23, 1942, pp. 1, 7.

"Torrington Youth and Six Others on Missing Rickenbacker Plane," *Hartford Courant*, October 26, 1942, p. 7.

"Town Holds Celebration," *Scranton (PA) Times-Tribune*, November 14, 1942, p. 15.

Tremaine, Frank. "Rickenbacker Pilot Safe; Hunt Renewed," *New York Daily News*, November 14, 1942, pp. 3, 9.

Trohan, Walter. "Rickenbacker's Pilot Picked Up; Hope for Others," *Chicago Tribune*, November 14, 1942, p. 3.

——————. "Gull Alights as 8 on Rafts Pray for Food," *Chicago Tribune*, December 20, 1942, pp. 1, 4.

"20th Anniversary of Johnny Bartek's Harrowing Experiences on Raft at Sea," *Freehold (NJ) Transcript and Monmouth Inquirer*, December 13, 1962, p. 25.

"T. W. A. Plane Crosses U.S. in Record Time of 13 Hours," *Pittsburgh Post-Gazette*, February 20, 1934, p. 11.

"2 Aces of First World War Pay Visit to Langley Field," *Newport News (VA) Daily Press*, April 8, 1942, p. 11.

"Two Atlantans, Five Others Die as Ship Falls," *Atlanta Constitution*, February 28, 1941, pp. 1, 7.

"Two Auto Events to Rickenbacher," *Chicago Tribune*, August 10, 1913, p. 21.

"U.S. Flyers Press Search for Rickenbacker in Pacific," *St. Louis Post-Dispatch*, October 24, 1942, p. 2.

Vance, Henry. "The Coal Bin," *Birmingham (AL) News*, March 4, 1941, p. 8.

"Vet of 94 Hopes to See His Hero—Rickenbacker!" *Chicago Tribune*, November 15, 1942, p. 4.

"Victory Corps," *Time*, October 5, 1942. Found at http://content.time.com /time/subscriber/article/0,33009,773765,00.html. Accessed February 8, 2021.

"Waiting for News of Dad," *Fort Worth Star-Telegram*, October 27, 1942, p. 1.

"War Apathy Flayed by Rickenbacker; Public Letting Army Down, He Says," *Los Angeles Times*, March 26, 1942, p. 6.

"War Hero Finds Home Folks Are Just as Heroic," *Chicago Tribune*, February 25, 1943, p. 4.

"Westbound Planes Search for 'Rick,'" *New York Daily News*, November 2, 1942, p. 44.

Whittaker, Lt. James C., as told to Charles Leavelle. "How 8 Men Fought the Elements—and 7 Won," *Chicago Tribune*, January 12, 1943, pp. 1–2. Installment #1 of 13.

——————. "Crashes Rickenbacker Plane in Sea Without Losing Man," *Chicago Tribune*, January 13, 1943, pp. 1, 6. Installment #2 of 13.

——————. "Tells of First 2 Days Adrift in Pacific with Rickenbacker," *Chicago Tribune*, January 14, 1943, pp. 1, 4. Installment #3 of 13.

——————. "How Rickenbacker and Drifting Crew Snare First Meal," *Chicago Tribune*, January 15, 1943, pp. 1–2. Installment #4 of 13.

——————. "Rickenbacker Crew Saved by Rain on Eighth Day Adrift," *Chicago Tribune*, January 16, 1943, pp. 1–2. Installment #5 of 13.

——————. "Rick's Pilot Hooks Shark and Battles It to Death," *Chicago Tribune*, January 17, 1943, pp. 1–2. Installment #6 of 13.

——————. "Whittaker Tells Tragic Burial from Raft at Sea," *Chicago Tribune*, January 18, 1943, pp. 1, 4. Installment #7 of 13.

——————. "Rickenbacker's Cussing Boosts Morale on Raft," *Chicago Tribune*, January 19, 1943, p. 2. Installment #8 of 13.

——————. "18th Day! Plane Fails to Notice Rick's 3 Rafts," *Chicago Tribune*, January 20, 1943, p. 2. Installment #9 of 13.

——————. "21st Day's Dawn Brings Land to 3 of Rick's Crew," *Chicago Tribune*, January 21, 1943, p. 3. Installment #10 of 13.

——————. "Natives Rescue 3 of Rick's Lost Crew on Island," *Chicago Tribune*, January 22, 1943, p. 2. Installment #11 of 13.

——————. "Natives' Chicken Broth Revives Three on Island," *Chicago Tribune*, January 23, 1943, p. 4. Installment #12 of 13.

——————. "Ordeal at End, 'Iron Man' Has 3 Malted Milks," *Chicago Tribune*, January 24, 1943, p. 2. Installment #13 of 13.

"Whole Town Cheered by Rescue of Pilot Cherry, Lost at Sea 23 Days," *Abilene Reporter-News*, November 14, 1942, p. 1.

"Wife Never Lost Faith That He Would Return," *Charlotte Observer*, November 15, 1942, p. 6.

"Wife Sure 'Eddie Will Turn Up,'" *Chicago Tribune*, October 24, 1942, p. 2.

"Wife to Keep on Building Planes," *Abilene Reporter-News*, November 13, 1942, p. 1.

"Wife Waits by Phone to Hear of Ace," *New York Daily News*, October 24, 1942, p. 3.

"Wife Worried About Sunburn," *Los Angeles Times*, November 15, 1942, p. 2.

"Will Welcome Ace Today," *Los Angeles Times*, June 21, 1919, p. 1.

Williams, Harry A. "On the Way to Berlin," *Los Angeles Times*, June 16, 1918, p. 6

"William T. Cherry, Jr.," *Fort Worth Star-Telegram*, September 15, 2000, p. 42.

Winchell, Walter. "East Side, West Side," *St. Louis Post-Dispatch*, November 22, 1942, p. 3I.

"With the American Armies in France," *Chicago Tribune*, June 16, 1918, p. 1.

"World War Ace: Down in Pacific," *Oklahoma County Register* (Luther, OK), November 12, 1942, p. 2.

"Would Name Field for Rickenbacker," *New York Daily News*, October 28, 1942, p. B13.

"Yesterday Made Their Prayers Come True," *Fort Worth Star-Telegram*, November 14, 1942, p. 1.

INDEX

Note: Page numbers in *italics* indicate illustrations.

ABOUT THE AUTHOR

John Wukovits is a military expert and an authority on US history in the Pacific Theater of World War II. He is the author of *Pacific Alamo: The Battle for Wake Island*, as well as several military biographies and many articles for publications such as *WWII History*, *Naval History*, *World War II*, *Journal of Military History*, *Naval War College Review*, and *Air Power History*.